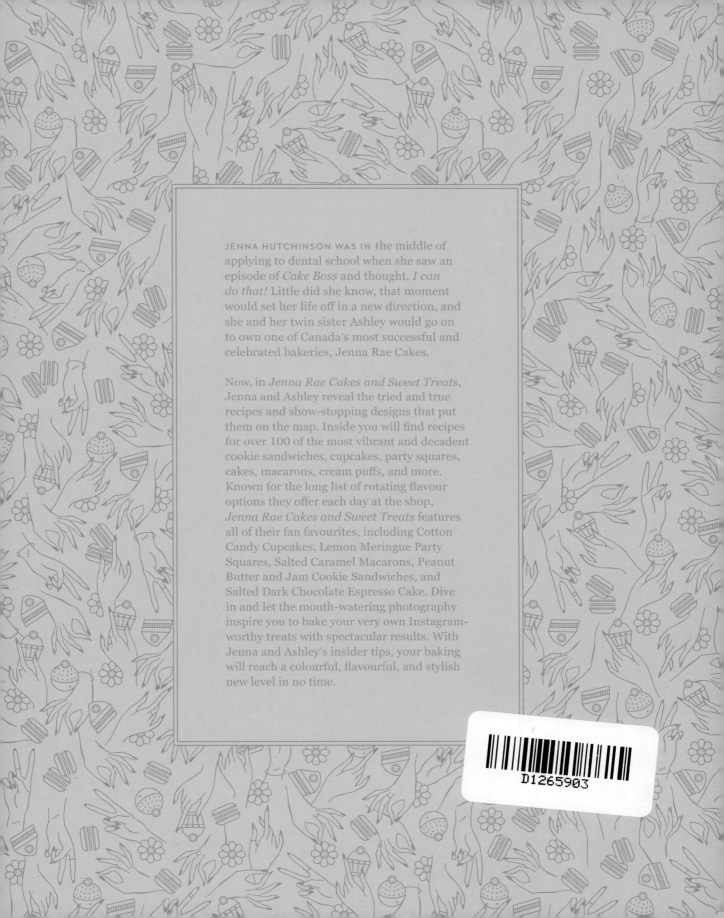

JENNA HUTCHINSON WAS IN the middle of
applying to dental school when she saw an
episode of *Cake Boss* and thought, *I can
do that!* Little did she know, that moment
would set her life off in a new direction, and
she and her twin sister Ashley would go on
to own one of Canada's most successful and
celebrated bakeries, Jenna Rae Cakes.

Now, in *Jenna Rae Cakes and Sweet Treats*,
Jenna and Ashley reveal the tried and true
recipes and show-stopping designs that put
them on the map. Inside you will find recipes
for over 100 of the most vibrant and decadent
cookie sandwiches, cupcakes, party squares,
cakes, macarons, cream puffs, and more.
Known for the long list of rotating flavour
options they offer each day at the shop,
Jenna Rae Cakes and Sweet Treats features
all of their fan favourites, including Cotton
Candy Cupcakes, Lemon Meringue Party
Squares, Salted Caramel Macarons, Peanut
Butter and Jam Cookie Sandwiches, and
Salted Dark Chocolate Espresso Cake. Dive
in and let the mouth-watering photography
inspire you to bake your very own Instagram-
worthy treats with spectacular results. With
Jenna and Ashley's insider tips, your baking
will reach a colourful, flavourful, and stylish
new level in no time.

JENNA RAE CAKES AND SWEET TREATS

OVER 100 RECIPES FOR THE MODERN BAKER

ASHLEY KOSOWAN AND JENNA HUTCHINSON

WITH JORDAIN HOUDAYER | PHOTOGRAPHY BY BRITTANY MAHOOD

PENGUIN

an imprint of Penguin Canada, a division of Penguin Random House Canada Limited

Canada • USA • UK • Ireland • Australia • New Zealand • India • South Africa • China

First published 2020

www.penguinrandomhouse.ca

Library and Archives Canada Cataloguing in Publication

Title: Jenna Rae Cakes and Sweet Treats : over 100 recipes for the modern
baker / Jenna Hutchinson and Ashley Kosowan.
Names: Hutchinson, Jenna, author. | Kosowan, Ashley, author.
Identifiers: Canadiana (print) 20200173588 | Canadiana (ebook)
20200173618 | ISBN 9780735236745 (hardcover) | ISBN 9780735236752 (HTML)
Subjects: LCSH: Cake. | LCSH: Desserts. | LCSH: Baking. | LCGFT: Cookbooks.
Classification: LCC TX771 .H88 2020 | DDC 641.86/53—dc23

Cover and book design by Ashley Kosowan with Five Seventeen
Cover and interior photography by Brittany Mahood
Photography on page 4 and 310 by Charles R. Venzon
Food and prop styling by Ashley Kosowan

Printed and bound in China

10 9 8 7 6 5 4 3 2 1

Penguin
Random House
PENGUIN CANADA

TO OUR MOM, GRANNY, AND BABA
for baking with us and inspiring us
from a very young age

TO OUR HUSBANDS AND KIDS
for being our rocks and our biggest fans

TO OUR JENNA RAE CAKES TEAM, PAST AND PRESENT
this book would not exist without you

TO OUR CLIENTS AND TO YOU
for allowing us to be a small, sweet
part of your most special occasions

CUSTOM CAKES AND SWEET TREATS

580
ACADEMY ROAD
———
jenna@jennaraecakes.com
jennaraecakes.com
204·691·4222

CONTENTS

COOKIE SANDWICHES

CUPCAKES

PARTY SQUARES

CAKES

CREAM PUFFS

MACARONS

CANDIES & CONFECTIONS

FILLINGS & BUTTERCREAM

OUR STORY

THE STORY OF JENNA RAE CAKES BEGINS LIKE MOST, in the little moments that shape your childhood, long before you realize what the future will hold. The two of us have been baking together since we were two years old in our Fisher-Price Kitchen. When we grew taller, we stood on stools to reach the countertop and baked side by side with our mom, measuring ingredients, mixing batter, and rolling out dough. We brought creativity into the kitchen (and some mess, like most excited children do), and we both truly believed a lesson taught to us from an early age: nothing beats the satisfaction of creating something from scratch with your own two hands. Especially when that something provides pure joy to whoever consumes it!

After watching an episode of *Cake Boss* in 2010, Jenna thought, "I can do that," and decided to reignite her natural talent for baking. She tried her hand at creating cakes that were more like works of edible art than the basic sheet cakes you find at a grocery store. After learning from cookbooks and YouTube tutorials, and after plenty of trial and error, Jenna started volunteering to bring a cake to just about every celebration we had with family and friends. She posted pictures of her homemade cakes on Facebook and soon orders and requests started rolling in at an overwhelming rate. Jenna knew she was on to something special. As Ashley helped Jenna's budding business look more polished with some initial branding, a website, and a lot of cheerleading, Jenna plunged into renting a commercial kitchen space to make Jenna Rae Cakes more official.

Before long, the cake business was booming, and Jenna couldn't keep up. She was on a track to pursue studies in dentistry, and her days were spent studying while she worked as a server in the evenings and pulled overnight shifts to make breathtaking cakes that rivalled those seen in wedding magazines. The all-nighters began to wear on Jenna, forcing her to make a decision: Should she be safe and stick with dentistry? Or should she be bold and pursue a career in cake design? Jenna has always been the kind of woman to take a leap and gracefully learn to fly in the very moment others would panic. She pursued her calling and gave herself fully to Jenna Rae Cakes. Ashley had recently left her job at a local wedding magazine, so it was the perfect time to join forces and see what they could create.

When the doors of our little flagship location—which was meant to be a place where locals could pick up a few treats and Jenna could meet with bubbly brides eager to taste mouth-watering cake samples—opened in the spring of 2014, we really had no idea what was in store. The cute shop for cake consults quickly turned into utter chaos, and we were completely blown away by the public's reaction. The first time we saw a line of excited customers outside the door before we opened we felt a mix of elation and terror. We had hundreds of people visiting us daily, creating lineups that lasted for hours and leaving our coolers bare of all prepared sweet treats. Sixteen-hour days and all-nighters were the norm for us in those early years as we struggled to keep up with the surprising demand from our customers. Although we felt fortunate to have the problem of not being able to keep up with demand, it was stressful trying to figure out how to make more and make it fast, because tomorrow was another day and we needed to turn on the *Open* sign.

Somehow, we managed to get through it, and the last six years have been a fun, exciting, and challenging adventure. The business has evolved and grown with us through marriages and children—from one woman pulling all-nighters to employing more than 30 people who love the brand like it's their own. A true "pinch me" moment was when Ashley and Trevor's wedding was featured in the coveted *Martha Stewart Weddings* magazine, with our macarons and beautiful cake front and centre. There have been as many bumps on the road as successes, but we thank our lucky stars every day because, when it comes down to it, we get to build this company together as sisters and best friends.

For years we have been bombarded on social media by bakers asking us to help them with their macarons, cake decorating, and buttercream. These comments led to one resounding request—for a cookbook! We know bakers are hungry for the honest-to-goodness truth behind mastering tricky macarons, creating crisp cake edges, and making treats that young and old alike would love to devour, and that's exactly what you'll find in these pages: the tried-and-true recipes that put Jenna Rae Cakes on the map. Detailed tutorials, helpful suggestions, and breathtaking images will make you drool as you flip through the pages of your new go-to dessert cookbook.

We love how creative baking allows you to be: you can layer different flavours and textures and decorate in your own way to create the perfect finishing touches. With no conventional baking backgrounds, we didn't feel confined to tradition, and that left the door wide open for us and our team to have fun creating whimsical flavours that no one else was doing yet. You shouldn't feel confined to anything in this book either. Allowing imagination to spur on creativity is what led us to where we are today. Who knows where it might lead you. So, switch up the flavours, change up the decorations, and put your own personal stamp on the desserts in this book. Don't be afraid to make them your own! We can't wait to see where the next few years will take Jenna Rae Cakes, and we are happy that you are now part of that wild ride.

Enjoy!

ashley & jenna xo

HOW TO USE THIS BOOK

TO MAKE THE MOST OF THIS BOOK, we recommend taking time to read and understand all of the helpful tips and tricks we've provided. Our General Baker's Notes (page 15) at the beginning of the book comprise the most helpful tips and tricks that our team of knowledgeable and skilled bakers has to offer. In addition, each section provides Baker's Notes specific to that part of the book, including suggestions for troubleshooting. You can reference these notes as you work through the cookbook—and you might even find tips that help you execute recipes in other books that you've had trouble with. You'll find any recipe-specific Baker's Notes at the bottom of each recipe. Save yourself a lot of time, money, and headaches by flipping to our notes any time you need guidance.

To ensure that you'll have the ingredients needed for successful baking, we've created a section called Stocking Your Fridge & Pantry (page 7), which gives insight into the ingredients we use in our kitchen. It explains why we like some items more than others and also addresses the importance of using quality ingredients to make the most scrumptious desserts. For our recommendations on the basic yet important tools to have readily available in your kitchen, reference Tools & Equipment (page 11), and to master a variety of piping techniques, flip to All About Piping (page 15). From decorating cupcakes to filling cookies to putting the final touches on cakes, this section will be your go-to for learning how to pipe like the pros.

STYLING SWEET TREATS

We know that part of the fun of creating a batch of beautiful baked goods is being able to proudly display them at your next dinner party or event or to share photos of them with friends and family. Here, Ashley shares her top tips for styling your sweet treats so that they're photo ready.

Use Natural Light

I can't recommend this one enough! Ninety-five percent of our photography is shot on my iPhone using natural light. When setting up your photo, make sure you're close to a window to get the best results.

Styling for Social Media

I always have my grid in mind when I'm planning our social media content for the upcoming weeks. I try to balance a busy photo with a simpler one and ensure that two busy photos or two photos with similar backgrounds won't end up stacked on top of each other in the grid. If you want your entire grid to feel harmonious and well branded, you need to plan ahead. Use a post planning app to make your life easier.

How to Use Props

You always want to keep the attention on your sweet treats in a photo. The tendency when styling flat lays (photos you're shooting from above) is to add a bunch of extra "stuff," which can look really beautiful if done right but can also be too much. It's a fine balance! Make sure that whatever you add to your photo to emphasize and complement the food makes sense. Interesting utensils, napkins, or some fresh florals from a centrepiece work well.

Show Off the Beauty of the Food

Does the centre of the macaron you just made ooze with salted caramel goodness? Bite into it to capture an appetizing view that will make everyone who sees it want a bite too. Does a step in the baking process, such as whipping the Meringue Marshmallow Fluff, cutting into a cake for the first time, or spreading frosting on your freshly baked party square, capture something special? Take some photos to give people a behind-the-scenes view of all of the hard work and turn the act of baking into a beautiful piece of art as well. With their vibrant colours and delicate garnishes, it won't take much to make the desserts in this book shine in a photo!

STOCKING YOUR FRIDGE & PANTRY

WONDERING WHICH INGREDIENTS you should always have stocked? Flour, butter, granulated sugar, icing sugar, eggs, high-quality vanilla, and milk will get you pretty far, but there are some other useful ingredients when making our recipes. Generally, using quality ingredients in your baking can make a big difference in the taste, texture, and overall presentation of your baked goods, but that's not always true. Lining the shelves of our kitchen are a combination of ingredients ordered from high-end providers and ingredients from the grocery store that do the trick without any fuss! Here, we let you know when it's important to spend a few extra dollars and when you should just save your money. As much as possible, we recommend using fresh ingredients because everything has an expiration date (just ask anyone who has tried using baking powder or baking soda that has lost its leavening power!). Read through our recommended ingredients and let our tips guide you as you stock your own pantry at home.

FLOUR We use all-purpose flour in a lot of our baking. Over the years, we've tried recipes with different types of flours—even some more expensive varieties—but we find that all-purpose gives the best results. You can use cake flour if it's what you have around (except in our Pâte à Choux, pages 200 and 203), but we do recommend all-purpose flour.

When it comes to recipes that call for almond flour, you may need to do some experimenting. Each variety of almond flour is a little different. We've tried countless brands, and each one yields a slightly different result when making delicate treats like macarons. Factors including how finely the flour is ground, the quality of the almond crop, and the amount of humidity in the air will affect the end product. The brands that work best for us are Mandelin and Treehouse, but there isn't necessarily a superior brand out there, in our opinion. You'll have to do some testing on your own to see what works best for you and the climate where you live. Grocery store brands will work just fine.

Some of our raw dough recipes call for heat-treated flour. Flour is a raw ingredient, and it must be toasted to kill any bacteria before consuming it. To make heat-treated flour, follow the directions below.

HEAT-TREATED FLOUR Preheat the oven to 350°F. Line a baking sheet with parchment paper. Spread the flour in an even layer on the prepared baking sheet. Bake for 10 to 15 minutes, or until the flour starts to turn an ivory colour. Let cool to room temperature and sift. Store in an airtight container at room temperature until ready to use.

BUTTER We use butter made at a local creamery because the freshness of local butter cannot be beat. For most recipes, it is important to soften the butter before using it! When baking, make sure your butter is at room temperature, or slightly warmer, but not melted. In each recipe, we give our recommendation for salted or unsalted butter, but you can adjust the recipe depending on what you have on hand. Just keep in mind that if you use salted butter where we call for unsalted, you should use a touch less salt.

SUGAR Granulated sugar is used in most of our baked goods. Caster sugar (or berry sugar) is a super-fine grind used for meringues, and icing sugar is most commonly used in recipes for buttercream because it helps to achieve a smooth, creamy, sweet flavour and texture.

EGGS Every recipe in this book that calls for eggs requires large eggs. Try to buy local eggs if you can—they're always the freshest. Egg whites, when called for, should be from fresh eggs. Carton egg whites can be used in some cases, like in our Vanilla Cupcakes (page 60), but we don't recommend them for recipes where the egg whites provide stability, like in our Macaron Shells (page 236), Mini Meringues (page 289), and Meringue Marshmallow Fluff (page 300). They just don't work as well as fresh egg whites do to create stiffness. When separating the whites from the yolks, take care to not break the yolks! Any yolk in the whites will prevent them from whipping up, and they won't be as stable. We recommend cracking the full egg into a dish, then using your clean hands to carefully scoop out the egg yolk. This makes for the least amount of breakage. Any extra yolks or whites can be saved in airtight containers in the fridge for a few days—there are so many ways to use them up! Our favourite way to use up egg whites is by making Mini Meringues (page 289), and egg yolks can be used up in our Lemon Curd (page 302) or Mocha Cream Puffs (page 211).

VANILLA We use vanilla bean paste in our butter-creams and in straight-up vanilla baked goods like our Vanilla Cupcakes (page 60). Paste adds beautiful flecks of vanilla to your baking, and you really can't beat the taste. We use the Neilsen-Massey brand. If you don't have vanilla bean paste on hand, substitute an equal amount of pure vanilla extract and scrape out the seeds from one vanilla bean (often available at bulk food stores). If you can't find a vanilla bean to scrape out, an equal amount of pure vanilla extract will work well. High-quality pure vanilla extract is preferred, but it has become quite pricey in recent years. Grocery store brands will taste delicious in our recipes—especially in recipes that have strong flavours, such as birthday cake, cotton candy, and fruit flavours.

MILK We only use whole (3.25%) milk for baking because fat equals flavour. Whatever milk you have in your fridge will work if needed (even milk substitutes like soy milk or other non-dairy milks will do the job), but if you can, use 3.25% cow's milk.

CREAM You cannot substitute anything for heavy cream in a recipe and achieve the same results—especially in our ganaches (pages 298 and 299) and the fillings for our cream puffs!

BAKING POWDER AND BAKING SODA No secrets here. We use the grocery store brands to give our cookies and cakes lift. To test if your baking soda has expired, sprinkle ½ teaspoon baking soda into a small glass with equal parts hot water and vinegar. If it bubbles up and fizzes, it is still good! To test baking powder, sprinkle ½ teaspoon baking powder into a small glass of hot water and look for the same fizzing and bubbling reaction to be sure it's still good to use.

CHOCOLATE Chocolate is an ingredient you do not want to skimp on. Whether milk, dark, or white chocolate, the flavour of high-quality chocolate can't be beat, and it bakes beautifully too. We often use Callebaut Callets and recommend you do as well; it's convenient to use and weigh because you don't need to chop it, but you can chop a high-quality bar of chocolate and get the same results.

COUVERTURE CHOCOLATE When tempering chocolate for our Truffles (pages 285 and 286) and Peanut Caramel Nougat Bites (page 282), we use couverture chocolate. During the production process, it's ground to a finer texture and contains more cocoa butter, which results in a superior flavour, glossy shine, and satisfying snap when you bite into it.

MELTING WAFERS If tempering chocolate is intimidating, you can skip it by using melting wafers (also known as candy wafers and coating chocolate). They're made for dipping, moulding, and coating without the need for tempering. A positive is that they come in plenty of fun colours and flavours, and they're very easy to melt down. A negative is that the cheaper options don't contain a lot of cocoa and can taste a little waxy. We use melting wafers to add a thin, colourful decorative drizzle to some baked goods.

CHOCOLATE CHIPS We use chocolate chips only in recipes where we want the chocolate to hold its shape and texture throughout the baking process, like in our Chocolate Chip Cookie Sandwiches (page 39). We like the small chocolate chips so that you get a good amount in every bite! Chips should not be used when we call for baking chocolate, as they are not the same thing.

COCOA POWDER Quality cocoa powder is the key to fudgy, chocolatey desserts! It is worth it to head to your nearest specialty grocery store to get the good stuff. If you can't find it there, you can always order it online. As with chocolate, we recommend the Callebaut brand.

PEANUT BUTTER We recommend using smooth peanut butter. Take your pick of natural or creamy peanut butter—as long as the texture is smooth, it will be ideal.

OILS Vegetable and canola oils are our preference for the recipes in this book because they are flavourless and easy to find in stores. They are very similar in their texture and flavour, which is why they can be used interchangeably in baking. For cooking spray, we use a canola oil–based spray.

FLAVOURING We believe that flavouring should be used sparingly, and only in cases where another paste or ingredient cannot be made from scratch. It was hard to find good quality flavourings that provided the results we were looking for, so we have had our own all-natural flavourings custom made for our two most popular flavours at the shop—cake batter and cotton candy—and they can be purchased on our website. Our JRC Liquid Cake Batter flavouring gives a nostalgic "lick-the-spatula" flavour to our buttercream and batters, and people with a sweet tooth love it. The secret ingredient in our cotton candy baked goods (pages 40, 68, 103, 146, 221, and 255) is our JRC Liquid Cotton Candy flavouring—trust us when we say that you need to have some of our original flavour on hand if you plan to make a recipe that calls for it! Another flavour essential is peach, to create baked goods that taste like your favourite peach candies. Sour peach candies don't taste like biting into fresh fruit, which is why we use the flavouring oil instead. Wherever you see a flavouring in this book, it's there to serve a purpose.

FOOD COLOURING We love colour at Jenna Rae Cakes, and we believe that you can have vibrantly coloured treats without losing quality flavour and texture. We use AmeriColor Soft Gel Paste because you only need a very small amount to achieve vibrant colour. Our biggest tip when it comes to food colouring is to avoid substituting liquid colouring for gel food colouring—it's simply not the same. If you're looking for more intense colour, use powdered food colouring to avoid adding extra liquid.

FRESH FRUIT VS. FRUIT PURÉES In this book, you'll see that we make our own fruit reductions using either fresh fruit or fruit that has been frozen in its most ripe state. We live in the middle of Canada, and the window for fresh fruit in our province is not large. If you want to save time, we suggest using store-bought fruit purées as a substitute. Boiron and Capfruit are our favourite brands. Just keep in mind that you'll need to reduce and thicken them so you're not adding too much moisture to the recipe.

SOUR CREAM Follow the rule "fat equals flavour" and use full-fat sour cream whenever possible.

NUTS Chopped instead of whole nuts are usually best to purchase, since most of our recipes call to break them down anyway. To get the longest shelf life out of them, store your nuts in the fridge if you're not going to use them right away.

OATS Make sure the oats you buy for baking aren't instant or quick-cooking. Large flake oats work wonderfully for our oatmeal cookies and oat-based crumbles!

SALT Iodized table salt and fine-grind kosher salt will both work well for the recipes in this book. Fine-grind sea salt will also work. No matter what kind of salt you use, be sure to use fine-grind.

SPICES Spices lose their vibrancy if they've been sitting in your cupboard for ages. Make sure that your spices are nice and fresh before using them in our recipes. Our amounts are guidelines, so be sure to taste along the way to adjust the amounts to your preference.

TOOLS & EQUIPMENT

WE'VE STRIPPED DOWN our selection of tools and equipment over the years and now stick to the essentials. We recommend splurging a bit on quality tools—they'll stand the test of time, which means you'll be able to get nice and acquainted with them! Read on for all of our top recommendations.

STAND MIXER You'll need a stand mixer with the paddle and whisk attachments for almost every recipe in this book.

PIPING BAGS AND TIPS Always err on the larger side when purchasing piping bags. It's much easier to manage a piping bag that is half full than a small one that is filled to the brim. We recommend cloth or canvas bags or heavy-duty plastic bags that you can use more than once. For piping tips, we use Wilton. They have a large selection for every purpose.

BAKING SHEETS You'll need 13- × 18-inch baking sheets (also called half sheet pans) that are heavy and rimmed. We suggest you keep two or three on hand. It's always disappointing when you're forced to throw out extra batter because you don't have an extra baking sheet to bake it on. Warped baking sheets will result in warped baked goods, so try to keep them in good condition. If you have only smaller pans available, that's okay. You'll just need to prepare more of them.

CUPCAKE PANS AND CUPCAKE LINERS You'll need to invest in two standard 12-cupcake pans to make the cupcake recipes in our book. We use gold foil cupcake liners in our shop, but any paper or silicone ones will do.

CAKE PANS You'll need two cake pans that are 6 inches in diameter and 3 inches deep to make the cake recipes in this book. At this height, each baked cake will yield two layers. Find cake pans at your local bulk food or craft store.

CAKE SCRAPER A cake scraper is essential for decorating cakes. We recommend purchasing a cake scraper that is taller than one of our standard cakes (about 4 to 5 inches) to help make your buttercream smooth and straight. If you don't want to purchase a specialty scraper, which you will likely need to order online, you can purchase a bench scraper from a cookware or bulk food store instead. Take care to purchase one with a handle that is even with the blade. If the handle sticks out on either side of the blade, you risk not being able to smooth the bottom edge of the cake.

OFFSET SPATULAS Offset spatulas are an important tool for decorating cakes. Large ones are great for applying a single colour of buttercream to a cake, and small ones are best for applying multiple colours, like when you're creating an ombre effect.

SPATULA We recommend investing in at least one heat-resistant spatula. It is a necessity when making candy and caramel, and it can be used in much of your day-to-day cooking as well—like when you're making scrambled eggs for your kids!

THERMOMETERS We regularly use two different kinds of thermometers: a candy thermometer and an oven thermometer. We recommend you invest in a digital candy thermometer because they're efficient and precise, which is especially important when making small batches. Bonus points for getting one that has a clip so that you don't have to hold it over hot candy! Using an oven thermometer will ensure even baking results every time, as every oven is different. Always go with the reading on your oven thermometer rather than the temperature you set your oven to.

PARCHMENT PAPER We use sheets of parchment paper that are cut to fit our baking sheets perfectly. Using parchment paper from a roll works well—just be sure it fits nicely. You can substitute parchment paper with a Silpat mat if you have one.

COOKIE SCOOP If you want to achieve round, uniform cookies, you'll need a cookie scoop. We use a medium scoop (1½ tablespoons).

SCALE A digital kitchen scale that measures to the nearest gram will help you to make macarons that turn out perfect every time. The macaron recipes are the only ones in this book in which we strongly encourage you to weigh the ingredients, and that's because precision is important. A kitchen scale can be purchased at any home store.

FAN BRUSH In this book, fan brushes are used for splattering cakes and for brushing macarons with gold.

KNIVES Paring knives are great for almost everything you'll do while using this book. You'll also need a large serrated knife, more commonly known as a bread knife, to level out cake layers. In our kitchen, we use an 8-inch bread knife. Our party squares and cakes require a chef's knife for clean cuts and can also be used to cut a cake before serving.

ROLLING PIN You'll only need this to roll out the craquelin in this book—you won't find any rolled cookies here—but it will come in handy throughout your baking adventures with pastries, breads, and shaped cookies.

FOOD PROCESSOR No big secrets here! We use ours for chopping nuts and puréeing the crème brûlée filling for our Earl Grey Crème Brûlée Macarons (page 249). Any old food processor will work well.

FINE-MESH SIEVE OR CHINOIS STRAINER We use a fine-mesh sieve for sifting our dry ingredients. A chinois comes to a point and is great for straining fruit purées.

STORAGE CONTAINERS Use food-safe containers with an airtight seal to store your baked goods and any leftover frostings and fillings. You should have large airtight containers on hand that are tall enough to fit decorated cupcakes and other baked goods that need a good seal to preserve freshness. Cakes should be stored in a tall cake box, which can be purchased at most bulk food stores.

GENERAL BAKER'S NOTES

OUR BAKERY IS A PLACE where each baker is valued for the knowledge and skills they bring. This section, as well as the section-specific Baker's Notes throughout the book, is where you'll find the most helpful tips and tricks to guide you through all of our recipes. We've also included recipe-specific tips at the end of each recipe. It's impossible to be overprepared heading into a recipe, especially if it's a complicated one for macarons or cream puffs!

OVENS

Every oven is different. In our kitchens, we use convection ovens. This means that the air is circulated with a fan to help distribute the heat evenly for even and consistent baking no matter where a tray happens to be placed inside the oven. If you don't have a convection oven at home, or if your oven doesn't have a "convection" setting, set your baking temperature 25°F higher than our recipes suggest, or increase the bake time by a couple of minutes at a time.

MISE EN PLACE

Mise en place is a French term that translates to "everything in its place." To prepare your mise en place, set out everything you'll need before you start following the recipe's method. Check that you have all necessary tools and that they are clean and readily available. Make sure that all ingredients are on the counter and that any butter or cream cheese is softened, eggs are separated, nuts are chopped, and so on. Having everything prepared in advance will make the recipes in the book—and any other ones you attempt—flow smoothly. It will also ensure that you don't have to run to the store to get a missing ingredient at a crucial point in the process. Setting your mise en place is a great habit to adopt no matter what you're making in the kitchen.

TIME

Anything new takes time to learn. Even in our kitchen, a new recipe takes some getting used to before it becomes second nature for our bakers. The first time you try any recipe, take time to read through the recipe carefully and reference our Baker's Notes and Baker's Tips if needed. Block off a few hours and make creating one of our treats a sweet afternoon activity, allowing yourself to enjoy the process. Be sure to leave enough time to premeasure the ingredients, for the butter to soften, and for things to chill properly.

ALL ABOUT PIPING

Our tagline says "sweet treats" for a reason! We have a sweet tooth (as do most of our customers), so we use classic American buttercream as the base for so many of our frostings and fillings—and we use it often.

Piping is a wonderful skill you will hone as you decorate cakes with piped touches that will elevate their final look. The range of shapes and effects you can achieve when piping fillings is massive. Some of the techniques used in this book have a practical purpose (piping rings of buttercream for cookie sandwiches creates a well for additional filling to sit in), and some are used purely to create a show-stopping visual effect (piping a crown of buttercream dollops on top of a cake).

But before you start decorating, knowing the best way to use a piping bag is going to be helpful. Below, we share our best practices for filling and holding a piping bag, as well as our best advice for piping perfect swirls and dollops. Refer to these pages whenever you need to pipe something and you'll be off to the races, or follow the instructions below to practise your piping skills with any leftover buttercream.

Filling a Piping Bag

It can be tempting to fill a piping bag to the top. For a piping bag that is easier to hold, squeeze, and control, we recommend using a larger piping bag and filling it halfway so that you don't end up dealing with buttercream or macaron batter seeping out of the top of the bag.

Start by fitting the piping bag with a tip, if needed. Grasp the middle of the piping bag with one hand. Fold the top half of the bag over your hand to open the bag and form a cuff that covers your hand before adding the filling. If it feels awkward filling a piping bag with only one hand, place the bag in a tall glass with the tip at the bottom. Fold the loose edges of the bag over the edges of the glass and use a spatula to scoop the filling into the piping bag.

Once the bag is half full, grab the loose edges and remove it from the glass. Gather the piping bag together just above the filling and give it a twist. Hold the bag over a spare mixing bowl or the bowl of the remaining filling and apply a small amount of pressure to push out any air bubbles before you start decorating. A bit of filling may plop out with the trapped air before it really starts to flow. The filling is now ready to be piped.

Holding a Piping Bag

For the most control when piping, hold the bag toward the top, at the twist, with your non-dominant hand. Use your dominant hand to help guide the bag near the bottom and hold it steady as you pipe.

Applying Pressure

It is important to apply slow, even pressure when piping. Even pressure will create even, professional-looking designs. Try piping your buttercream on a piece of parchment or wax paper for practice. As your piping skills improve, you can apply more pressure and start to move more quickly, but starting slow is the best way to perfect your skills.

Dollops

The technique used to pipe buttercream dollops onto a cake is the same one you will use to fill macarons with dollops of buttercream. The only difference is that you'll want to make sure that any dollops piped onto a cake look more pristine.

To pipe a dollop, hold the piping bag 1 inch above the cake or baked good in a vertical orientation and apply even pressure until a dollop forms. Release the

pressure from the piping bag and quickly pull it straight up to create a point.

Rings

A ring of buttercream is used to fill many cookie sandwiches or macarons that call for an additional filling. The buttercream ring creates a small well in which the second filling can sit.

To pipe a buttercream ring, hold the piping bag with an even pressure and begin to pipe the buttercream in a circular shape. When you reach the starting point, release the pressure from the bag and continue to trace the circle of buttercream, allowing the tail of the buttercream to fall into the ring you have already piped for a smooth finish. The thickness of each buttercream ring will depend on what you are filling—a larger item, like a cookie sandwich, will need a thicker ring to fill it, whereas a macaron will need a thinner ring.

Rosettes

Rosettes are a beautiful way to decorate the crown of a cake or the exterior buttercream. It takes practice to be able to create uniform rosettes, so do a test run on a sheet of parchment paper before piping onto your cake.

To pipe a rosette, move the piping tip in a circle about the size of a quarter while holding the bag with an even pressure. When you've completed the circle, release pressure from the piping bag and continue to move your hand in a circular motion to blend the end tip of buttercream into the rosette.

Nests

We teach our cupcake staff the "nest" technique. It's a style of frosting cupcakes unique to Jenna Rae Cakes and is how Jenna first started decorating her cupcakes.

To make a buttercream nest, pipe buttercream onto each cupcake with an even pressure, starting from the middle and swirling in a circular motion until you round the cupcake twice. Release pressure from the piping bag and pull it away for a clean finish. There should be a small "nest" in the middle of the buttercream. For best results, move your entire arm in a circular motion to create a consistent-looking swirl.

Swirls

We love a good swirl of buttercream on top of a fluffy, moist cupcake! One nice thing about piping buttercream onto cupcakes is that if you are unhappy with how it looks, you can simply use an offset spatula to remove the buttercream and try again!

To create a perfect buttercream swirl, pipe buttercream onto each cupcake with an even pressure, starting at the outer edge and swirling in a circular motion while moving inward until you round the cupcake twice. Release pressure from the piping bag and pull it upward for a clean finish.

COOKIE SANDWICHES

BAKER'S NOTES

From our Kitchen to yours
xo

ONE DAY IN EARLY 2014, when Jenna, Ashley, and their sister Chelsea were working a long shift filling cookies with ice cream, one of them said, "Why don't we fill these with buttercream?" And with that simple question, the JRC Cookie Sandwich was born. Whether Jenna or Chelsea came up with the idea is still up for debate. There are two votes for Chelsea and one vote for Jenna. We'll let you be the judge. Since then, these cookie sandwiches have been on the menu every day, and each staff member has played a part in creating the lineup of delicious and creative flavour combinations.

At first, our cookie sandwiches may appear to have a lot of moving parts—but the extra work is always worth it! Short on time? Our cookies are great on their own, no filling required. Read on to learn our tips and tricks for creating perfectly round and mouth-watering cookies.

SCOOPING AND PRESSING

We use a medium cookie scoop, equal to 1½ tablespoons, to size our cookies. Then we press each cookie to 2½ inches in diameter. Cookies will expand slightly during the baking process but will maintain roughly the same size and shape, so be sure to flatten each cookie the way you'd like it to bake. Adjust the baking time for larger or smaller cookies.

BAKING TIME

"How do you know when a cookie is done?"

"When it's done!"

Vague directions like this are all too common, but if the middle of a cookie looks wet and sunken while it's in the oven, it needs a little more time. When a cookie is baked to chewy perfection, the entire cookie will puff up, and the middle will sink back down when you take it out of the oven while the outside edge remains slightly raised and golden. You know a cookie is overbaked when it is more crispy than chewy and the middle doesn't sink down as it cools.

OVEN

If you find that your cookies always come out looking wet in the middle while the edges are beginning to look dark brown, try lowering the temperature of your oven by 25°F. We suggest always setting your timer for the shortest bake time listed. If the cookies need more time, simply pop them back into the oven until they're just right.

SUBSTITUTIONS

Don't have the ingredients to make a specific filling or garnish? Want to get creative in the kitchen and create your own cookie sandwich flavour? When substituting add-ons, such as sprinkles, Skor bits, or nuts, we recommend maintaining the same quantity.

If you want to use margarine instead of butter when making the cookies, press your cookies to a slightly smaller diameter. Margarine spreads more than butter does during baking.

If you don't have buttermilk at home, make your own by combining the milk of your choice with white vinegar or lemon juice. You should add 1 tablespoon of white vinegar or lemon juice for every 1 cup of milk. Allow the mixture to curdle for 5 minutes before measuring the amount you'll need for the recipe.

COLOURING THE DOUGH

Colouring your cookie dough is a fun way to be creative and customize a cookie for any special occasion. We recommend using gel food colouring. Although liquid colouring can be found in grocery stores, it doesn't give as vibrant a hue. It can also contribute a bad taste and should be counted as additional liquid in the recipe. Gel colour creates beautiful colours without adding extra liquid. A little goes a long way, and often a drop from a toothpick is enough to give an entire batch of dough a vibrant colour that really pops! As with liquid food colouring, too much can leave a bad taste in your mouth, so be mindful of that. We use AmeriColor gel food colouring. The exception to this rule is our red velvet items. You'll need to use liquid food colouring for them because we account for the extra liquid in the recipe.

TROUBLESHOOTING

We find that the most common error with cookie sandwiches is overmixing the dough. If your baked cookies seem to have a tough or cakey texture, there is either too much flour in the dough or the dough has been overmixed. If the dough tastes or feels gummy, it has also probably been overmixed. For best results, mix cookie dough just until it comes together.

If your cookies are spreading too much, there may not be enough flour, or you may have added too much of a flavour ingredient that spreads. For example, adding extra Skor bits may sound like a good idea, but they melt during baking and cause additional spreading.

VANILLA SPRINKLE COOKIE SANDWICHES

SUGAR COOKIES

1¼ cups granulated sugar

½ cup unsalted butter, room temperature

¼ cup buttermilk

1 egg

¾ teaspoon pure vanilla extract

2¼ cups all-purpose flour

¾ teaspoon baking soda

¼ teaspoon salt

½ teaspoon baking powder

3 tablespoons + 2 cups long sprinkles, divided, more for garnish

VANILLA BUTTERCREAM

½ batch (page 296)

A simple yet perfect cookie sandwich for kids' parties or to please a crowd. These cookie sandwiches have a classic vanilla flavour, and the sprinkles add party flair, colour, and an extra crunch. They are so chewy and delicious, you will be tempted to eat them before you get a chance to fill them with buttercream. Stay strong!

SUGAR COOKIES

1. Preheat the oven to 350°F. Line 2 baking sheets with parchment paper.

2. In the bowl of a stand mixer fitted with the paddle attachment, cream the sugar and butter on medium speed for 2 to 3 minutes, until the mixture looks white, light, and fluffy.

3. In a small bowl, whisk together the buttermilk, egg, and vanilla. With the mixer on low speed, slowly pour the buttermilk mixture into the butter mixture and mix until fully incorporated. Scrape the bottom of the bowl with a spatula and mix for an additional 15 to 30 seconds, until combined.

4. Add the flour, baking soda, salt, baking powder, and 3 tablespoons sprinkles to the wet ingredients and mix on low speed until just combined. The dough is fully mixed when it comes together and pulls clean away from the sides of the bowl. If the mixture is dry, add a teaspoon of buttermilk at a time, until you can easily scoop it.

5. Using a medium cookie scoop, scoop the cookies onto the prepared baking sheets 1 to 2 inches apart. Using the base of your palm, flatten the cookies to the desired size and shape. Top each cookie with a pinch of sprinkles.

6. Bake for 5 to 6 minutes, or until the edges of the cookies begin to brown. Let cool on the baking sheets for 5 minutes before transferring them to a wire rack to cool completely.

VANILLA BUTTERCREAM

7. Prepare ½ batch Vanilla Buttercream.

ASSEMBLY

8. Transfer the Vanilla Buttercream to a piping bag fitted with a No. 8B tip. Flip over half of the cookies and pipe the buttercream onto each with an even pressure, starting from the inside of the cookie and swirling outward in a circular motion until the middle of the cookie is completely covered in buttercream. Leave a ½-inch ring of cookie around the exterior edge.

9. Place the remaining cookies, right side up, on top of the buttercream and press down gently to help them stick. The buttercream will spread slightly to the edges of the cookies.

10. Fill a medium bowl with 2 cups sprinkles. Roll the edge of each cookie sandwich in the sprinkles.

11. Place the finished cookie sandwiches in the fridge to chill for easier handling. Store cookie sandwiches in an airtight container in the fridge for up to 4 days.

BAKER'S TIP

If you want to make only a handful of cookie sandwiches for an occasion, freeze the leftover cookies until you're ready to fill them with buttercream.

TOFFEE SALTED CARAMEL COOKIE SANDWICHES

TOFFEE SUGAR COOKIES

1 batch Sugar Cookies
(page 25), without the
long sprinkles
2 tablespoons toffee bits,
more for garnish

SALTED CARAMEL

½ batch (page 299)

**SALTED CARAMEL
BUTTERCREAM**

½ batch Vanilla Buttercream
(page 296)
½ cup Salted Caramel

The cookie sandwich that started it all—our signature Toffee Salted Caramel Cookie Sandwich—is a menu staple available every day at Jenna Rae Cakes (and it's Jenna's personal favourite, too!). The salted caramel makes this cookie pop, adding a touch of saltiness to this delectable sweet treat.

TOFFEE SUGAR COOKIES

1. Prepare 1 batch Sugar Cookies, substituting the long sprinkles for the toffee bits.

SALTED CARAMEL

2. Prepare ½ batch Salted Caramel. Let cool to room temperature.

SALTED CARAMEL BUTTERCREAM

3. Prepare ½ batch Vanilla Buttercream.
4. Add ½ cup Salted Caramel to the buttercream. Whisk on high speed until combined.

ASSEMBLY

5. Transfer the Salted Caramel Buttercream to a piping bag fitted with a No. 8B tip. Flip over half of the cookies and pipe the buttercream onto each with an even pressure, starting from the inside of the cookie and swirling outward in a circular motion until the middle of the cookie is completely covered in buttercream. Leave a ½-inch ring of cookie around the exterior edge.
6. Transfer the remaining Salted Caramel to a piping bag. Cut a small opening in the tip of the bag. Drizzle the caramel in a zigzag pattern across the buttercream.
7. Place the remaining cookies, right side up, on top of the filling and press down gently to help them stick. The buttercream will spread slightly to the edges of the cookies.
8. Place the finished cookie sandwiches in the fridge to chill for easier handling. Store cookie sandwiches in an airtight container in the fridge for up to 4 days.

BAKER'S TIP

Salted Caramel can be made in advance and stored in a sealed container in the fridge for up to 2 weeks. Use it to sweeten your favourite coffee or as a dip for fruit. Trust us, it won't last long!

PEANUT BUTTER MARSHMALLOW COOKIE SANDWICHES

Makes 12 cookie sandwiches

SUGAR COOKIES

1 batch Sugar Cookies
   (page 25) , without the
   long sprinkles
Sequin sprinkles, for garnish

**PEANUT BUTTER
MARSHMALLOW SQUARES**

1 batch (page 307)

**PEANUT BUTTER TOFFEE
BUTTERCREAM**

½ batch Vanilla Buttercream
   (page 296)
½ cup creamy peanut butter
¼ teaspoon toffee flavouring

Toffee flavouring is the secret ingredient added to the peanut butter buttercream that gives every bite of this cookie sandwich the rich flavour of melt-in-your-mouth peanut butter marshmallow squares (PBMS). Use this recipe to transform a dainty tray staple into a cookie sandwich that will leave everyone feeling like they are a kid again! As in all of our PBMS-inspired treats, we have you make a full pan of the squares since we reckon you'll want extras to snack on.

SUGAR COOKIES

1. Prepare 1 batch Sugar Cookies, omitting the long sprinkles. Before baking, sprinkle each cookie with a pinch of sequin sprinkles.

PEANUT BUTTER MARSHMALLOW SQUARES

2. Prepare 1 batch Peanut Butter Marshmallow Squares. Cut into 1- × ½-inch pieces.

PEANUT BUTTER TOFFEE BUTTERCREAM

3. Prepare ½ batch Vanilla Buttercream.

4. Add the peanut butter and toffee flavouring to the buttercream. Whisk on high speed until combined.

ASSEMBLY

5. Transfer the Peanut Butter Toffee Buttercream to a piping bag fitted with a No. 8B tip. Flip over half of the cookies and pipe the buttercream onto each with an even pressure, creating a 1-inch ring. There should be a "hole" in the middle of each ring and a ½-inch ring of cookie around the exterior edge.

6. Place 1 Peanut Butter Marshmallow Square in the middle of each buttercream ring.

7. Place the remaining cookies, right side up, on top of the filling and press down gently to help them stick. The buttercream will spread slightly to the edges of the cookies.

8. Place the finished cookie sandwiches in the fridge to chill for easier handling. Store cookie sandwiches in an airtight container in the fridge for up to 4 days.

BAKER'S TIP

1. Peanut Butter Marshmallow Squares are delicious all on their own! Indulge in leftover squares as bite-size dainties to enjoy. They look great in little paper baking cups, served on a pretty plate.
2. Do you really love peanut butter? Swap out the Sugar Cookies for our Peanut Butter Cookies (page 36) instead!

BROWNIE BATTER
COOKIE SANDWICHES

BROWNIE COOKIES

1½ cups (330 g) chopped
   dark baking chocolate
¼ cup unsalted butter,
   room temperature
2 eggs
2 teaspoons pure vanilla
   extract
1 cup packed brown sugar
1¼ cups all-purpose flour
½ teaspoon baking powder
¼ teaspoon baking soda
½ teaspoon salt
½ cup mini semi-sweet
   chocolate chips
   (see Baker's Tip)

**CHOCOLATE LOVER'S
BUTTERCREAM**

½ batch (page 297)

BROWNIE BATTER

½ batch (page 301)

**DARK CHOCOLATE GANACHE
(OPTIONAL)**

1 batch (page 298)

These Brownie Batter Cookie Sandwiches are for serious chocolate lovers. Each cookie sandwich contains a centre of gooey brownie batter for an extra-satisfying chocolate experience.

BROWNIE COOKIES

1. Preheat the oven to 325°F. Line 2 baking sheets with parchment paper.

2. In a medium heat-resistant bowl, melt the dark chocolate and butter in a microwave in 30-second intervals, stirring after each interval, until smooth.

3. In the bowl of a stand mixer fitted with the whisk attachment, whisk the eggs and vanilla on high speed for 2 minutes, until the mixture has doubled in size. Add the brown sugar and continue to whisk on high for 3 minutes, until the mixture doubles in size again. Reduce the speed to low, slowly pour the melted chocolate mixture into the bowl, and whisk until fully incorporated. Scrape the bottom of the bowl with a spatula and mix for an additional 15 to 30 seconds, until combined. Add the flour, baking powder, baking soda, salt, and chocolate chips. Mix on low speed until just combined. Scrape the bottom of the bowl again and mix for an additional 15 to 30 seconds, until combined.

4. Using a medium cookie scoop, scoop the cookies onto the prepared baking sheets 1 to 2 inches apart. Using the base of your palm, flatten the cookies to the desired size and shape (see Baker's Tip).

5. Bake for 6 to 8 minutes, or until the cookies begin to crack slightly on top. Let cool on the baking sheets for 5 minutes before transferring them to a wire rack to cool completely.

CHOCOLATE LOVER'S BUTTERCREAM

6. Prepare ½ batch Chocolate Lover's Buttercream.

BROWNIE BATTER

7. Prepare ½ batch Brownie Batter.

DARK CHOCOLATE GANACHE

8. Prepare 1 batch Dark Chocolate Ganache, if using.

ASSEMBLY

9. Transfer the Chocolate Lover's Buttercream to a piping bag fitted with a No. 8B tip. Flip over half of the cookies and pipe buttercream onto each with an even pressure, creating a 1-inch ring. There should be a "hole" in the middle of each ring and a ½-inch ring of cookie around the exterior edge.

10. Transfer the Brownie Batter to a piping bag and cut off the tip. Pipe 1 to 2 tablespoons batter into the middle of each buttercream ring.

11. Pour the Dark Chocolate Ganache into a squeeze bottle or piping bag. Heat in the microwave until a pipable consistency is achieved, about 30 seconds. Drizzle the ganache in a zigzag pattern over the filling.

12. Place the remaining cookies, right side up, on top of the filling and press down gently to help them stick. The buttercream will spread slightly to the edges of the cookies.

13. Place the finished cookie sandwiches in the fridge to chill for easier handling. Store cookie sandwiches in an airtight container in the fridge for up to 4 days.

BAKER'S TIP

1. For an extra-decadent treat, try adding ¼ cup mini white chocolate chips to the cookie batter in place of the mini semi-sweet chocolate chips. **2.** If the cookies are tacky after being scooped and are hard to flatten, let them sit for 10 minutes to form a skin before pressing them down.

APPLE CRUMBLE COOKIE SANDWICHES

SUGAR AND SPICE COOKIES

1¼ cups granulated sugar

½ cup unsalted butter, room temperature

2 tablespoons whole (3.25%) milk

1 egg

¾ teaspoon pure vanilla extract

2¼ cups all-purpose flour

½ teaspoon cinnamon, more for garnish

Pinch of ground nutmeg

¾ teaspoon baking soda

½ teaspoon baking powder

¼ teaspoon salt

SALTED CARAMEL

1 batch (page 299)

SALTED CARAMEL BUTTERCREAM

½ batch Vanilla Buttercream (page 296)

½ cup Salted Caramel

APPLE FILLING

½ batch (page 302)

OAT CRUMBLE

⅔ cup all-purpose flour

⅓ cup rolled oats

½ cup packed brown sugar

½ teaspoon cinnamon

Pinch of salt

¼ cup unsalted butter, melted

The perfect fall treat, our customers anticipate this cookie sandwich on our menu every year when the days begin to get chilly and spice is in the air. The homemade apple pie filling is what sets this recipe apart. With a gooey salted caramel drizzle and a buttery oat crumble, this recipe will be hard to beat for the pie lovers in your life.

SUGAR AND SPICE COOKIES

1. Preheat the oven to 350°F. Line 2 baking sheets with parchment paper.

2. In the bowl of a stand mixer fitted with the paddle attachment, cream the sugar and butter on medium speed for 2 to 3 minutes, until the mixture looks white, light, and fluffy.

3. In a small bowl, whisk together the milk, egg, and vanilla. With the mixer on low speed, slowly pour the milk mixture into the butter mixture and mix until fully incorporated. Scrape the bottom of the bowl with a spatula and mix for an additional 15 to 30 seconds, until combined.

4. Add the flour, cinnamon, nutmeg, baking soda, baking powder, and salt to the wet ingredients and mix on low speed until just combined. The dough is fully mixed when it comes together and pulls clean away from the sides of the bowl.

5. Using a medium cookie scoop, scoop the cookies onto the prepared baking sheets 1 to 2 inches apart. Using the base of your palm, flatten the cookies to the desired size and shape. Sprinkle with a light dusting of cinnamon.

6. Bake for 5 to 6 minutes, or until the edges of the cookies begin to brown. Let cool for 5 minutes on the baking sheets before transferring them to a wire rack to cool completely.

SALTED CARAMEL

7. Prepare 1 batch Salted Caramel. Let cool to room temperature.

SALTED CARAMEL BUTTERCREAM

8. Prepare ½ batch Vanilla Buttercream.

9. Add ½ cup Salted Caramel to the buttercream. Whisk on high speed until combined.

APPLE FILLING

10. Prepare ½ batch Apple Filling. Let cool to room temperature.

OAT CRUMBLE

11. Preheat the oven to 350°F. Line a baking sheet with parchment paper.

12. In a medium bowl, stir together the flour, oats, brown sugar, cinnamon, and salt. Pour in the butter and stir until the dry ingredients are evenly coated.

13. Spread the mixture in an even layer on the prepared baking sheet. Bake for 5 minutes. Remove from the oven and stir. Bake for an additional 2 to 4 minutes, until golden brown. Let cool to room temperature before using.

CONTINUED

ASSEMBLY

14. Transfer the Salted Caramel Buttercream to a piping bag fitted with a No. 8B tip. Flip over half of the cookies and pipe the buttercream onto each with an even pressure, creating a 1-inch ring. There should be a "hole" in the middle of each ring and a ½-inch ring of cookie around the exterior edge.

15. Place a heaping tablespoon of Apple Filling in the middle of each buttercream ring. Sprinkle 1 tablespoon Oat Crumble on top.

16. Transfer the remaining Salted Caramel to a piping bag and cut off the tip. Drizzle the caramel in a zigzag pattern over the filling.

17. Place the remaining cookies, right side up, on top of the filling and press down gently to help them stick. The buttercream will spread slightly to the edges of the cookies.

18. Place the finished cookie sandwiches in the fridge to chill for easier handling. Store cookie sandwiches in an airtight container in the fridge for up to 4 days.

BAKER'S TIP

Store leftover Oat Crumble in an airtight container in the freezer for up to 1 month. Use the crumble anytime you want to make these cookie sandwiches. For a delicious breakfast, add any leftover Apple Filling and Oat Crumble to a bowl of oatmeal!

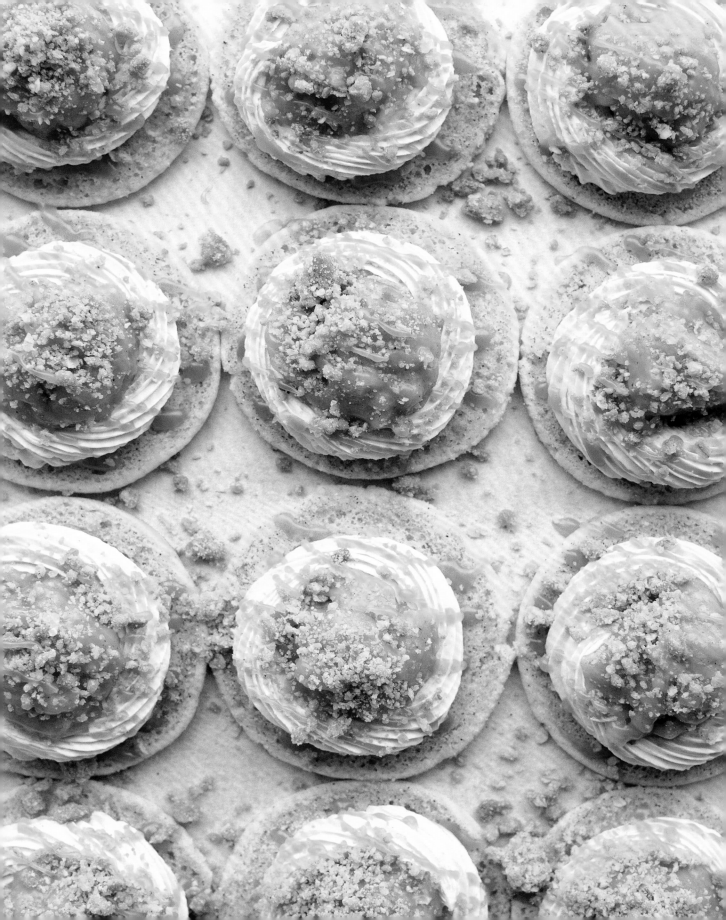

PEANUT BUTTER AND JAM COOKIE SANDWICHES

STRAWBERRY JAM

½ batch (page 304)

PEANUT BUTTER COOKIES

1⅓ cups packed brown sugar
1 cup creamy peanut butter
½ cup unsalted butter, room
    temperature
1 egg
¾ teaspoon pure vanilla
    extract
1½ cups all-purpose flour
1 teaspoon baking soda
Chopped peanuts, for garnish

**PEANUT BUTTER
BUTTERCREAM**

½ batch Vanilla Buttercream
    (page 296)
½ cup creamy peanut butter

Is there a better combination than peanut butter and jelly? With such a clear match made in heaven, it's no surprise that we turned it into a cookie sandwich. The Strawberry Jam in this recipe needs to set overnight. If you're running short on time, use your favourite store-bought jam to fill these cookie sandwiches.

STRAWBERRY JAM

1. Prepare ½ batch Strawberry Jam the day before you plan to assemble the cookie sandwiches.

PEANUT BUTTER COOKIES

2. Preheat the oven to 350°F. Line 2 baking sheets with parchment paper.

3. In the bowl of a stand mixer fitted with the paddle attachment, cream the sugar, peanut butter, and butter on medium speed for 2 to 3 minutes, until the mixture looks light and fluffy. Reduce the speed to low. Slowly add the egg and vanilla and mix until fully incorporated. Scrape the bottom of the bowl with a spatula and mix for an additional 15 to 30 seconds, until combined. Add the flour and baking soda and mix on low speed until just combined.

4. Using a medium cookie scoop, scoop the cookies onto the prepared baking sheets 1 to 2 inches apart. Using the base of your palm, flatten the cookies to the desired size and shape. They will spread a lot while baking, so keep that in mind when shaping them. Sprinkle with the chopped peanuts.

5. Bake for 5 to 6 minutes, or until the edges of the cookies begin to brown. Let cool for 5 minutes on the baking sheets before transferring them to a wire rack to cool completely.

PEANUT BUTTER BUTTERCREAM

6. Prepare ½ batch Vanilla Buttercream.

7. Add ½ cup peanut butter to the buttercream. Whisk on high speed until combined.

ASSEMBLY

8. Transfer the Peanut Butter Buttercream to a piping bag fitted with a No. 8B tip. Flip over half of the cookies and pipe the buttercream onto each with an even pressure, creating a 1-inch ring. There should be a "hole" in the middle of each ring and a ½-inch ring of cookie around the exterior edge.

9. Transfer the Strawberry Jam to a piping bag and cut off the tip. Pipe a generous dollop (1 to 2 tablespoons) of jam into the middle of each buttercream ring.

10. Place the remaining cookies, right side up, on top of the filling and press down gently to help them stick. The buttercream will spread slightly to the edges of the cookies.

11. Place the finished cookie sandwiches in the fridge to chill for easier handling. Store cookie sandwiches in an airtight container in the fridge for up to 4 days.

BAKER'S TIP

1. We call for a ½ batch of Strawberry Jam in this recipe, but you can still make a full batch and spread the leftovers on toast or add to your morning oatmeal! 2. Another popular cookie sandwich we make with our Peanut Butter Cookies is the Peanut Butter Cup Cookie Sandwich. Swap out the Peanut Butter Buttercream for our Chocolate Lover's Buttercream (page 297) and fill the centre with our Peanut Butter Filling (page 64) instead of the jam for a decadent makeover.

CHOCOLATE CHIP COOKIE SANDWICHES

Makes 12 cookie sandwiches

CHOCOLATE CHIP COOKIES

⅓ cup granulated sugar
¾ cup packed brown sugar
¾ cup unsalted butter, room temperature
1 egg
½ teaspoon pure vanilla extract
1 cup mini milk or semi-sweet chocolate chips (see Baker's Tip)
2 cups all-purpose flour
¾ teaspoon salt
¾ teaspoon baking soda

VANILLA BUTTERCREAM

½ batch (page 296)

DARK CHOCOLATE GANACHE (OPTIONAL)

½ batch (page 298)

Who doesn't love chocolate chip cookies? These are the go-to cookies in Ashley's household; flattening the cookies is her son's favourite part of the recipe. Eating this cookie sandwich is like eating an oven-fresh chocolate chip cookie dipped in a refreshing glass of milk. This is what childhood memories are made of. Mini chocolate chips in the cookies allow each bite to be filled with melty chocolatey goodness.

CHOCOLATE CHIP COOKIES

1. Preheat the oven to 350°F. Line 2 baking sheets with parchment paper.
2. In the bowl of a stand mixer fitted with the paddle attachment, cream the granulated sugar, brown sugar, and butter on medium speed for 2 to 3 minutes, until the mixture looks light and fluffy. Reduce the speed to low. Slowly add the egg and vanilla and mix until fully incorporated. Scrape the bottom of the bowl with a spatula, add the chocolate chips, and mix for an additional 15 to 30 seconds, until combined. Add the flour, salt, and baking soda and continue to mix on low speed until just combined.
3. Using a medium cookie scoop, scoop the cookies onto the prepared baking sheets 1 to 2 inches apart. Using the base of your palm, flatten the cookies to the desired size and shape.
4. Bake for 5 to 6 minutes, or until the edges of the cookies begin to brown. Let cool for 5 minutes on the baking sheets before transferring them to a wire rack to cool completely.

VANILLA BUTTERCREAM

5. Prepare ½ batch Vanilla Buttercream.

DARK CHOCOLATE GANACHE

6. Prepare ½ batch Dark Chocolate Ganache, if using.

ASSEMBLY

7. Transfer the Vanilla Buttercream to a piping bag fitted with a No. 8B tip. Flip over half of the cookies and pipe the buttercream onto each with an even pressure, starting from the inside of the cookie and swirling outward in a circular motion until the middle of the cookie is completely covered in buttercream. Leave a ½-inch ring of cookie around the exterior edge.
8. Pour the Dark Chocolate Ganache into a squeeze bottle. Heat in the microwave until a pipable consistency is achieved, about 30 seconds. Drizzle the ganache in a zigzag pattern over the filling.
9. Place the remaining cookies, right side up, on top of the filling and press down gently to help them stick. The buttercream will spread slightly to the edges of the cookies.
10. Place the finished cookie sandwiches in the fridge to chill for easier handling. Store cookie sandwiches in an airtight container in the fridge for up to 4 days.

BAKER'S TIP

Can't decide if you love the taste of milk or semi-sweet chocolate chips more? Try using a combination for a rich flavour experience. Ashley likes these cookies when they're a bit salty, so she sprinkles sea salt on them before baking.

COTTON CANDY COOKIE SANDWICHES

Makes 12 cookie sandwiches

COTTON CANDY SUGAR COOKIES

1 batch Sugar Cookies (page 25, steps 1 to 4), without the pure vanilla extract

¾ teaspoon JRC Liquid Cotton Candy or cotton candy flavouring

1 drop soft pink gel food colouring

1 drop sky blue gel food colouring

COTTON CANDY BUTTERCREAM

½ batch Vanilla Buttercream (page 296)

2 teaspoons JRC Liquid Cotton Candy or cotton candy flavouring

1 drop soft pink gel food colouring

1 drop sky blue gel food colouring

Cotton candy has become an iconic flavour at Jenna Rae Cakes. It took us a while to find the perfect flavour, but it was worth it: people line up and plan their trips to our locations on days when the menu calls for anything that has "cotton candy" in the name. These cookie sandwiches are a pastel-coloured dream and are as delicious as they are beautiful.

COTTON CANDY SUGAR COOKIES

1. Prepare 1 batch Sugar Cookies, following steps 1 to 4 of the recipe on page 25, substituting the cotton candy flavouring for the vanilla extract in step 3.

2. Divide the cookie dough evenly between 2 medium bowls. To one bowl, add the soft pink food colouring with a toothpick and knead the colour into the dough using your hands, until it is mostly pink. To the other bowl, add the sky blue food colouring with a toothpick and knead the colour into the dough, until it is mostly blue. Place the pink dough and the blue dough into a medium bowl and mix by hand, until the colours are swirled together, being careful not to overmix.

3. Using a medium cookie scoop, scoop the cookies onto the prepared baking sheets 1 to 2 inches apart. Using the base of your palm, flatten the cookies to the desired size and shape.

4. Bake for 5 to 6 minutes, or until the edges of the cookies begin to brown. Let cool on the baking sheets for 5 minutes before transferring them to a wire rack to cool completely.

COTTON CANDY BUTTERCREAM

5. Prepare ½ batch Vanilla buttercream.

6. Add the cotton candy flavouring to the buttercream. Whisk on high speed until combined.

7. Divide the buttercream evenly between 2 medium bowls. To one bowl, add the soft pink food colouring and mix with a spatula until the colour is uniform. To the other bowl, add the sky blue food colouring and mix with a spatula until the colour is uniform.

ASSEMBLY

8. Transfer the Cotton Candy Buttercream to a piping bag fitted with a No. 8B tip by adding small scoops to the bag, alternating between the pink and blue buttercream (see Baker's Tip). Flip over half of the cookies and pipe the buttercream onto each with an even pressure, starting from the inside of the cookie and swirling outward in a circular motion until the middle of the cookie is completely covered in buttercream. Leave a ½-inch ring of cookie around the exterior edge.

9. Place the remaining cookies, right side up, on top of the buttercream and press down gently to help them stick. The buttercream will spread slightly to the edges of the cookies.

10. Place the finished cookie sandwiches in the fridge to chill for easier handling. Store cookie sandwiches in an airtight container in the fridge for up to 4 days.

BAKER'S TIP

Achieving swirled buttercream can take time and practice. Alternating scoops of pink and blue buttercream when filling the piping bag will ensure that the colours stay separate. Only fill about a quarter of the piping bag at a time to prevent the colours from combining as you put pressure on the piping bag.

S'MORES COOKIE SANDWICHES

Makes 12 cookie sandwiches

GRAHAM CRACKER COOKIES

1¼ cups packed brown sugar
½ cup unsalted butter, room temperature
2 tablespoons whole (3.25%) milk
1 egg
1 teaspoon fancy molasses
¾ teaspoon pure vanilla extract
1½ cups whole wheat flour
¾ cup all-purpose flour
¾ teaspoon baking soda
¼ teaspoon salt
½ teaspoon baking powder
⅛ teaspoon cinnamon

MILK CHOCOLATE BUTTERCREAM

½ batch (page 296)

MERINGUE MARSHMALLOW FLUFF

½ batch (page 300) or 2 (7.5-ounce) jars store-bought marshmallow spread

MILK CHOCOLATE GANACHE (OPTIONAL)

1 batch (page 298)

Truly a labour of love that is worth every moment, our S'mores Cookie Sandwiches are one of the more involved treats on our menu, with a number of homemade elements. Trust us: one bite into these cookie sandwiches and you'll find they were well worth the effort you put in for that gooey toasted marshmallow, milk chocolate drizzle, and graham flavour that bring the campfire anywhere you go.

GRAHAM CRACKER COOKIES

1. Preheat the oven to 350°F. Line 2 baking sheets with parchment paper.
2. In the bowl of a stand mixer fitted with the paddle attachment, cream the sugar and butter on medium speed for 2 to 3 minutes, until the mixture looks light and fluffy.
3. In a medium bowl, mix the milk, egg, molasses, and vanilla. With the mixer on low speed, slowly add the milk mixture to the butter mixture and mix until fully incorporated. Scrape the bottom of the bowl with a spatula and mix for an additional 15 to 30 seconds, until combined.
4. Add the whole wheat flour, all-purpose flour, baking soda, salt, baking powder, and cinnamon to the wet ingredients. Mix on low speed until just combined.
5. Using a medium cookie scoop, scoop the cookies onto the prepared baking sheets 1 to 2 inches apart. Using the base of your palm, flatten the cookies to the desired size and shape. Use a fork to poke 2 or 3 rows of holes in each one.
6. Bake for 5 to 6 minutes, or until the edges of the cookies begin to brown. Let cool for 5 minutes on the baking sheets before transferring them to a wire rack to cool completely.

MILK CHOCOLATE BUTTERCREAM

7. Prepare ½ batch Milk Chocolate Buttercream.

MERINGUE MARSHMALLOW FLUFF

8. Prepare ½ batch Meringue Marshmallow Fluff. Let cool to room temperature.

MILK CHOCOLATE GANACHE

9. Prepare 1 batch Milk Chocolate Ganache, if using.

ASSEMBLY

10. Transfer the Milk Chocolate Buttercream to a piping bag fitted with a No. 8B tip. Flip over half of the cookies and pipe the buttercream onto each with an even pressure, creating a 1-inch ring. There should be a "hole" in the middle of each ring and a ½-inch ring of cookie around the exterior edge.
11. Transfer the Meringue Marshmallow Fluff to a piping bag and cut off the tip. Pipe a generous dollop (1 to 2 tablespoons) of fluff into the middle of each buttercream ring. Using a handheld torch on the low setting, toast the fluff.
12. Pour the Milk Chocolate Ganache into a squeeze bottle. Heat in the microwave until a pipable consistency is achieved, about 30 seconds. Drizzle the ganache in a zigzag pattern over the filling.
13. Place the remaining cookies, right side up, on top of the filling and press down gently to help them stick. The buttercream will spread slightly to the edges of the cookies.
14. Place the finished cookie sandwiches in the fridge to chill for easier handling. Store cookie sandwiches in an airtight container in the fridge for up to 4 days.

BAKER'S TIP

1. Instead of using Milk Chocolate Ganache, try drizzling your cookie sandwiches with Salted Caramel (page 299) to give them an added touch of salt. 2. If you have any leftover marshmallow fluff, we love spreading it on toast or using it as a dip for fresh fruit.

LEMON MERINGUE COOKIE SANDWICHES

Makes 12 cookie sandwiches

LEMON SUGAR COOKIES

1¼ cups granulated sugar
½ cup unsalted butter
1 tablespoon buttermilk
2 tablespoons fresh
  lemon juice
1 egg
¾ teaspoon pure vanilla
  extract
1 drop yellow gel food
  colouring
2¼ cups all-purpose flour
Zest from 2 lemons (about
  2 tablespoons)
¾ teaspoon baking soda
½ teaspoon baking powder
¼ teaspoon salt
Round white sprinkles,
  for garnish

MERINGUE MARSHMALLOW FLUFF

½ batch (page 300)

LEMON CURD

½ batch (page 302)

Inspired by Jenna's favourite pie, these cookie sandwiches have a generous filling of tangy lemon curd surrounded by toasted meringue fluff. They are the perfect treat for a summer BBQ! The lemon curd filling can be prepared in advance and stored in the fridge for a few days before you're ready to use it.

LEMON SUGAR COOKIES

1. Preheat the oven to 350°F. Line 2 baking sheets with parchment paper.
2. In the bowl of a stand mixer fitted with the paddle attachment, cream the sugar and butter on medium speed for 2 to 3 minutes, until the mixture looks white, light, and fluffy.
3. In a small bowl, mix the buttermilk, lemon juice, egg, vanilla, and food colouring. With the mixer on low speed, slowly pour the buttermilk mixture into the butter mixture and mix until fully incorporated. Scrape the bottom of the bowl with a spatula and mix for an additional 15 to 30 seconds, until combined.
4. In a medium bowl, mix the flour and lemon zest. Use your hands to coat the lemon zest with flour to ensure that there are no chunks. Add the flour mixture, baking soda, baking powder, and salt to the wet ingredients and mix on low speed until just combined. The dough is fully mixed when it comes together and pulls clean away from the sides of the mixing bowl. If the mixture is dry, add a teaspoon of buttermilk at a time, until you can easily scoop it.
5. Using a medium cookie scoop, scoop the cookies onto the prepared baking sheets 1 to 2 inches apart. Using the base of your palm, flatten the cookies to the desired size and shape. Top with the sprinkles.
6. Bake for 5 to 6 minutes, or until the edges of the cookies begin to brown. Let cool for 5 minutes on the baking sheets before transferring them to a wire rack to cool completely.

MERINGUE MARSHMALLOW FLUFF

7. Prepare ½ batch Meringue Marshmallow Fluff.

LEMON CURD

8. Prepare ½ batch Lemon Curd. Transfer to an airtight container and store in the fridge for up to 1 week until ready to use.

ASSEMBLY

9. Transfer the Meringue Marshmallow Fluff to a piping bag fitted with a No. 8B tip. Flip over half of the cookies and pipe the fluff onto each with an even pressure, creating a 1-inch ring. There should be a "hole" in the middle of each ring and a ½-inch ring of cookie around the exterior edge.
10. Transfer the Lemon Curd to a piping bag and cut off the tip. Pipe a generous dollop (1 to 2 tablespoons) into the middle of each fluff ring.
11. Place the remaining cookies, right side up, on top of the filling and press down gently to help them stick. The fluff will spread slightly to the edges of the cookies. Using a handheld torch, toast the edges of the fluff, being careful not to burn the cookies.
12. Place the finished cookie sandwiches in the fridge to chill for easier handling. Store cookie sandwiches in an airtight container in the fridge for up to 4 days.

BAKER'S TIP

To create mini lemon meringue pies, fill homemade or store-bought tart shells with lemon curd and top with meringue fluff. Use a handheld torch to toast the meringue.

STRAWBERRY SHORTCAKE COOKIE SANDWICHES

This take on a classic strawberry shortcake is a delightful treat packed full of strawberry flavour with a pretty pink colour palette. The chewy shortbread cookies sandwich fresh-tasting strawberry buttercream, then the whole thing is rolled in pastel pink shortbread crumble for extra texture and colour.

SHORTBREAD COOKIES

1 cup unsalted butter, room temperature
½ cup vegetable oil
½ teaspoon pure vanilla extract
1½ cups icing sugar
3 cups all-purpose flour
2 tablespoons cornstarch
½ teaspoon salt

STRAWBERRY BUTTERCREAM

½ batch Vanilla Buttercream (page 296)
½ batch Strawberry Compote (page 303)

SHORTBREAD CRUMBLE

1 batch (page 305)

SHORTBREAD COOKIES

1. Preheat the oven to 350°F. Line 2 baking sheets with parchment paper.

2. In the bowl of a stand mixer fitted with the paddle attachment, cream the butter on high speed for 3 minutes, scraping down the bowl and paddle every 45 seconds. Reduce the speed to low and slowly pour in the vegetable oil and vanilla. Scrape the sides of the bowl, increase the speed to high, and cream for an additional 2 minutes. Add the icing sugar, and cream on medium speed for 2 to 3 minutes, until the mixture looks light and fluffy. Scrape the bottom of the bowl with a spatula and mix for an additional 15 to 30 seconds, until combined. Add the flour, cornstarch, and salt and mix on low speed until just combined. The dough should be crumbly. Do not overmix.

3. Using a medium cookie scoop, scoop the cookies onto the prepared baking sheets 1 to 2 inches apart. Using the base of your palm, flatten the cookies to the desired size and shape.

4. Bake for 5 to 6 minutes, or until the cookies begin to look puffed and the edges are still white (see Baker's Tip). Let cool for 5 minutes on the baking sheets before transferring them to a wire rack to cool completely.

STRAWBERRY BUTTERCREAM

5. Prepare ½ batch Vanilla Buttercream.

6. Prepare ½ batch Strawberry Compote.

7. Add the compote to the buttercream. Whisk on medium speed until well combined.

SHORTBREAD CRUMBLE

8. Prepare 1 batch Shortbread Crumble, making sure to add the electric pink gel food colouring. Set aside to cool.

ASSEMBLY

9. Transfer the Strawberry Buttercream to a piping bag fitted with a No. 8B tip. Flip over half of the cookies and pipe the buttercream onto each with an even pressure, starting from the inside of the cookie and swirling outward in a circular motion until the middle of the cookie is completely covered in buttercream. Leave a ½-inch ring of cookie around the exterior edge.

10. Place the remaining cookies, right side up, on top of the buttercream and press down gently to help them stick. The buttercream will spread slightly to the edges of the cookies.

11. Place the Shortbread Crumble on a medium plate. Roll the edge of each cookie sandwich in the crumble until the buttercream is completely covered.

12. Place the finished cookie sandwiches in the fridge to chill for easier handling. Store cookie sandwiches in an airtight container in the fridge for up to 4 days.

BAKER'S TIP

When baking shortbread cookies, you don't want them to brown along the edges. If they start to brown, they have been in the oven for too long and will become dry and crumbly. These cookies are Jenna and Ashley's favourite by themselves—it's impossible not to steal one or two right out of the oven!

MONSTER OATMEAL COOKIE SANDWICHES

MONSTER OATMEAL COOKIES

⅔ cup creamy peanut butter

¼ cup packed brown sugar

⅓ cup granulated sugar

⅓ cup unsalted butter, room temperature

1 egg

2 tablespoons whole (3.25%) milk

1¼ cups large flake oats

½ cup all-purpose flour

1 teaspoon baking soda

½ cup mini Smarties (or mini M&Ms), more for garnish

¼ cup sultana raisins

¼ cup chopped peanuts

¼ cup mini semi-sweet chocolate chips

VANILLA BUTTERCREAM

½ batch (page 296)

DARK CHOCOLATE GANACHE (OPTIONAL)

1 batch (page 298)

There's something for everyone in a monster cookie. This is our mom's recipe, and it's one of the first cookies we learned to bake when we were kids. Filled with oats, chocolate chips, creamy peanut butter, raisins, Smarties, and peanuts, these cookie sandwiches are a delicious combination of salty and sweet and hold a dear place in our hearts.

MONSTER OATMEAL COOKIES

1. Preheat the oven to 350°F. Line 2 baking sheets with parchment paper.

2. In the bowl of a stand mixer fitted with the paddle attachment, cream the peanut butter, brown sugar, granulated sugar, and butter on medium speed for 2 to 3 minutes, until the mixture looks light and fluffy. Reduce the speed to low, add the egg and milk, and mix until fully incorporated. Scrape the bottom of the bowl with a spatula and mix for an additional 15 to 30 seconds, until combined. Add the oats, flour, baking soda, Smarties, raisins, peanuts, and chocolate chips and continue to mix on low speed until just combined.

3. Using a medium cookie scoop, scoop the cookies onto the prepared baking sheets 1 to 2 inches apart. Using the base of your palm, flatten the cookies to the desired size and shape. Gently press 5 to 6 Smarties into the top of each cookie.

4. Bake for 5 to 6 minutes, or until the edges of the cookies begin to brown. Let cool for 5 minutes on the baking sheets before transferring them to a wire rack to cool completely.

VANILLA BUTTERCREAM

5. Prepare ½ batch Vanilla Buttercream.

DARK CHOCOLATE GANACHE

6. Prepare 1 batch Dark Chocolate Ganache.

ASSEMBLY

7. Transfer the Vanilla Buttercream to a piping bag fitted with a No. 8B tip. Flip over half of the cookies and pipe the buttercream onto each with an even pressure, starting from the inside of the cookie and swirling outward in a circular motion until the middle of the cookie is completely covered in buttercream. Leave a ½-inch ring of cookie around the exterior edge.

8. Pour the Dark Chocolate Ganache into a squeeze bottle. Heat in the microwave until a pipable consistency is achieved, about 30 seconds. Drizzle the ganache in a zigzag pattern over the buttercream.

9. Place the remaining cookies, right side up, on top of the filling and press down gently to help them stick. The buttercream will spread slightly to the edges of the cookies.

10. Place the finished cookie sandwiches in the fridge to chill for easier handling. Store cookie sandwiches in an airtight container in the fridge for up to 4 days.

BAKER'S TIP

Our mom made Monster Oatmeal Cookies for us all the time as kids. Her best piece of advice: "Be sure not to overbake these cookies or the Smarties will crack!"

RED VELVET
COOKIE SANDWICHES

Makes 12 cookie sandwiches

RED VELVET COOKIES

1⅓ cups granulated sugar
⅓ cup unsalted butter,
    room temperature
¼ cup buttermilk
1 tablespoon red liquid
    food colouring
1¼ teaspoons pure vanilla
    extract
1¼ teaspoons apple cider
    vinegar
1 egg
2½ cups all-purpose flour
2 tablespoons cocoa powder,
    sifted
1¼ teaspoons cornstarch
½ teaspoon baking soda
¼ teaspoon salt

**CREAM CHEESE
BUTTERCREAM**

½ batch (page 297)

Perfect for your sweetheart on Valentine's Day, our Red Velvet Cookie Sandwiches are a modern take on the classic cake. Not a fan of cream cheese frosting? Swap it out for vanilla or milk chocolate buttercream for an equally tasty treat.

RED VELVET COOKIES

1. Preheat the oven to 350°F. Line 2 baking sheets with parchment paper.

2. In the bowl of a stand mixer fitted with the paddle attachment, cream the sugar and butter on medium speed for 2 to 3 minutes, until the mixture looks white, light, and fluffy.

3. In a medium bowl, whisk together the buttermilk, food colouring, vanilla, apple cider vinegar, and egg. Slowly pour the buttermilk mixture into the butter mixture and mix on low speed until fully incorporated. Scrape the bottom of the bowl with a spatula and mix for an additional 15 to 30 seconds, until combined.

4. Add the flour, cocoa powder, cornstarch, baking soda, and salt to the wet ingredients. Mix on low speed until just combined. Scrape the bottom of the bowl again and mix for an additional 15 to 30 seconds, until combined.

5. Using a medium cookie scoop, scoop the cookies onto the prepared baking sheets 1 to 2 inches apart. Using the base of your palm, flatten the cookies to the desired size and shape. They will spread a lot while baking, so you may want to press them to a slightly smaller size.

6. Bake for 5 to 6 minutes, or until the edges of the cookies begin to brown. Let cool for 5 minutes on the baking sheet before transferring them to a wire rack to cool completely.

CREAM CHEESE BUTTERCREAM

7. Prepare ½ batch Cream Cheese Buttercream.

ASSEMBLY

8. Transfer the Cream Cheese Buttercream to a piping bag fitted with a No. 8B tip. Flip over half of the cookies and pipe the buttercream onto each with an even pressure, starting from the inside of the cookie and swirling outward in a circular motion until the middle of the cookie is completely covered in buttercream. Leave a ½-inch ring of cookie around the exterior edge.

9. Place the remaining cookies, right side up, on top of the buttercream and press down gently to help them stick. The buttercream will spread slightly to the edges of the cookies.

10. Place the finished cookie sandwiches in the fridge to chill for easier handling. Store cookie sandwiches in an airtight container in the fridge for up to 4 days.

BAKER'S TIP

To make these cookies Christmas ready, simply add a drop of green gel food colouring to the Cream Cheese Buttercream when whipping. You can also top the Red Velvet Cookies with red and green sprinkles before baking for an extra festive touch!

COOKIE DOUGH BROWNIE COOKIE SANDWICHES

Makes 12 cookie sandwiches

BROWNIE COOKIES

1 batch (page 30, steps
   1 to 4), without the
   chocolate chips
Chocolate sprinkles, for
   garnish

VANILLA BUTTERCREAM

½ batch (page 296)
2 drops ivory gel food
   colouring

COOKIE DOUGH

½ batch (page 301)

If you're like us, you probably can't resist eating at least a little bit of cookie dough before you pop your cookies in the oven. These Cookie Dough Brownie Cookie Sandwiches are filled with cookie dough, making them the stuff your childhood dreams were made of.

BROWNIE COOKIES

1. Prepare 1 batch Brownie Cookies, following steps 1 to 4 of the recipe on page 30, omitting the chocolate chips in step 3.
2. Top each cookie with a pinch of chocolate sprinkles.
3. Bake for 5 to 6 minutes, or until the cookies begin to crack slightly on top. Let cool for 5 minutes on the baking sheets before transferring them to a wire rack to cool completely.

VANILLA BUTTERCREAM

4. Prepare ½ batch Vanilla Buttercream.
5. Add the food colouring to the buttercream. Whisk for 1 minute on high speed, until fully incorporated.

COOKIE DOUGH

6. Prepare ½ batch Cookie Dough.

ASSEMBLY

7. Transfer the Vanilla Buttercream to a piping bag fitted with a No. 8B tip. Flip over half of the cookies and pipe the buttercream onto each with an even pressure, creating a 1-inch ring. There should be a "hole" in the middle of each ring and a ½-inch ring of cookie around the exterior edge.
8. Scoop 1 to 2 tablespoons Cookie Dough into the middle of each buttercream ring.
9. Place the remaining cookies, right side up, on top of the filling and press down gently to help them stick. The buttercream will spread slightly to the edges of the cookies.
10. Place the finished cookie sandwiches in the fridge to chill for easier handling. Store cookie sandwiches in an airtight container in the fridge for up to 4 days.

BAKER'S TIP

1. Store any extra Cookie Dough in an airtight container in the fridge for up to 4 days. We won't judge you if you eat it with a spoon! **2.** If you want to double up on the chocolate chip cookie dough experience, swap out the Brownie Cookies for our Chocolate Chip Cookies (page 39).

OATMEAL PIE
COOKIE SANDWICHES

Makes 12 cookie sandwiches

OATMEAL COOKIES

½ cup granulated sugar

½ cup packed brown sugar

⅓ cup unsalted butter, room temperature

2 tablespoons whole (3.25%) milk

1 egg

1½ teaspoons pure vanilla extract

1½ cups all-purpose flour

1 cup large flake oats

1½ teaspoons cinnamon

½ teaspoon baking soda

¼ teaspoon salt

⅛ teaspoon ground cloves

½ cup sultana raisins (optional, see Baker's Tip)

VANILLA BUTTERCREAM

½ batch (page 296)

If you ask us, oatmeal cookies don't get as much attention as they deserve. We love soft, chewy oatmeal cookies that are lightly spiced with cinnamon and cloves and made extra sweet with some raisins. There's something comforting about these simple yet classic flavours that make you feel like you're at grandma's house. Simple and flavourful, these cookies will be a crowd pleaser for those young and old.

OATMEAL COOKIES

1. Preheat the oven to 350°F. Line 2 baking sheets with parchment paper.

2. In the bowl of a stand mixer fitted with the paddle attachment, cream the granulated sugar, brown sugar, and butter on medium speed for 2 to 3 minutes, until the mixture looks light and fluffy.

3. In a small bowl, whisk together the milk, egg, and vanilla. With the mixer on low speed, slowly pour the milk mixture into the butter mixture and mix until fully incorporated. Scrape the bottom of the bowl with a spatula and mix for an additional 15 to 30 seconds, until combined.

4. Add the flour, oats, cinnamon, baking soda, salt, cloves, and raisins, if using, to the wet ingredients and mix on low speed until just combined. The dough is fully mixed once all of the dry ingredients have been incorporated.

5. Using a medium cookie scoop, scoop the cookies onto the prepared baking sheets 1 to 2 inches apart. Using the base of your palm, flatten the cookies to the desired size and shape.

6. Bake for 5 to 6 minutes, or until the edges of the cookies begin to brown. Let cool for 5 minutes on the baking sheets before transferring them to a wire rack to cool completely.

VANILLA BUTTERCREAM

7. Prepare ½ batch Vanilla Buttercream.

ASSEMBLY

8. Transfer the Vanilla Buttercream to a piping bag fitted with a No. 8B tip. Flip over half of the cookies and pipe the buttercream onto each with an even pressure, starting from the inside of the cookie and swirling outward in a circular motion until the middle of the cookie is completely covered in buttercream. Leave a ½-inch ring of cookie around the exterior edge.

9. Place the remaining cookies, right side up, on top of the buttercream and press down gently to help them stick. The buttercream will spread slightly to the edges of the cookies.

10. Place the finished cookie sandwiches in the fridge to chill for easier handling. Store cookie sandwiches in an airtight container in the fridge for up to 4 days.

BAKER'S TIP

If you aren't a fan of raisins but are looking for a little something extra to add to your oatmeal cookies, try replacing the raisins with an equal amount of shredded coconut or chocolate chips.

CUPCAKES

BAKER'S
NOTES

From our
Kitchen to yours
xo

WHEN JENNA RAE CAKES first opened its doors, we can clearly recall people being amazed by our cupcakes. With the additions of fillings, crusts, and various homemade toppings, a Jenna Rae Cakes cupcake isn't your average cupcake; it's truly a special treat that could easily replace a cake for a special occasion.

A go-to cupcake recipe is important for every baker. Our cupcakes appear to have a lot going on—many are stuffed with flavourful fillings, topped with light and fluffy buttercream, and decorated with drizzles of salted caramel, dollops of colourful ganache, sprinkles, glitter, gold leaf flakes, and sometimes bite-size treats—but the foundation of each one is a tried-and-true cupcake recipe. We spent a lot of time tweaking our recipes until we settled on the ones you'll find in this section.

Taking time to adequately prepare your mise en place (see page 15) will really help you succeed when making cupcakes. Allowing adequate time for baking and decorating cupcakes will ensure that you don't feel rushed. Read on to learn all of our tips and tricks so that you can recreate our perfectly moist and heavenly cupcakes at home.

SCOOPING

A standard-size cupcake scoop (1.3 ounces) will be very useful in making cupcakes that are the same size. Run the entire top of your scoop against the edge of your bowl so that each and every portion of batter is nice and even. Be sure not to fill cupcake liners more than three-quarters full, including any crust you may be required to make, or the batter will spill over the liner while baking.

BAKING TIME

One of the keys to a moist cupcake is to not overbake it. When baking your cupcakes, leave them in the oven for about 15 to 18 minutes, then insert a toothpick in the middle of a cupcake to check if it is done. When it's ready, a toothpick inserted in the middle will come out clean, or with just a few crumbs on it, and the top will bounce back when touched with the tip of your finger. You can also look for lightly browned edges and a well-defined, puffed-up shape.

If you decide to make mini cupcakes, or if you have a giant cupcake pan you'd like to use instead, note that you will need to adjust your baking time. Mini cupcakes can be baked for around 8 minutes, and larger ones will need 20-plus minutes.

OVEN TIPS

If you find that your cupcakes look wet in the middle while the edges are beginning to turn dark brown, try lowering the temperature of your oven by 25°F.

SUBSTITUTIONS

We've tweaked our recipes for years before finding the ones that produce consistent, moist, and universally crowd-pleasing cupcakes. For best results, we recommend sticking to the recipe, but if you don't have sour cream on hand, you can substitute an equal amount of plain full-fat yogurt. Using sour cream is one way to keep your cupcakes extra moist.

We encourage creativity in the kitchen. If you want to pair one of our cupcake base flavours with a different buttercream flavour, go ahead! We want you to feel empowered to make any cupcake you dream up a reality.

DECORATING

A Jenna Rae Cakes cupcake is quite the display of decadence. Many recipes will encourage you to decorate with specific sprinkles if you want to mimic our design, but you always have the option to decorate with your favourite combinations. Head to your local bulk food store or craft supply store and pick up some sprinkles you've always wanted to try and incorporate them into your next cupcake—let your creativity shine! Adding your own artistry will take your cupcakes to the next level and will be sure to impress every crowd.

TROUBLESHOOTING

We find that the most common error with cupcakes is simply overmixing. Our recipes for Vanilla Cupcakes (page 60) and Red Velvet Cupcakes (page 87) are meant to be slightly lumpy. If you overmix the batter, they just won't turn out the same.

Always take extra care to scrape down the sides of the bowl to incorporate any ingredients that may have stuck to the sides.

VANILLA CUPCAKES

VANILLA CUPCAKES

1 ¾ cups all-purpose flour

1 cup granulated sugar

1 teaspoon baking powder

¼ teaspoon baking soda

¼ teaspoon salt

¾ cup unsalted butter, room
  temperature, cut into cubes

⅓ cup egg whites (about
  2 eggs)

¼ cup sour cream

½ cup whole (3.25%) milk

1 tablespoon pure vanilla
  extract (see Baker's Tip)

VANILLA BUTTERCREAM

1 batch (page 296)

1 to 2 drops soft pink gel
  food colouring

Finding a good recipe for vanilla cupcakes can be like finding a needle in a haystack. The cupcakes need to be moist and flavourful, and the buttercream needs to be sweet—but not so sweet that it overpowers the vanilla flavour of the cupcake. Welcome to your new favourite vanilla cupcake recipe. Make these once and every person who takes a bite will be asking you to share the recipe with them.

VANILLA CUPCAKES

1. Preheat the oven to 350°F. Line 2 cupcake pans with 16 cupcake liners.

2. In the bowl of a stand mixer fitted with the paddle attachment, combine the flour, sugar, baking powder, baking soda, and salt. Mix on low speed for 30 seconds. Add the butter and continue to mix on low speed for 2 minutes, or until the mixture has the texture of wet sand. Do not overmix. Slowly pour in the egg whites and mix until just combined. Scrape down the sides of the bowl. Add the sour cream and mix until just combined.

3. In a measuring cup, whisk together the milk and vanilla. With the mixer on low speed, slowly pour the milk mixture into the bowl and mix until just combined. Scrape down the sides of the bowl and mix again for 10 to 15 seconds. The batter will look a little lumpy.

4. Divide the batter evenly among the cupcake liners, filling each three-quarters full. Bake for 15 to 18 minutes, or until a toothpick inserted in the middle of a cupcake comes out clean. Let cool for 5 minutes in the pans before transferring the cupcakes to a wire rack to cool completely.

VANILLA BUTTERCREAM

5. Prepare 1 batch Vanilla Buttercream.

6. Add the food colouring to the buttercream. Whisk on high speed until well combined.

ASSEMBLY

7. Transfer the Vanilla Buttercream to a piping bag fitted with a No. 8B tip. Pipe the buttercream onto each cupcake with an even pressure, starting from the middle and swirling in a circular motion until you round the cupcake twice. Release pressure from the piping bag and pull it away for a clean finish.

8. For maximum freshness and deliciousness, serve cupcakes on the day they are made. If you want to bake the cupcakes a day in advance, store the baked, undecorated cupcakes in an airtight container at room temperature until ready to decorate and serve.

BAKER'S TIP

For the richest possible vanilla flavour, we recommend adding the seeds of one vanilla bean to the pure vanilla extract called for in the recipe. To collect the seeds, use a small paring knife to cut a vanilla bean in half lengthwise. Using the dull side of the paring knife, scrape the seeds out of the vanilla bean. Add the seeds to the measuring cup with the whole (3.25%) milk and pure vanilla extract in step 3. Stir well and continue making the cupcake batter as instructed.

CUSTOM CAKES AND SWEET TREATS

JENNA *Rae* CAKES

580 ACADEMY ROAD | WINNIPEG, MB

CHOCOLATE LOVER'S CUPCAKES

Makes 16 cupcakes

CHOCOLATE CUPCAKES

1¼ cups all-purpose flour
1 cup granulated sugar
⅓ cup cocoa powder, sifted
1 teaspoon baking soda
1½ teaspoons baking powder
1 teaspoon cornstarch
¾ teaspoon salt
¾ cup buttermilk
⅓ cup vegetable oil
⅓ cup strong brewed coffee
    (see Baker's Tip)
1 egg
2 tablespoons egg whites
    (about 1 egg)
2 teaspoons pure vanilla
    extract
2 tablespoons sour cream

**CHOCOLATE LOVER'S
BUTTERCREAM**

1 batch (page 297)

**DARK CHOCOLATE GANACHE
(OPTIONAL)**

1 batch (page 298)

We all know someone who loves—and I mean loves—chocolate. For Jenna, her husband's most frequent request is for one of these velvety chocolate cupcakes that's topped with Chocolate Lover's Buttercream and Dark Chocolate Ganache. For the chocolate lover in your life, this will be the cupcake they request over and over again.

CHOCOLATE CUPCAKES

1. Preheat the oven to 350°F. Line 2 cupcake pans with 16 cupcake liners.
2. In the bowl of a stand mixer fitted with the paddle attachment, mix the flour, sugar, cocoa powder, baking soda, baking powder, cornstarch, and salt on low speed for 1 minute until combined.
3. In a measuring cup, whisk together the buttermilk, oil, coffee, egg, egg whites, and vanilla. With the mixer on low speed, slowly pour the buttermilk mixture into the bowl and mix until just combined. Add the sour cream and mix on medium-high speed for 2 minutes. Scrape down the sides of the bowl and continue mixing for 10 to 15 seconds. The batter will look thin and runny.
4. Divide the batter evenly among the cupcake liners, filling each three-quarters full. Bake for 15 to 18 minutes, or until a toothpick inserted in the middle of a cupcake comes out clean. Let cool for 5 minutes in the pans before transferring the cupcakes to a wire rack to cool completely.

CHOCOLATE LOVER'S BUTTERCREAM

5. Prepare 1 batch Chocolate Lover's Buttercream.

DARK CHOCOLATE GANACHE

6. Prepare 1 batch Dark Chocolate Ganache, if using.

ASSEMBLY

7. Transfer the Chocolate Lover's Buttercream to a piping bag fitted with a No. 8B tip. Pipe the buttercream onto each cupcake with an even pressure, starting from the middle and swirling in a circular motion until you round the cupcake twice. Release pressure from the piping bag and pull it away for a clean finish.
8. Pour the Dark Chocolate Ganache into a squeeze bottle. Heat in the microwave until a pipable consistency is achieved, about 30 seconds. Drizzle the ganache in a zigzag pattern over the buttercream.
9. For maximum freshness and deliciousness, serve cupcakes on the day they are made. If you want to bake the cupcakes a day in advance, store the baked, undecorated cupcakes in an airtight container at room temperature until ready to decorate and serve.

BAKER'S TIP

If you don't want to brew an entire pot of coffee for this recipe, dissolve 2 tablespoons instant coffee in ⅓ cup hot water to make the exact amount you'll need.

STUFFED PEANUT BUTTER CUPCAKES

Makes 16 cupcakes

PEANUT BUTTER CUPCAKES

1 ¾ cups all-purpose flour
1 cup granulated sugar
1 teaspoon baking powder
¼ teaspoon baking soda
¼ teaspoon salt
¾ cup unsalted butter, room temperature, cut into cubes
⅓ cup egg whites (about 2 eggs)
½ cup whole (3.25%) milk
½ cup creamy peanut butter
1 tablespoon pure vanilla extract

PEANUT BUTTER BUTTERCREAM

1 batch Vanilla Buttercream (page 296)
½ cup creamy peanut butter

PEANUT BUTTER FILLING (OPTIONAL, SEE BAKER'S TIP)

1 cup creamy peanut butter
2 tablespoons unsalted butter, melted
2 teaspoons pure vanilla extract
1 cup icing sugar
2 tablespoons whole (3.25%) milk

BAKER'S TIP

1. If you want to simplify this recipe, exchange the homemade Peanut Butter Filling for smooth peanut butter. **2.** Peanut Butter Filling can easily be transformed into the perfect party treat. After preparing the filling, scoop it into bite-size balls. Roll each ball in mini chocolate chips and serve as a chocolate peanut butter truffle.

These cupcakes were created for the person who likes to slather peanut butter on just about everything. Each one is stuffed with a peanut butter filling like the one found in chocolate peanut butter cups. Just in case that isn't enough, we swirl Peanut Butter Buttercream on top and finish each cupcake with another scoop of Peanut Butter Filling. Too much peanut butter? Never! Just have a glass of milk handy.

PEANUT BUTTER CUPCAKES

1. Preheat the oven to 350°F. Line 2 cupcake pans with 16 cupcake liners.
2. In the bowl of a stand mixer fitted with the paddle attachment, combine the flour, sugar, baking powder, baking soda, and salt. Mix on low speed for 30 seconds. Add the butter and continue to mix on low speed for 2 minutes, or until the mixture has the texture of wet sand. Do not overmix. Slowly pour in the egg whites and mix until just combined. Scrape down the sides of the bowl.
3. In a measuring cup, whisk together the milk, peanut butter, and vanilla. With the mixer on low speed, slowly pour the milk mixture into the bowl and mix until just combined. Scrape down the sides of the bowl and mix again for 10 to 15 seconds. The batter will look a little lumpy.
4. Divide the batter evenly among the cupcake liners, filling each three-quarters full. Bake for 15 to 18 minutes, or until a toothpick inserted in the middle of a cupcake comes out clean. Let cool for 5 minutes in the pans before transferring the cupcakes to a wire rack to cool completely.

PEANUT BUTTER BUTTERCREAM

5. Prepare 1 batch Vanilla Buttercream.
6. Add the peanut butter to the buttercream. Whisk on medium-high speed until well combined.

PEANUT BUTTER FILLING (IF USING)

7. In the bowl of a stand mixer fitted with the paddle attachment, cream the peanut butter, butter, and vanilla on high speed until light and creamy. Reduce the speed to low. Add the icing sugar, increase the speed to medium, and mix until fully combined. Scrape down the sides of the bowl. Add the milk and mix on medium speed for an additional minute, until smooth and creamy.

ASSEMBLY

8. Transfer the Peanut Butter Filling to a piping bag and cut off the tip. Wearing a glove, use a finger to poke a hole in the centre of each cupcake. Pipe filling into each hole.
9. Transfer the Peanut Butter Buttercream to a piping bag fitted with a No. 8B tip. Pipe the buttercream onto each cupcake with an even pressure, starting from the middle and swirling in a circular motion until you round the cupcake twice. Release pressure from the piping bag and pull it away for a clean finish. There should be a small "nest" in the middle of the buttercream.
10. Scoop 16 tablespoon-size chunks of Peanut Butter Filling and roll them into balls. Place 1 ball in each "nest."
11. For maximum freshness and deliciousness, serve cupcakes on the day they are made. If you want to bake the cupcakes a day in advance, store the baked, undecorated cupcakes in an airtight container at room temperature until ready to decorate and serve.

CARROT CAKE CUPCAKES

Makes 16 cupcakes

CARROT CAKE CUPCAKES

1 ¾ cups all-purpose flour
1 cup granulated sugar
1 tablespoon cinnamon
1 teaspoon baking powder
¼ teaspoon baking soda
¼ teaspoon ground nutmeg
¼ teaspoon salt
¾ cups unsalted butter,
   room temperature,
   cut into cubes
1 egg
¼ cup sour cream
½ cup whole (3.25%) milk
1 tablespoon pure vanilla
   extract
2 cups grated carrots
½ cup raisins (optional)

**CREAM CHEESE
BUTTERCREAM**

1 batch (page 297)
1 to 2 drops peach gel food
   colouring

**SPICED CANDIED PECANS
(OPTIONAL, SEE BAKER'S
TIP)**

1 batch (page 307)

We love the combination of our spiced carrot cake, cream cheese buttercream, and crunchy spiced pecans. A favourite especially around Easter, Carrot Cake Cupcakes bring fresh flavours back into your home after a long winter.

CARROT CAKE CUPCAKES

1. Preheat the oven to 350°F. Line 2 cupcake pans with 16 cupcake liners.

2. In the bowl of a stand mixer fitted with the paddle attachment, combine the flour, sugar, cinnamon, baking powder, baking soda, nutmeg, and salt. Mix on low speed for 2 minutes, until combined. Add the butter and continue to mix on low speed for 1 to 2 minutes, or until the mixture has the texture of wet sand. Do not overmix. Add the egg and mix until just combined. Add the sour cream and mix until just combined. Scrape down the sides of the bowl.

3. In a measuring cup, whisk together the milk and vanilla. With the mixer on low speed, slowly pour the milk mixture into the bowl and mix until just combined. Add the carrots and raisins (if using) and mix until combined. Scrape down the sides of the bowl and mix again for 10 to 15 seconds. The batter will look a little lumpy.

4. Divide the batter evenly among the cupcake liners, filling each three-quarters full. Bake for 15 to 18 minutes, or until a toothpick inserted in the centre comes out clean. Let cool for 5 minutes in the pans before transferring the cupcakes to a wire rack to cool completely.

CREAM CHEESE BUTTERCREAM

5. Prepare 1 batch Cream Cheese Buttercream.

6. Add the food colouring to the buttercream and mix until well combined.

SPICED CANDIED PECANS

7. Prepare 1 batch Spiced Candied Pecans.

ASSEMBLY

8. Transfer the Cream Cheese Buttercream to a piping bag fitted with a No. 8B tip. Pipe the buttercream onto each cupcake with an even pressure, starting from the middle and swirling in a circular motion until you round the cupcake twice. Release pressure from the piping bag and pull it away for a clean finish. There should be a small "nest" in the middle of the buttercream. Sprinkle a generous amount of Spiced Candied Pecans (if using) in each "nest."

9. For maximum freshness and deliciousness, serve cupcakes on the day they are made. If you want to bake the cupcakes a day in advance, store the baked, undecorated cupcakes in an airtight container at room temperature until ready to decorate and serve.

BAKER'S TIP

If you're not a fan of pecans, try substituting walnut or almond pieces for the pecan pieces when making the spiced candied nuts.

KEEP IT FRESH

COTTON CANDY CUPCAKES

Close your eyes and imagine yourself at a carnival watching cotton candy being freshly spun before your eyes. Take a deep breath and inhale the mouth-watering smell of warm sugar, feel the warm breeze, and hear the carnival sounds, then make every moment feel like that when you create our perfectly pastel, Instagram-worthy Cotton Candy Cupcakes.

COTTON CANDY CUPCAKES

1¾ cups all-purpose flour

1 cup granulated sugar

1 teaspoon baking powder

¼ teaspoon baking soda

¼ teaspoon salt

¾ cup unsalted butter, room temperature, cut into cubes

⅓ cup egg whites (about 2 eggs)

¼ cup sour cream

½ cup whole (3.25%) milk

2 teaspoons vanilla extract

1 teaspoon JRC Liquid Cotton Candy or cotton candy flavouring

2 drops soft pink gel food colouring

2 drops sky blue gel food colouring

COTTON CANDY BUTTERCREAM

1 batch Vanilla Buttercream (page 296)

2 teaspoons JRC Liquid Cotton Candy or cotton candy flavouring

2 drops soft pink gel food colouring

2 drops sky blue gel food colouring

GARNISH

½ cup sprinkle mix of your choice (we use long sprinkles and ball sprinkles in various sizes and edible glitter)

COTTON CANDY CUPCAKES

1. Preheat the oven to 350°F. Line 2 cupcake pans with 16 cupcake liners.
2. In the bowl of a stand mixer fitted with the paddle attachment, combine the flour, sugar, baking powder, baking soda, and salt. Mix on low speed for 1 minute until combined. Add the butter and continue to mix on low speed for 1 to 2 minutes, or until the mixture has the texture of wet sand. Do not overmix. Slowly pour in the egg whites and mix until just combined. Add the sour cream and mix until just combined. Scrape down the sides of the bowl.
3. In a measuring cup, whisk together the milk, vanilla, and cotton candy flavouring. With the mixer on low speed, slowly pour the milk mixture into the bowl and mix until just combined. Scrape down the sides of the bowl and mix again for 10 to 15 seconds. The batter will look a little lumpy.
4. Divide the batter evenly between 2 small bowls. To one bowl, add the soft pink food colouring and mix with a spatula until the colour is uniform. To the other bowl, add the sky blue food colouring and mix with a spatula until the colour is uniform. Pour the pink batter into the bowl with the blue batter. Using a spatula, gently fold the two colours together 3 to 4 times. The batter should look marbled.
5. Divide the batter evenly among the cupcake liners, filling each three-quarters full. Bake for 15 to 18 minutes, or until a toothpick inserted in the middle of a cupcake comes out clean. Let cool for 5 minutes in the pans before transferring the cupcakes to a wire rack to cool completely.

COTTON CANDY BUTTERCREAM

6. Prepare 1 batch Vanilla Buttercream.
7. Add the cotton candy flavouring to the buttercream. Whisk on medium-high speed until combined.
8. Divide the buttercream evenly between 2 medium bowls. To one bowl, add the soft pink food colouring and mix with a spatula until the colour is uniform. To the other bowl, add the sky blue food colouring and mix with a spatula until the colour is uniform.

ASSEMBLY

9. Transfer the Cotton Candy Buttercream to a piping bag fitted with a No. 8B tip by adding small scoops to the bag, alternating between the pink and blue buttercream (see Baker's Tip). Pipe the buttercream onto each cupcake with an even pressure, starting from the middle and swirling in a circular motion until you round the cupcake twice. Release pressure from the piping bag and pull it away for a clean finish. Garnish with the sprinkle mix.
10. For maximum freshness and deliciousness, serve cupcakes on the day they are made. If you want to bake the cupcakes a day in advance, store the baked, undecorated cupcakes in an airtight container at room temperature until ready to decorate and serve.

BAKER'S TIP

Alternating scoops of pink and blue buttercream when filling the piping bag will ensure that the colours stay separate. Only fill about a quarter of the piping bag at a time to prevent the colours from combining as you put pressure on the piping bag.

S'MORES CUPCAKES

Sweet and melty marshmallows, decadent and creamy milk chocolate, and crisp graham crust—are we talking about all the fixings for a traditional s'more or a S'mores Cupcake? What makes our S'mores Cupcakes unique is the graham crust pressed into the bottom of the cupcake liner before the batter is added. This crunch ensures that each bite has the essential flavour of graham crackers.

GRAHAM CRACKER CRUST

¾ cup graham cracker crumbs
2 tablespoons unsalted butter, melted
Pinch of cinnamon (optional)
Pinch of salt

GRAHAM CRACKER CUPCAKES

1½ cups whole wheat flour
¼ cup all-purpose flour
½ cup granulated sugar
½ cup packed brown sugar
1 teaspoon baking powder
1 teaspoon cinnamon
¼ teaspoon baking soda
¼ teaspoon salt
¾ cup unsalted butter, room temperature, cut into cubes
⅓ cup egg whites (about 2 eggs)
¾ cup whole (3.25%) milk
1 tablespoon pure vanilla extract

MERINGUE MARSHMALLOW FLUFF

½ batch (page 300) or 2 (7.5-ounce) jars store-bought marshmallow spread

MILK CHOCOLATE BUTTERCREAM

1 batch (page 296)

BAKER'S TIP

For best results, make the Meringue Marshmallow Fluff on the day you plan to use it so that it remains stiff and easy to pipe. If you have any leftover fluff, we love dipping fresh fruit in it, or simply eat it with a spoon on some peanut butter! Trust us, it's delicious.

GRAHAM CRACKER CRUST

1. Preheat the oven to 350°F. Line 2 cupcake pans with 16 cupcake liners.

2. In a small bowl, use a wooden spoon to stir together the graham cracker crumbs, butter, cinnamon (if using), and salt until evenly coated.

3. Scoop 2 teaspoons crust into the bottom of each cupcake liner and press firmly to create a dense crust.

GRAHAM CRACKER CUPCAKES

4. In the bowl of a stand mixer fitted with the paddle attachment, combine the whole wheat flour, all-purpose flour, granulated sugar, brown sugar, baking powder, cinnamon, baking soda, and salt. Mix on low speed for 2 minutes. Add the butter and mix for 1 to 2 minutes, or until the mixture has the texture of wet sand. Do not overmix. Slowly pour the egg whites into the bowl and mix until just combined. Scrape down the sides of the bowl.

5. In a measuring cup, whisk together the milk and vanilla. With the mixer on low speed, slowly pour the milk mixture into the bowl and mix until just combined. Scrape down the sides of the bowl and mix again for 10 to 15 seconds. The batter will look a little lumpy.

6. Divide the batter evenly among the cupcake liners, filling each three-quarters full. Bake for 15 to 18 minutes, or until a toothpick inserted in the middle of a cupcake comes out clean. Let cool for 5 minutes in the pans before transferring the cupcakes to a wire rack to cool completely.

MERINGUE MARSHMALLOW FLUFF

7. Prepare ½ batch Meringue Marshmallow Fluff.

MILK CHOCOLATE BUTTERCREAM

8. Prepare 1 batch Milk Chocolate Buttercream.

ASSEMBLY

9. Transfer the Meringue Marshmallow Fluff to a piping bag and cut off the tip. Wearing a glove, use a finger to poke a hole in the centre of each cupcake. Pipe fluff into each hole.

10. Transfer the Milk Chocolate Buttercream to a piping bag fitted with a No. 8B tip. Pipe the buttercream onto each cupcake with an even pressure, starting from the middle and swirling in a circular motion until you round the cupcake twice. Release pressure from the piping bag and pull it away for a clean finish. There should be a small "nest" in the middle of the buttercream.

11. Fill each "nest" with a dollop of fluff. Use a handheld torch to toast the top of the fluff, taking care not to melt the buttercream.

12. For maximum freshness and deliciousness, serve cupcakes on the day they are made. If you want to bake the cupcakes a day in advance, store the baked, undecorated cupcakes in an airtight container at room temperature until ready to decorate and serve.

SALTED CARAMEL COCONUT CUPCAKES

Taste the tropics, where the sweet, exotic flavour of toasted coconut meets sticky salted caramel in this vacation-worthy treat. Our mom requests one of these whenever they're on the menu at the shop—they're her favourite!

SALTED CARAMEL

1 batch (page 299), divided

TOASTED COCONUT

2 cups sweetened shredded coconut

SALTED CARAMEL COCONUT CUPCAKES

1¾ cups all-purpose flour
1 cup granulated sugar
1 teaspoon baking powder
¼ teaspoon baking soda
¼ teaspoon salt
¼ cup sweetened shredded coconut, more for garnish
¾ cup butter, room temperature, cut into cubes
⅓ cup egg whites (about 2 eggs)
¼ cup sour cream
½ cup canned coconut milk
1 tablespoon pure vanilla extract
¼ cup Salted Caramel

SALTED CARAMEL COCONUT BUTTERCREAM

1 batch Vanilla Buttercream (page 296)
½ cup Salted Caramel
¼ to ½ teaspoon coconut emulsion (see Baker's Tip)

SALTED CARAMEL

1. Prepare 1 batch Salted Caramel. Let cool to room temperature.

TOASTED COCONUT

2. Preheat the oven to 350°F. Line a baking sheet with parchment paper.

3. Sprinkle the coconut in an even layer on the prepared baking sheet. Toast in the oven for 6 to 8 minutes, stirring halfway. Remove from the oven when lightly toasted and golden brown. Let cool on the baking sheet until ready to use. Keep the oven at 350°F.

SALTED CARAMEL COCONUT CUPCAKES

4. Line 2 cupcake pans with 16 cupcake liners.

5. In the bowl of a stand mixer fitted with the paddle attachment, combine the flour, sugar, baking powder, baking soda, salt, and coconut. Mix on low speed for 2 minutes. Add the butter and mix for 1 to 2 minutes, or until the mixture has the texture of wet sand. Do not overmix. Slowly pour in the egg whites and mix until just combined. Add the sour cream and mix until just combined. Scrape down the sides of the bowl.

6. In a measuring cup, whisk together the coconut milk and vanilla. With the mixer on low speed, slowly pour the coconut milk mixture into the bowl and mix until just combined. Scrape down the sides of the bowl and mix again for 10 to 15 seconds. Gently fold in ¼ cup Salted Caramel until the batter is swirled with caramel streaks. The batter will look a little lumpy.

7. Divide the batter evenly among the cupcake liners, filling each three-quarters full. Sprinkle each cupcake with coconut. Bake for 15 to 18 minutes, or until a toothpick inserted in the middle of a cupcake comes out clean. Let cool for 5 minutes in the pans before transferring the cupcakes to a wire rack to cool completely.

SALTED CARAMEL COCONUT BUTTERCREAM

8. Prepare 1 batch Vanilla Buttercream. Add ½ cup Salted Caramel and coconut emulsion to the buttercream. Whisk on medium speed until well combined.

ASSEMBLY

9. Transfer the remaining Salted Caramel to a piping bag and cut off the tip. Wearing a glove, use a finger to poke a hole in the centre of each cupcake. Pipe caramel into each hole.

10. Transfer the Salted Caramel Coconut Buttercream to a piping bag fitted with a No. 8B tip. Pipe the buttercream onto each cupcake with an even pressure, starting from the middle and swirling in a circular motion until you round the cupcake twice. Release pressure from the piping bag and pull it away for a clean finish.

11. Place the Toasted Coconut in a small bowl. Holding each cupcake by its base, roll the buttercream in the toasted coconut until it is covered evenly and a dome shape forms.

12. For maximum freshness and deliciousness, serve cupcakes on the day they are made. If you want to bake the cupcakes a day in advance, store the baked, undecorated cupcakes in an airtight container at room temperature until ready to decorate and serve.

BAKER'S TIP

Coconut emulsion is quite strong! If you love coconut and want to add more flavour, start with ¼ teaspoon and taste the buttercream before mixing in more.

NANAIMO CUPCAKES

Makes 16 cupcakes

NANAIMO CRUST

3 tablespoons unsalted butter, room temperature

¼ teaspoon pure vanilla extract

2 tablespoons sifted cocoa powder

2 tablespoons granulated sugar

½ cup graham cracker crumbs

¼ cup unsweetened shredded coconut

CHOCOLATE CUPCAKES

1 batch (page 62), baked in crusted liners

NANAIMO FILLING

¼ cup whole (3.25%) milk

¼ cup vanilla custard powder or vanilla pudding powder

2 cups icing sugar

½ cup unsalted butter, room temperature

3 drops yellow gel food colouring

CHOCOLATE LOVER'S BUTTERCREAM

1 batch (page 297)

CHOCOLATE TOPPING

3 cups (660 g) chopped dark baking chocolate

¼ cup canola oil

What makes a Nanaimo bar so delicious is all the layers—the chocolate base filled with coconut and graham cracker crumbs, then a layer of delicious vanilla custard, and smooth, silky chocolate to finish it all off. Our Nanaimo Cupcakes incorporate each of these decadent elements.

NANAIMO CRUST

1. In a small heat-resistant bowl, melt the butter in the microwave. Add the vanilla.

2. In a medium bowl, whisk together the cocoa powder, sugar, graham cracker crumbs, and coconut. Pour the melted butter mixture into the dry ingredients and mix to combine.

3. Line 2 cupcake pans with 16 liners. Scoop 2 teaspoons crust into the bottom of each cupcake liner and press firmly to create a dense crust.

CHOCOLATE CUPCAKES

4. Prepare 1 batch Chocolate Cupcakes. Bake the batter in the liners prepared with Nanaimo Crust.

NANAIMO FILLING

5. Heat the milk in a medium saucepan over medium-high heat. Once the milk is steaming, add the custard powder and whisk to dissolve. Set aside.

6. In the bowl of a stand mixer fitted with the paddle attachment, beat the icing sugar and butter on medium speed until combined. Reduce the speed to low, add the milk mixture, and mix until smooth and creamy. Add the food colouring and beat on medium speed until the colour is uniform. If the mixture is too thick, add 1 tablespoon milk at a time until a pipable consistency is achieved.

CHOCOLATE LOVER'S BUTTERCREAM

7. Prepare 1 batch Chocolate Lover's Buttercream.

CHOCOLATE TOPPING

8. In a deep heat-resistant bowl, melt the chocolate in the microwave in 30-second intervals, stirring after each interval, until melted and smooth. Add the oil and stir well to combine.

ASSEMBLY

9. Transfer the Nanaimo Filling to a piping bag and cut off the tip. Wearing a glove, use a finger to poke a hole in the centre of each cupcake. Pipe filling into each hole.

10. Transfer the Chocolate Lover's Buttercream to a piping bag fitted with a No. 8B tip. Pipe the buttercream onto each cupcake with an even pressure, starting from the middle and swirling in a circular motion until you round the cupcake twice. Release pressure from the piping bag and pull it away for a clean finish. Place iced cupcakes in the fridge for 30 minutes to set.

11. Once the cupcakes are cool, reheat the Chocolate Topping in the microwave in 10-second intervals until melted and smooth. Holding each cupcake by its base, slowly turn it upside down and dip it into the topping until the buttercream is completely covered. Place dipped cupcakes on a plate to dry.

12. For maximum freshness and deliciousness, serve cupcakes on the day they are made. If you want to bake the cupcakes a day in advance, store the baked, undecorated cupcakes in an airtight container at room temperature until ready to decorate and serve.

BAKER'S TIP

Feel free to add a sprinkle of shredded coconut to each cupcake before the chocolate topping dries for a bit of decoration.

PISTACHIO ROSE CUPCAKES

PISTACHIO CUPCAKES

1 ¾ cups all-purpose flour

1 cup granulated sugar

½ cup + ¼ cup chopped
   pistachios, divided

1 teaspoon baking powder

¼ teaspoon baking soda

¼ teaspoon salt

¾ cup unsalted butter, room
   temperature, cut into cubes

⅓ cup egg whites (about
   2 eggs)

¼ cup sour cream

½ cup whole (3.25%) milk

1 tablespoon pistachio paste

1 tablespoon pure vanilla
   extract

ROSE BUTTERCREAM

1 batch Vanilla Buttercream
   (page 296)

¼ to ½ teaspoon rose extract

1 drop soft pink gel food
   colouring

The distinct flavour of pistachio flawlessly combines with the light, floral taste of rose in this cupcake designed for a more sophisticated palette. Perfect for a summer tea party, garnish your cupcakes with a candied rose petal for a whimsical, enchanting look.

PISTACHIO CUPCAKES

1. Preheat the oven to 350°F. Line 2 cupcake pans with 16 cupcake liners.

2. In the bowl of a stand mixer fitted with the paddle attachment, combine the flour, sugar, ½ cup pistachios, baking powder, baking soda, and salt on low speed for 2 minutes. Add the butter and mix for 1 to 2 minutes, or until the mixture has the texture of wet sand. Do not overmix. With the mixer on low, slowly pour in the egg whites and mix until just combined. Add the sour cream and mix until just combined. Scrape down the sides of the bowl.

3. In a measuring cup, whisk together the milk, pistachio paste, and vanilla. With the mixer on low speed, slowly pour the milk mixture into the bowl and mix until just combined. Scrape down the sides of the bowl and mix again for 10 to 15 seconds. The batter will look a little lumpy.

4. Divide the batter evenly among the cupcake liners, filling each three-quarters full. Bake for 15 to 18 minutes, or until a toothpick inserted in the middle of a cupcake comes out clean. Let cool for 5 minutes in the pans before transferring the cupcakes to a wire rack to cool completely.

ROSE BUTTERCREAM

5. Prepare 1 batch Vanilla Buttercream.

6. Add the rose extract and food colouring to the buttercream. Whisk on medium speed until well combined.

ASSEMBLY

7. Transfer the Rose Buttercream to a piping bag fitted with a No. 8B tip. Pipe the buttercream onto each cupcake with an even pressure, starting from the middle and swirling in a circular motion until you round the cupcake twice. Release pressure from the piping bag and pull it away for a clean finish. Sprinkle each cupcake with about 1 teaspoon of chopped pistachios.

8. For maximum freshness and deliciousness, serve cupcakes on the day they are made. If you want to bake the cupcakes a day in advance, store the baked, undecorated cupcakes in an airtight container at room temperature until ready to decorate and serve.

BAKER'S TIP

If you want to make the Rose Buttercream even bolder by adding more rose extract, be mindful that the flavour of buttercream will often get stronger as it sits, and even a light rose taste will become more prominent as the decorated cupcakes wait to be devoured.

LEMON BAR CUPCAKES

A classic found on many a dessert tray, lemon bars offer the perfect combination of sweet and tart. Our take on lemon bars transforms this staple into delicious cupcakes that bring together lemony freshness and sweet buttery shortbread in a dessert you'll make over and over again.

SHORTBREAD CRUMBLE

2 batches (page 305, step 2), without the food colouring

LEMON CUPCAKES

1¾ cups all-purpose flour
1 cup granulated sugar
1 teaspoon baking powder
¼ teaspoon baking soda
¼ teaspoon salt
¾ cup butter, room temperature, cut into cubes
1 egg
¼ cup sour cream
Zest and juice of 2 lemons
1 tablespoon pure vanilla extract

LEMON CURD

1 batch (page 302), divided

LEMON BUTTERCREAM

1 batch Vanilla Buttercream (page 296)
1 cup Lemon Curd

GARNISH

½ cup icing sugar

SHORTBREAD CRUMBLE

1. Preheat the oven to 350°F. Line 2 cupcake pans with 16 cupcake liners.

2. Prepare 2 batches Shortbread Crumble, following step 2 of the recipe on page 305. Scoop 2 teaspoons crumble into the bottom of each cupcake liner and press firmly to create a dense crust.

3. Bake the remaining crumble following step 3 of the recipe on page 305.

LEMON CUPCAKES

4. In the bowl of a stand mixer fitted with the paddle attachment, combine the flour, sugar, baking powder, baking soda, and salt on low speed for 2 minutes. Add the butter and mix on low speed for 1 to 2 minutes, or until the mixture has the texture of wet sand. Do not overmix. Slowly pour the egg into the bowl and mix until just combined. Add the sour cream, lemon zest and juice, and vanilla and mix until just combined. Scrape down the sides of the bowl. The batter will look a little lumpy.

5. Divide the batter evenly among the cupcake liners, filling each three-quarters full. Bake for 15 to 18 minutes, or until a toothpick inserted in the middle of a cupcake comes out clean. Let cool for 5 minutes in the pans before transferring the cupcakes to a wire rack to cool completely.

LEMON CURD

6. Prepare 1 batch Lemon Curd.

LEMON BUTTERCREAM

7. Prepare 1 batch Vanilla Buttercream.

8. Add 1 cup Lemon Curd to the buttercream. Whisk on medium-high speed until well combined.

ASSEMBLY

9. Transfer the remaining Lemon Curd to a piping bag and cut off the tip. Wearing a glove, use a finger to poke a hole in the centre of each cupcake. Pipe lemon curd into each hole.

10. Transfer the Lemon Buttercream to a piping bag and cut off the tip. Pipe the buttercream onto each cupcake with an even pressure, starting from the middle and swirling in a circular motion until you round the cupcake twice. Release pressure from the piping bag and pull it away for a clean finish.

11. Transfer the baked Shortbread Crumble to a small bowl. Holding each cupcake by its base, roll the buttercream in the crumble until it is covered evenly and a dome shape forms.

12. Place the cupcakes on a piece of parchment paper and sift a generous amount of icing sugar over top.

13. For maximum freshness and deliciousness, serve cupcakes on the day they are made. If you want to bake the cupcakes a day in advance, store the baked, undecorated cupcakes in an airtight container at room temperature until ready to decorate and serve.

BAKER'S TIP

To make these cupcakes a summery treat, try folding 1 cup fresh raspberries into the batter after all of the wet ingredients have been incorporated.

COOKIE DOUGH CUPCAKES

No need to sneak some cookie dough when no one is looking, since each of these cupcakes is stuffed with cookie dough and then garnished with cookie dough, too! Get your cookie dough fix and share these cupcakes with every cookie dough lover you know—they'll be over the moon.

CHOCOLATE CHIP CUPCAKES

1¾ cups all-purpose flour
1 cup granulated sugar
1 teaspoon baking powder
¼ teaspoon baking soda
¼ teaspoon salt
¾ cup unsalted butter, room temperature, cut into cubes
⅓ cup egg whites (about 2 eggs)
¼ cup sour cream
½ cup buttermilk
1 tablespoon pure vanilla extract
½ cup mini chocolate chips

VANILLA BUTTERCREAM

1 batch (page 296)
2 drops ivory gel food colouring (optional)

COOKIE DOUGH

1 batch (page 301)

CHOCOLATE CHIP CUPCAKES

1. Preheat the oven to 350°F. Line 2 cupcake pans with 16 cupcake liners.
2. In the bowl of a stand mixer fitted with the paddle attachment, combine the flour, sugar, baking powder, baking soda, and salt on low speed for 1 minute. Add the butter and mix for an additional 1 to 2 minutes, or until the mixture has the texture of wet sand. Do not overmix. Add the egg whites and mix until just combined. Add the sour cream and mix until just combined. Scrape down the sides of the bowl.
3. In a measuring cup, whisk together the buttermilk and vanilla. With the mixer on low speed, slowly pour in the milk mixture and mix until just combined. Scrape down the sides of the bowl and mix again for 10 to 15 seconds. The batter will look a little lumpy. Using a spatula, gently fold in the chocolate chips.
4. Divide the batter evenly among the cupcake liners, filling each three-quarters full. Bake for 15 to 18 minutes, or until a toothpick inserted in the middle of a cupcake comes out clean. Let cool for 5 minutes in the pans before transferring the cupcakes to a wire rack to cool completely.

VANILLA BUTTERCREAM

5. Prepare 1 batch Vanilla Buttercream.
6. Add the food colouring (if using) to the buttercream. Whisk on high speed until the colour is uniform.

COOKIE DOUGH

7. Prepare 1 batch Cookie Dough.

ASSEMBLY

8. Wearing a glove, use a finger to poke a hole in the centre of each cupcake. Stuff about 2 teaspoons cookie dough into each hole and pat down.
9. Transfer the Vanilla Buttercream to a piping bag fitted with a No. 8B tip. Pipe the buttercream onto each cupcake with an even pressure, starting from the middle and swirling in a circular motion until you round the cupcake twice. Release pressure from the piping bag and pull it away for a clean finish. There should be a small "nest" in the middle of the buttercream.
10. Scoop 16 tablespoon-size chunks of Cookie Dough and roll them into balls. Place 1 ball in each "nest."
11. For maximum freshness and deliciousness, serve cupcakes on the day they are made. If you want to bake the cupcakes a day in advance, store the baked, undecorated cupcakes in an airtight container at room temperature until ready to decorate and serve.

BAKER'S TIP

Leftover Cookie Dough can be scooped and rolled into tablespoon-size balls, then rolled in mini chocolate chips to create cookie dough truffles.

PUMPKIN SPICE CUPCAKES

As soon as the temperature dips and fall knocks on your door, get these cupcakes exploding with pumpkin spice flavour in the oven! Topped with a dreamy Cream Cheese Buttercream that complements the spice of the cupcake, baker beware: if you make these once, you'll be asked to make them again and again.

PUMPKIN SPICE CUPCAKES

1¾ cups all-purpose flour
1 cup granulated sugar
1 tablespoon cinnamon
1 teaspoon baking powder
1 teaspoon pumpkin pie spice
¼ teaspoon baking soda
¼ teaspoon salt
¾ cup unsalted butter, room
    temperature, cut into cubes
1 egg
½ cup whole (3.25%) milk
½ cup canned pure pumpkin
    purée
1 tablespoon pure vanilla
    extract

**CREAM CHEESE
BUTTERCREAM**

½ batch (page 297)

SUGAR AND SPICE CRUMBLE

½ batch (page 306)

SALTED CARAMEL

½ batch (page 299)

PUMPKIN SPICE CUPCAKES

1. Preheat the oven to 350°F. Line 2 cupcake pans with 16 cupcake liners.

2. In the bowl of a stand mixer fitted with the paddle attachment, combine the flour, sugar, cinnamon, baking powder, pumpkin pie spice, baking soda, and salt on low speed for 1 minute. Add the butter and mix for an additional 1 to 2 minutes, or until the mixture has the texture of wet sand. Do not overmix. Add the egg and mix until just combined.

3. In a measuring cup, whisk together the milk, pumpkin purée, and vanilla. With the mixer on low speed, slowly pour in the milk mixture and mix until just combined. Scrape down the sides of the bowl and mix again for 10 to 15 seconds. The batter will look a little lumpy.

4. Divide the batter evenly among the cupcake liners, filling each three-quarters full. Bake for 15 to 18 minutes, or until a toothpick inserted in the middle of a cupcake comes out clean. Let cool for 5 minutes in the pans before transferring the cupcakes to a wire rack to cool completely.

CREAM CHEESE BUTTERCREAM

5. Prepare ½ batch Cream Cheese Buttercream.

SUGAR AND SPICE CRUMBLE

6. Prepare ½ batch Sugar and Spice Crumble.

SALTED CARAMEL

7. Prepare ½ batch Salted Caramel. Let cool to room temperature.

ASSEMBLY

8. Transfer the Cream Cheese Buttercream to a piping bag fitted with a No. 8B tip. Pipe the buttercream onto each cupcake with an even pressure, starting from the middle and swirling in a circular motion until you round the cupcake twice. Release pressure from the piping bag and pull it away for a clean finish.

9. Sprinkle a generous amount of Sugar and Spice Crumble on top of each cupcake.

10. Transfer the Salted Caramel to a piping bag and cut off the tip. Drizzle each cupcake with caramel.

11. For maximum freshness and deliciousness, serve cupcakes on the day they are made. If you want to bake the cupcakes a day in advance, store the baked, undecorated cupcakes in an airtight container at room temperature until ready to decorate and serve.

BAKER'S TIP

Leftover Sugar and Spice Crumble is delicious sprinkled on top of oatmeal, granola, pancakes, or waffles!

WILDBERRY CUPCAKES

Put summer's abundance of fresh berries to use in our Wildberry Cupcakes. These feature a combination of the rich, velvety texture you desire from a cupcake and fresh, bursting summer flavours. Make them when celebrating the person who would rather eat fruit than cake to please every palette in the room.

WILDBERRY REDUCTION

1 batch (page 304)

WILDBERRY CUPCAKES

1¾ cups + 2 tablespoons
   all-purpose flour, divided
1 cup granulated sugar
1 teaspoon baking powder
¼ teaspoon baking soda
¼ teaspoon salt
¾ cup unsalted butter, room
   temperature, cut into cubes
⅓ cup egg whites (about
   2 eggs)
¼ cup sour cream
½ cup whole (3.25%) milk
1 tablespoon pure vanilla
   extract
1 cup mixed berries (we
   like a combination of
   blueberries, raspberries,
   and strawberries,
   hulled and quartered),
   more for garnish

WILDBERRY BUTTERCREAM

1 batch Vanilla Buttercream
   (page 296)
1 cup Wildberry Reduction

GARNISH (OPTIONAL)

Edible gold leaf flakes

WILDBERRY REDUCTION

1. Prepare 1 batch Wildberry Reduction.

WILDBERRY CUPCAKES

2. Preheat the oven to 350°F. Line 2 cupcake pans with 16 cupcake liners.

3. In the bowl of a stand mixer fitted with the paddle attachment, combine 1¾ cups flour, sugar, baking powder, baking soda, and salt on low speed for 1 minute. Add the butter and mix for an additional 1 to 2 minutes, or until the mixture has the texture of wet sand. Do not overmix. Slowly pour in the egg whites and mix until just combined. Scrape down the sides of the bowl. Add the sour cream and mix until just combined. Scrape down the sides of the bowl.

4. In a measuring cup, whisk together the milk and vanilla. With the mixer on low speed, slowly pour the milk mixture into the bowl and mix until just combined. Scrape down the sides of the bowl and mix again for 10 to 15 seconds.

5. Place the remaining 2 tablespoons flour in a medium bowl. Add the berries and toss to coat. Using a spatula, gently fold the berries into the batter. The batter will look a little lumpy.

6. Divide the batter evenly among the cupcake liners, filling each three-quarters full. Bake for 15 to 18 minutes, or until a toothpick inserted in the middle of a cupcake comes out clean. Let cool for 5 minutes in the pans before transferring the cupcakes to a wire rack to cool completely.

WILDBERRY BUTTERCREAM

7. Prepare 1 batch Vanilla Buttercream.

8. Add the Wildberry Reduction to the buttercream. Whisk until well combined.

ASSEMBLY

9. Transfer the Wildberry Buttercream to a piping bag fitted with a No. 8B tip. Pipe the buttercream onto each cupcake with an even pressure, starting from the middle and swirling in a circular motion until you round the cupcake twice. Release pressure from the piping bag and pull it away for a clean finish.

10. Top each cupcake with a fresh raspberry, a fresh blueberry, and a quarter of a fresh strawberry. Sprinkle gold leaf flakes on top, if using.

11. For maximum freshness and deliciousness, serve cupcakes on the day they are made. If you want to bake the cupcakes a day in advance, store the baked, undecorated cupcakes in an airtight container at room temperature until ready to decorate and serve.

BAKER'S TIP

We suggest making a double batch of the Wildberry Reduction—it is delicious drizzled over French toast or pancakes. You can also serve it over whipped cream as a simple dessert!

RED VELVET CUPCAKES

Makes 16 cupcakes

RED VELVET CUPCAKES

1½ cups all-purpose flour

1¼ cups granulated sugar

3 tablespoons cornstarch

1 tablespoon cocoa powder, sifted

¾ teaspoon salt

½ cup unsalted butter, room temperature, cut into cubes

1 egg

2 tablespoons egg whites (about 1 egg)

¾ cup buttermilk

2 tablespoons red liquid food colouring

1½ teaspoons pure vanilla extract

¼ cup sour cream

¾ teaspoon baking soda

¾ teaspoon apple cider vinegar

CREAM CHEESE BUTTERCREAM

1 batch (page 297)

GARNISH (OPTIONAL)

Edible gold leaf flakes

As velvety as you would expect a cupcake with the word "velvet" in its name to be, these rich, cocoa-filled cupcakes are paired with silky-smooth Cream Cheese Buttercream for a treat Ashley simply cannot resist. Just ask her how often she steals one from the pastry case. Be sure to stand guard when you make them—you might find people in your kitchen trying to sneak them before it's time for dessert.

RED VELVET CUPCAKES

1. Preheat the oven to 350°F. Line 2 cupcake pans with 16 cupcake liners.

2. In the bowl of a stand mixer fitted with the paddle attachment, combine the flour, sugar, cornstarch, cocoa powder, and salt on low speed for 1 minute. Add the butter and mix for an additional 1 to 2 minutes, or until the mixture has the texture of wet sand. Do not overmix. Add the egg and egg whites and mix until just combined.

3. In a measuring cup, whisk together the buttermilk, food colouring, and vanilla. With the mixer on low speed, slowly pour in the buttermilk mixture and mix until just combined. Add the sour cream and mix until just combined. Scrape down the sides of the bowl.

4. In a small bowl, whisk together the baking soda and apple cider vinegar. Pour into the batter immediately and mix on low speed until combined. Scrape down the sides of the bowl and mix again for 10 to 15 seconds. The batter will look a little lumpy.

5. Divide the batter evenly among the cupcake liners, filling each three-quarters full. Bake for 15 to 18 minutes, or until a toothpick inserted in the middle of a cupcake comes out clean. Let cool for 5 minutes in the pans before transferring the cupcakes to a wire rack to cool completely.

CREAM CHEESE BUTTERCREAM

6. Prepare 1 batch Cream Cheese Buttercream.

ASSEMBLY

7. Transfer the Cream Cheese Buttercream to a piping bag fitted with a No. 8B tip. Pipe the buttercream onto each cupcake with an even pressure, starting from the middle and swirling in a circular motion until you round the cupcake twice. Release pressure from the piping bag and pull it away for a clean finish. Garnish with the gold leaf flakes, if using.

8. For maximum freshness and deliciousness, serve cupcakes on the day they are made. If you want to bake the cupcakes a day in advance, store the baked, undecorated cupcakes in an airtight container at room temperature until ready to decorate and serve.

BAKER'S TIP

Not a fan of cream cheese buttercream? Substitute our classic Vanilla Buttercream (page 296), our Milk Chocolate Buttercream (page 296), or Ashley's favourite, our Strawberry Buttercream (page 138).

EARL GREY CUPCAKES

Makes 16 cupcakes

Bring the coffee shop home with these decadent cupcakes inspired by Earl Grey tea. We infuse both the cupcake batter and the buttercream with steeped Earl Grey tea for a bold and fragrant flavour that is comparable to a London fog— warm Earl Grey tea paired with vanilla and just the right amount of sweetness.

EARL GREY REDUCTION

3 cups whipping (35%) cream
1 cup loose leaf Earl Grey
   tea, more for garnish
   (see Baker's Tip)

EARL GREY CUPCAKES

1 ¾ cups all-purpose flour
1 cup granulated sugar
1 teaspoon baking powder
¼ teaspoon baking soda
¼ teaspoon salt
¾ cup unsalted butter, room
   temperature, cut into cubes
⅓ cup egg whites (about
   2 eggs)
¼ cup sour cream
½ cup whole (3.25%) milk
¼ cup Earl Grey Reduction
1 tablespoon pure vanilla
   extract

EARL GREY BUTTERCREAM

1 batch Vanilla Buttercream
   (page 296)
1 cup Earl Grey Reduction

GARNISH (OPTIONAL)

Edible gold leaf flakes

EARL GREY REDUCTION

1. In a small saucepan, bring the cream and tea to a boil over medium heat. Reduce the heat to low, stirring occasionally. Simmer for 10 minutes, or until reduced by about half.

2. Using a fine-mesh sieve, strain the mixture into an airtight container. Cover and refrigerate to cool. Discard the solids. Store the Earl Grey Reduction in an airtight container in the fridge for up to 1 week.

EARL GREY CUPCAKES

3. Preheat the oven to 350°F. Line 2 cupcake pans with 16 cupcake liners.

4. In the bowl of a stand mixer fitted with the paddle attachment, combine the flour, sugar, baking powder, baking soda, and salt on low speed for 1 minute. Add the butter and mix for an additional 1 to 2 minutes, or until the mixture has the texture of wet sand. Do not overmix. Slowly pour in the egg whites and mix until just combined. Add the sour cream and mix until just combined. Scrape down the sides of the bowl.

5. In a measuring cup, whisk together the milk, ¼ cup Earl Grey Reduction, and vanilla. With the mixer on low speed, slowly pour the milk mixture into the bowl and mix until just combined. Scrape down the sides of the bowl and mix again for 10 to 15 seconds. The batter will look a little lumpy.

6. Divide the batter evenly among the cupcake liners, filling each three-quarters full. Bake for 15 to 18 minutes, or until a toothpick inserted in the middle of a cupcake comes out clean. Let cool for 5 minutes in the pans before transferring the cupcakes to a wire rack to cool completely.

EARL GREY BUTTERCREAM

7. Prepare 1 batch Vanilla Buttercream.

8. Add 1 cup Earl Grey Reduction to the buttercream. Whisk on medium speed until well combined.

ASSEMBLY

9. Transfer the Earl Grey Buttercream to a piping bag fitted with a No. 8B tip. Pipe the buttercream onto each cupcake with an even pressure, starting from the middle and swirling in a circular motion until you round the cupcake twice. Release pressure from the piping bag and pull it away for a clean finish. Garnish each cupcake with a sprinkle of tea leaves and a pinch of gold leaf flakes, if using.

10. For maximum freshness and deliciousness, serve cupcakes on the day they are made. If you want to bake the cupcakes a day in advance, store the baked, undecorated cupcakes in an airtight container at room temperature until ready to decorate and serve.

BAKER'S TIP

1. Have a favourite tea at home you'd like to turn into a reduction? Simply swap out the Earl Grey tea in the recipe for the Earl Grey Reduction for an equal amount of the tea of your choice.
2. These are the perfect cupcakes for a cool fall evening. Serve with a hot cup of tea for a truly cozy experience.

PEANUT BUTTER BANANA CUPCAKES

Makes 16 cupcakes

BANANA CUPCAKES

1 ¾ cups all-purpose flour
1 cup granulated sugar
1 teaspoon baking powder
¼ teaspoon baking soda
¼ teaspoon cinnamon
¼ teaspoon salt
¾ cup unsalted butter, room
  temperature, cut into cubes
⅓ cup egg whites (about
  2 eggs)
½ cup mashed very
  ripe banana (about
  1 to 1½ bananas)
¼ cup sour cream
½ cup whole (3.25%) milk
1 tablespoon pure vanilla
  extract

SALTED CARAMEL

1 batch (page 299), divided

**PEANUT BUTTER SALTED
CARAMEL BUTTERCREAM**

1 batch Vanilla Buttercream
  (page 296)
½ cup Salted Caramel
2 tablespoons creamy peanut
  butter

PEANUT BUTTER FILLING

½ cup creamy peanut butter

BAKER'S TIP

The riper the bananas in
the Banana Cupcakes, the
stronger the flavour will be!
Save brown bananas that
you don't want to eat for
your next batch of Peanut
Butter Banana Cupcakes
by peeling and chopping
them, then storing them in
a zip-top bag in the freezer.

Just reading the name of these cupcakes is sure to make your mouth water! These perfectly combined flavours are a harmonious blend of creamy peanut butter, sweet banana cupcake, and lightly salted caramel.

BANANA CUPCAKES

1. Preheat the oven to 350°F. Line 2 cupcake pans with 16 cupcake liners.

2. In the bowl of a stand mixer fitted with the paddle attachment, combine the flour, sugar, baking powder, baking soda, cinnamon, and salt on low speed for 1 minute. Add the butter and mix for an additional 1 to 2 minutes, or until the mixture has the texture of wet sand. Do not overmix. Slowly pour in the egg whites and mix until just combined. Add the banana and sour cream and mix until just combined. Scrape down the sides of the bowl.

3. In a measuring cup, whisk together the milk and vanilla. With the mixer on low speed, slowly pour the milk mixture into the bowl and mix until just combined. Scrape down the sides of the bowl and mix again for 10 to 15 seconds. The batter will look a little lumpy.

4. Divide the batter evenly among the cupcake liners, filling each three-quarters full. Bake for 15 to 18 minutes, or until a toothpick inserted in the middle of a cupcake comes out clean. Let cool for 5 minutes in the pans before transferring the cupcakes to a wire rack to cool completely.

SALTED CARAMEL

5. Prepare 1 batch Salted Caramel. Let cool to room temperature.

PEANUT BUTTER SALTED CARAMEL BUTTERCREAM

6. Prepare 1 batch Vanilla Buttercream.

7. Add ½ cup Salted Caramel and 2 tablespoons peanut butter to the buttercream. Whisk on medium-high speed until combined.

PEANUT BUTTER FILLING

8. Fill a piping bag with ½ cup peanut butter and cut off the tip.

ASSEMBLY

9. Wearing a glove, use a finger to poke a hole in the centre of each cupcake. Pipe filling into each hole.

10. Transfer the Peanut Butter Salted Caramel Buttercream to a piping bag fitted with a No. 8B tip. Pipe the buttercream onto each cupcake with an even pressure, starting from the middle and swirling in a circular motion until you round the cupcake twice. Release pressure from the piping bag and pull it away for a clean finish. There should be a small "nest" in the middle of the buttercream. Pipe a dollop of Peanut Butter Filling into each "nest."

11. Transfer the remaining Salted Caramel to a piping bag and cut off the tip. Decorate each cupcake with a drizzle of caramel.

12. For maximum freshness and deliciousness, serve cupcakes on the day they are made. If you want to bake the cupcakes a day in advance, store the baked, undecorated cupcakes in an airtight container at room temperature until ready to decorate and serve.

PARTY SQUARES

BAKER'S NOTES

From our Kitchen to yours

xo

OUR PARTY SQUARES are probably the easiest items to make in this entire book. Many are classic treats that remind us of our childhood days when we would head to potlucks with family or whip up treats with friends. Using basic techniques, the directions are easy to follow, and the party squares themselves can often be prepared in a hurry. Read our tips below to ensure that your treats turn out perfect every time.

PRESSING

A number of our party squares include a base layer that is parbaked (partially baked) before the filling is added on top. Base layers should be firmly pressed into the bottom of the baking dish. We find that using our hands or the bottom of a plastic or stainless steel measuring cup works best.

BAKING TIME

When baking items like brownies and cheesecakes, it can be difficult to know when they are ready. These items are often so rich and creamy that they jiggle slightly when the pan is wiggled—even when they're ready to come out of the oven—causing the inexperienced baker to think they need more time. If you bake these items for longer than recommended, you risk them drying out and having less of the luxurious texture one expects when biting into a brownie or a slice of cheesecake.

Start by baking for the minimum time suggested. When testing, try tapping the pan with a knife or gently shaking the pan. If a brownie or cheesecake jiggles slightly, and if the middle no longer looks wet, it is probably ready to be pulled out of the oven. Let cheesecake cool in the warm oven with the door slightly ajar to prevent cracking and collapse. Placing a baking dish filled with water in the oven when baking your cheesecake will also help prevent cracking.

OVEN

Every oven is different. In our kitchens, we use convection ovens. This means that the air is circulated with a fan to help distribute the heat evenly for even and consistent baking no matter where a tray happens to be placed inside the oven. If you don't have a convection oven at home, or if your oven doesn't have a convection setting, start baking with your temperature 25°F higher than our recipes suggest or increase the bake time by a couple of minutes at a time.

LAYERS

Most of our squares have layers. Make sure that each layer has cooled to room temperature before you add a new one. This is especially true when the top layer is buttercream or something else that might melt if the layer underneath it is too warm. Be sure to follow the instructions carefully so that your squares hold their shape and are easy to cut.

CUTTING

Cutting your party squares with crisp, clean edges will make them stand out in a crowd! To create pristine edges, fill a tall glass or pitcher with hot water. Dip a long, sharp knife into the glass to heat it, then wipe off excess water with a soft cloth or paper towel. Use the warm, sharp knife to make the cuts, wiping any crumbs off the knife after each cut. Use a ruler to help you slice the bar into even squares to give your presentation an extra wow factor.

COOKIE DOUGH CHEESECAKE PARTY SQUARES

A perfect plain cheesecake is the creamy yet neutral base for these party squares. Then we've added irresistible cookie dough to combine two of everyone's favourite desserts into one rich and decadent treat you'll be taking to gatherings and potlucks regularly.

CHOCOLATE CHIP COOKIE BASE

¾ cup unsalted butter, room temperature
⅓ cup granulated sugar
⅓ cup packed brown sugar
2 eggs
¼ teaspoon pure vanilla extract
2 cups mini milk chocolate chips
2½ cups all-purpose flour
1 teaspoon baking soda
1 teaspoon salt

CHEESECAKE BATTER

2½ cups cream cheese, room temperature
¾ cup granulated sugar
3 eggs
½ cup whipping (35%) cream
1 teaspoon pure vanilla extract

COOKIE DOUGH

1 batch (page 301)

CHOCOLATE CHIP COOKIE BASE

1. Preheat the oven to 350°F. Spray a 13- × 9-inch baking dish with cooking spray. Line it with parchment paper.

2. In the bowl of a stand mixer fitted with the paddle attachment, cream the butter, granulated sugar, and brown sugar on high speed for 2 to 3 minutes, until the mixture looks light and fluffy. Reduce the speed to medium. Add the eggs and vanilla and mix until combined. Scrape down the sides of the bowl. Add the chocolate chips and mix on medium-low speed for 1 minute. Add the flour, baking soda, and salt and mix until just combined. Do not overmix.

3. Remove ½ cup of the dough from the bowl, wrap it in plastic wrap, and put it in the fridge to chill. You will use this when making the Cheesecake Batter. Transfer the remaining dough to the prepared baking dish and press it evenly into the bottom to create a base layer.

4. Bake for 5 to 8 minutes. Let cool to room temperature.

CHEESECAKE BATTER

5. Reduce the oven temperature to 300°F.

6. In the bowl of a stand mixer fitted with the whisk attachment, whip the cream cheese on medium-high speed for 3 to 4 minutes, scraping down the bowl at 30-second intervals, until it is smooth and creamy. Add the sugar and whip on high speed for 2 minutes, scraping down the bowl at 30-second intervals.

7. In a small bowl, whisk together the eggs, whipping cream, and vanilla. With the mixer on low speed, slowly pour the cream mixture into the bowl and whip until fully incorporated. Scrape down the sides of the bowl and continue whipping until no chunks remain. Do not overmix.

8. Pour the batter over the base layer. Unwrap the reserved portion of dough and crumble it over the batter. Press the dough pieces into the batter.

9. Place an oven-safe baking dish filled with at least 1 inch of water on the lower rack of the oven. Bake the squares on the rack above for 25 to 30 minutes, or until the top of the cheesecake is firm to the touch but the centre jiggles when the pan is tapped. Do not open the oven during the first 25 minutes of baking. Turn off the oven and let the squares cool for 5 to 10 minutes with the oven door slightly ajar before removing them from the oven to cool to room temperature. Cover and place in the fridge to chill for 30 minutes.

COOKIE DOUGH

10. Prepare 1 batch Cookie Dough.

ASSEMBLY

11. Transfer the squares to a cutting board by lifting the edges of the parchment paper. Pull the parchment paper away from the sides of the squares. Using a sharp chef's knife, cut into 12 equal squares.

12. Using a medium cookie scoop, scoop a generous dollop of Cookie Dough onto each square. Store in an airtight container in the fridge for up to 1 week.

BAKER'S TIP

Overmixing the cheesecake batter can cause it to crack in the oven, and cooling the cheesecake too quickly can cause it to collapse in the middle. Follow the directions carefully for an even, rich party square.

STRAWBERRY SHORTCAKE PARTY SQUARES

Makes 12 large squares

SHORTBREAD TOPPING

2 cups all-purpose flour
½ cup granulated sugar
¼ cup cornstarch
¾ cup unsalted butter, room temperature
2 drops soft pink gel food colouring
½ teaspoon pure vanilla extract

STRAWBERRY FILLING

10 cups fresh or frozen strawberries, hulled and cut into quarters
½ cup granulated sugar
2 tablespoons cornstarch
½ teaspoon vanilla bean paste

This dessert is more of a crumble than a square. When you cut it and lift a piece from the pretty baking dish, the filling will spill out all over the place. But with the rich, red colour of the strawberries and the lighter hue of the shortbread topping, it really does make a beautiful mess. Using strawberries from a local U-Pick will make these squares even more flavourful.

SHORTBREAD TOPPING

1. In a small bowl, whisk together the flour, sugar, and cornstarch.
2. In the bowl of a stand mixer fitted with the paddle attachment, cream the butter on high speed for 4 minutes, until it looks light and fluffy. Midway through, add the food colouring, scrape down the sides of the bowl, and continue mixing. Reduce the speed to low. Add the dry ingredients and the vanilla and mix until combined. It should have a crumbly texture.

STRAWBERRY FILLING

3. In a large bowl, use a spatula to evenly coat the strawberries with the sugar and cornstarch. Add the vanilla and mix to combine.

ASSEMBLY

4. Preheat the oven to 350°F. Line a 13- × 9-inch baking dish with parchment paper.
5. Pour the Strawberry Filling into the prepared baking dish. Use an offset spatula to spread it evenly in the bottom of the dish. Crumble the Shortbread Topping over the filling, allowing some pieces of strawberry to remain visible.
6. Bake for 15 minutes, or until the filling is bubbling around the edges of the pan. Let cool to room temperature.
7. Use a large spoon or lifter to serve. Store in an airtight container in the fridge for up to 4 days. Remove from the fridge 30 minutes before serving.

BAKER'S TIP

Strawberries are delicious, but if you'd prefer raspberry shortcake squares or blueberry shortcake squares, simply substitute an equal amount of your preferred fruit for the strawberries. Keep in mind that not all fruit is as sweet as strawberries, so you might want to add a teaspoon of extra sugar for fruit that's more on the tart side.

S'MORES PARTY SQUARES

VANILLA MARSHMALLOWS

1 batch (page 273)

GRAHAM CRACKER CRUST

3 cups graham cracker crumbs
½ cup packed brown sugar
⅛ teaspoon salt
¾ cup unsalted butter, melted

DARK CHOCOLATE GANACHE

3¼ cups (715 g) chopped dark
   baking chocolate
2½ cups whipping (35%) cream

Toasted marshmallow lovers unite! Your wildest marshmallow dreams come true with a thick layer of marshmallow atop a sizable layer of decadent chocolate ganache. Add a salty graham cracker crust to the mix and you have a bar that is going to have you dreaming of sweets all night long. Toast the marshmallow to irresistible ooey-gooey perfection before serving.

VANILLA MARSHMALLOWS

1. Prepare 1 batch Vanilla Marshmallows the day before you plan to make the rest of the S'mores Party Squares to ensure that it sets completely.

GRAHAM CRACKER CRUST

2. Preheat the oven to 350°F. Spray a 13- × 9-inch baking dish with cooking spray. Line it with parchment paper.

3. In a medium bowl, stir together the graham cracker crumbs, brown sugar, and salt. Add the butter and stir until evenly coated. Transfer the mixture to the prepared baking dish and press evenly into the bottom to create a base layer, using an offset spatula for an extra-smooth base.

4. Bake for 5 minutes. Let cool to room temperature.

DARK CHOCOLATE GANACHE

5. In a large heat-resistant bowl, melt the chocolate in the microwave in 30-second intervals, stirring after each interval, until smooth.

6. In a glass measuring cup, heat the cream in the microwave for 1 minute. Pour into the bowl with the melted chocolate and whisk until smooth.

ASSEMBLY

7. Pour the warm ganache over the Graham Cracker Crust. Cover with plastic wrap and place the baking dish in the fridge for 30 to 60 minutes, until the ganache has set.

8. Transfer the squares to a cutting board by lifting the edges of the parchment paper. Pull the parchment paper away from the sides of the squares. Using a sharp chef's knife, cut into 12 equal squares.

9. Flip the marshmallow onto a textured plastic cutting board (not a smooth or a wooden cutting board or else the marshmallow will stick). Using a chef's knife, cut the marshmallow into 12 equal squares. Use a wet towel to wipe the knife between cuts.

10. Top each square with an equal-size square of marshmallow. Use a handheld torch to toast the marshmallow before serving. Store in an airtight container in the fridge for up to 1 week.

BAKER'S TIP

We make this treat for the dessert menu at a local restaurant, and it is always a hit! We adjust our S'mores Party Squares seasonally by creating new marshmallow and ganache flavours. These squares are very versatile, so dream up new combinations and give them a try!

COTTON CANDY PARTY SQUARES

COTTON CANDY BLONDIE

2½ cups packed brown sugar
1½ cups unsalted butter, melted
3 eggs
2 egg yolks
2 teaspoons pure vanilla
    extract
1 teaspoon JRC Liquid Cotton
    Candy or cotton candy
    flavouring
3¾ cups all-purpose flour
1½ teaspoons cornstarch
1½ teaspoons salt
¾ teaspoon baking powder
1 drop electric pink gel food
    colouring
2 drops sky blue gel food
    colouring

**COTTON CANDY
BUTTERCREAM**

½ batch Vanilla Buttercream
    (page 296)
1 teaspoon JRC Liquid Cotton
    Candy or cotton candy
    flavouring
1 drop electric pink gel food
    colouring
1 drop sky blue gel food
    colouring

GARNISH (OPTIONAL)

1 cup (220 g) purple chocolate
    melting wafers
1 cup sprinkle mix of
    your choice (we use
    Sweetapolita's Wanderlust
    Twinkle Sprinkle Medley)

BAKER'S TIP

When checking if your blondies are done, you'll want your blondie to be fudgy in the centre (a little batter will stick to the knife, but it won't be wet, it will be a fudgy crumb). Don't confuse this with being underbaked, or you'll end up with a dry blondie!

Pink and blue blondie? Check. Cotton candy buttercream? Check. Rainbow sprinkles? Check. These unicorn-inspired squares will look gorgeous on your next party treats table and will be quickly snatched up by little hands who can't resist the pastel palette and the smell of warm spun sugar.

COTTON CANDY BLONDIE

1. Preheat the oven to 350°F. Spray a 13- × 9-inch baking dish with cooking spray. Line it with parchment paper.

2. In the bowl of a stand mixer fitted with the paddle attachment, cream the sugar and butter on low speed for 1 minute, or until combined. Add the eggs, egg yolks, vanilla, and cotton candy flavouring and mix until combined. Scrape down the sides of the bowl.

3. In a small bowl, mix the flour, cornstarch, salt, and baking powder. Add the dry ingredients to the wet ingredients and fold together with a spatula until there are no clumps.

4. Divide the batter evenly between 2 medium bowls. To one bowl, add the electric pink food colouring and use the spatula to gently fold in the colour until it is uniform. To the other bowl, add the sky blue food colouring and gently fold in until the colour is uniform.

5. Scoop the batter into the prepared baking dish, alternating large scoops of each colour. Run a butter knife through the batter to swirl the colours. Bake for 30 to 40 minutes, or until a knife inserted in the middle comes out almost clean (see Baker's Tip). Let cool to room temperature.

COTTON CANDY BUTTERCREAM

6. Prepare ½ batch Vanilla Buttercream.

7. Add the flavouring to the buttercream. Whisk on medium speed until fully incorporated.

8. Divide the buttercream evenly between 2 medium bowls. To one bowl, add the electric pink food colouring and use the spatula to fold in the colour until it is uniform. To the other bowl, add the sky blue food colouring and fold until the colour is uniform. Transfer all of the buttercream to one bowl and gently fold with the spatula 2 to 3 times to swirl the colours.

ASSEMBLY

9. Scoop the Cotton Candy Buttercream onto the Cotton Candy Blondie in heaping tablespoons to cover the blondie. Using an offset spatula, spread the buttercream into an even layer, taking care not to mix the buttercream too much and lose the swirl of colours. Cover with plastic wrap and place in the fridge for at least 1 hour to allow the buttercream to set.

10. Transfer the squares to a cutting board by lifting the edges of the parchment paper. Pull the parchment paper away from the sides of the squares. Using a sharp chef's knife, cut into 12 equal squares.

11. In a medium heat-resistant bowl, melt the chocolate wafers (if using) in the microwave in 30-second intervals, stirring after each interval, until smooth. Transfer the chocolate to a piping bag and cut off the tip. Drizzle half of each square with chocolate. Garnish with the sprinkle mix, if using.

12. Store in an airtight container in the fridge for up to 1 week. Remove from the fridge 30 minutes before serving.

BIRTHDAY CAKE PARTY SQUARES

Makes 12 large squares

BIRTHDAY CAKE BLONDIE

2½ cups packed brown sugar

1½ cups unsalted butter, melted

3 eggs

2 egg yolks

1 tablespoon pure vanilla extract

3¾ cups all-purpose flour

1½ teaspoons cornstarch

1½ teaspoons salt

¾ teaspoon baking powder

2 tablespoons round rainbow sprinkles

BIRTHDAY CAKE BATTER WHITE CHOCOLATE FUDGE

½ cup cream cheese, room temperature

2¼ cups icing sugar

½ teaspoon JRC Liquid Cake Batter or cake batter flavouring

½ teaspoon pure vanilla extract

1¼ cups (275 g) chopped white baking chocolate

2 to 4 drops soft pink gel food colouring

GARNISH

1 cup (220 g) pink chocolate melting wafers

1 cup sprinkle mix of your choice (we use Sweetapolita's Birthday Party Sprinkle Medley)

Close your eyes and imagine combining the tempting flavour of vanilla birthday cake with the fudgy texture of a traditional brownie. Seems almost too good to be true, right? This recipe will exceed your expectations with its seductive flavour combination.

BIRTHDAY CAKE BLONDIE

1. Preheat the oven to 350°F. Spray a 13- × 9-inch baking dish with cooking spray. Line it with parchment paper.

2. In the bowl of a stand mixer fitted with the paddle attachment, cream the sugar and butter on low speed for 1 minute, until the mixture looks light and fluffy. Add the eggs, egg yolks, and vanilla and mix until combined. Scrape down the sides of the bowl.

3. In a small bowl, mix the flour, cornstarch, salt, baking powder, and sprinkles. Add the dry ingredients to the wet ingredients and fold together with a spatula until there are no clumps.

4. Pour the batter into the prepared baking dish. Use an offset spatula or a spoon to spread it into an even layer. Bake for 30 to 40 minutes, or until a knife inserted in the middle comes out almost clean (see Baker's Tip). Let cool to room temperature.

BIRTHDAY CAKE BATTER WHITE CHOCOLATE FUDGE

5. In the bowl of a stand mixer fitted with the paddle attachment, beat the cream cheese on medium-high speed until smooth, about 4 or 5 minutes, scraping down the sides of the bowl every 60 seconds. Add the icing sugar, cake batter flavouring, and vanilla and beat for an additional 2 minutes until smooth, scraping down the sides of the bowl every 60 seconds.

6. In a heat-resistant bowl, melt the white chocolate in the microwave in 30-second intervals, stirring after each interval, until smooth. With the mixer on low speed, slowly add the chocolate. Add the food colouring and beat on medium speed for 2 to 4 minutes, until creamy and smooth. If you want your fudge to be a darker shade of pink, add more food colouring and mix again. The fudge must be used immediately.

ASSEMBLY

7. Pour the Birthday Cake Batter White Chocolate Fudge over the Birthday Cake Blondie. Use an offset spatula to spread the fudge over the blondie in an even layer. If you're having trouble spreading the fudge, warm the spatula by dipping it in a cup of hot water and drying it, then resume spreading. Continue dipping the spatula in hot water as needed. Cover with plastic wrap and place in the fridge for at least 30 minutes to set.

8. Transfer the squares to a cutting board by lifting the edges of the parchment paper. Pull the parchment paper away from the sides of the squares. Using a sharp chef's knife, cut into 12 equal squares.

9. In a heat-resistant bowl, melt the chocolate wafers in the microwave in 30-second intervals, stirring after each interval, until smooth. Transfer the chocolate to a piping bag and cut off the tip. Drizzle half of each square with chocolate. Garnish with the sprinkle mix.

10. Store in an airtight container in the fridge for up to 1 week. Remove from the fridge 30 minutes before serving.

BAKER'S TIP

When checking if your blondies are done, you'll want your blondie to be fudgy in the centre (a little batter will stick to the knife, but it won't be wet, it will be more of a fudgy crumb). Don't confuse this with being underbaked, or you'll end up with a dry blondie!

STICKY COCONUT BROWNIE PARTY SQUARES

Makes 12 large squares

STICKY CARAMELIZED COCONUT

½ cup unsalted butter, room temperature
½ cup packed brown sugar
⅓ cup white corn syrup
½ cup whipping (35%) cream
2¾ cups unsweetened shredded coconut
¼ teaspoon salt

CHOCOLATE BROWNIES

1 cup + 2 tablespoons melted butter
2 tablespoons vegetable oil
2½ cups granulated sugar
4 eggs
1 egg yolk
1 tablespoon pure vanilla extract
1¼ cups all-purpose flour
1 cup cocoa powder
¼ teaspoon salt

Chocolate and sticky caramelized coconut combine to make magical flavour alchemy in these party squares. When our book photographer, Brittany, tried one for the first time, she announced that it was the best thing we had ever made! We think a lot of coconut lovers will agree! Bring this to your next gathering for a special surprise.

STICKY CARAMELIZED COCONUT

1. In a small saucepan over medium-high heat, stir together the butter, sugar, and corn syrup. Cook until the mixture begins to bubble and thicken. Slowly pour in the cream and whisk to combine. Remove from the heat, add the coconut and salt, and stir to combine. Set aside.

CHOCOLATE BROWNIES

2. Preheat the oven to 350°F. Spray a 13- × 9-inch baking sheet with cooking spray. Line it with parchment paper.

3. In the bowl of a stand mixer fitted with the whisk attachment, whip the melted butter, oil, and sugar on high speed for 1 minute. Add the eggs, egg yolk, and vanilla and whip on medium-high speed for an additional minute, or until the mixture becomes lighter in colour.

4. Remove the bowl from the mixer and sift the flour and cocoa powder into the wet ingredients. Add the salt. Using a spatula, gently fold in the dry ingredients until just combined. Do not overmix.

5. Pour the batter into the prepared baking dish and use an offset spatula or the back of a spoon to spread it into an even layer. Bake for 25 to 35 minutes, or until a knife inserted in the middle comes out almost clean with moist crumbs (you don't want a clean knife for fudgy brownies). Keep the oven set at 350°F.

ASSEMBLY

6. Using your hands, carefully spread the Sticky Caramelized Coconut over the warm brownie and gently pat it down to create a solid layer of topping. Bake for 5 minutes. Let cool to room temperature.

7. Transfer the squares to a cutting board by lifting the edges of the parchment paper. Pull the parchment paper away from the sides of the squares. Using a sharp chef's knife, cut into 12 equal squares.

8. Store in an airtight container in the fridge for up to 1 week. Remove from the fridge 30 minutes before serving.

BAKER'S TIP

If you have leftover salted caramel in your fridge from our other delicious recipes, drizzle each square with salted caramel before serving.

NANAIMO PARTY SQUARES

Makes 12 large squares

NANAIMO BASE

½ cup + 2 tablespoons
   unsalted butter
½ cup cocoa powder, sifted
½ cup granulated sugar
1 egg
¼ teaspoon pure vanilla extract
3¼ cups graham cracker
   crumbs
1 cup unsweetened shredded
   coconut

CHOCOLATE BROWNIES

1 batch (page 107), baked
   with the Nanaimo Base

NANAIMO FILLING

3¼ cups icing sugar
⅔ cup unsalted butter, room
   temperature
¼ cup vanilla custard powder
   or vanilla pudding powder
¼ cup whole (3.25%) milk
4 drops yellow gel food
   colouring

CHOCOLATE TOPPING

1 cup (220 g) chopped dark
   baking chocolate
2 tablespoons unsalted butter,
   room temperature

GARNISH (OPTIONAL)

1 cup (220 g) yellow chocolate
   melting wafers
½ cup unsweetened shredded
   coconut

BAKER'S TIP

Don't know the history of the Nanaimo bar? Named after the British Columbia town of the same name, the Nanaimo bar is an iconic Canadian treat. It contains a soft layer of yellow custard sandwiched between rich chocolate ganache and a coconut–graham cracker crust and can be found on dainty trays nationwide—especially during the holidays!

The Jenna Rae Cakes take on a Nanaimo bar features the addition of an extravagant brownie layer to elevate these squares to epic party status. Find it too decadent for a dainty tray? Make this inspired rendition of the classic bar for your friends and family to enjoy around the holidays as a featured dessert.

NANAIMO BASE

1. Preheat the oven to 350°F. Spray a 13- × 9-inch baking dish with cooking spray. Line it with parchment paper.

2. In a small saucepan over low heat, melt the butter. In a small bowl, whisk together the cocoa powder and sugar, then add it to the saucepan. Stir to combine. In the same small bowl, whisk together the egg and vanilla. Slowly pour into the saucepan while whisking constantly. Stir the mixture over low heat for about 2 to 3 minutes, or until it thickens.

3. Remove from the heat. Add the graham cracker crumbs and coconut. Stir to combine. Transfer the Nanaimo Base to the prepared baking dish and press firmly to create an even layer.

CHOCOLATE BROWNIES

4. Prepare 1 batch Chocolate Brownies. Pour the batter over the Nanaimo Base. Using an offset spatula or the back of a spoon, spread it into an even layer. Bake for 30 to 40 minutes or until a knife inserted in the middle comes out almost clean with moist crumbs (you don't want a clean knife for fudgy brownies). Let cool to room temperature.

NANAIMO FILLING

5. In the bowl of a stand mixer fitted with the paddle attachment, beat the sugar, butter, and vanilla custard powder on medium speed until combined. Reduce the speed to low. Slowly add the milk, 1 tablespoon at a time, until the mixture is smooth and creamy. Add the food colouring and beat until the colour is uniform.

6. Using an offset spatula, spread the filling over the Chocolate Brownies in an even layer. Cover and place in the fridge for about 30 minutes to set.

CHOCOLATE TOPPING

7. In a medium heat-resistant bowl, melt the chocolate and butter in the microwave in 30-second intervals, stirring after each interval, until the mixture is smooth.

8. Once cool but malleable, pour the Chocolate Topping over the Nanaimo Filling. Using an offset spatula, spread it into an even layer. Cover and return to the fridge for at least 1 hour to set.

ASSEMBLY

9. Transfer the squares to a cutting board by lifting the edges of the parchment paper. Pull the parchment paper away from the sides of the squares. Using a sharp chef's knife, cut into 12 equal squares.

10. In a medium heat-resistant bowl, melt the chocolate wafers (if using) in the microwave in 30-second intervals, stirring after each interval, until smooth. Transfer to a piping bag and cut off the tip. Drizzle half of each square with chocolate and immediately top with a sprinkle of coconut, if using.

11. Store in an airtight container in the fridge for up to 1 week. Remove from the fridge 30 minutes before serving.

CASHEW PRALINE PARTY SQUARES

Makes 12 large squares

CASHEW PRALINE

1½ cups raw cashews
1 cup granulated sugar
2 tablespoons water

CASHEW PRALINE BLONDIE

2½ cups packed brown sugar
1½ cups melted unsalted
    butter
3 eggs
2 egg yolks
1 tablespoon pure vanilla
    extract
3¾ cups all-purpose flour
1 cup ground Cashew Praline
1½ teaspoons cornstarch
1½ teaspoons salt
¾ teaspoon baking powder

BROWNED BUTTER FUDGE

1 batch (page 300)

GARNISH (OPTIONAL)

½ batch Salted Caramel
    (page 299)
½ cup ground Cashew Praline

In this recipe, cashews are covered in a candy coating to create a praline that is added directly to the blondie before baking. This gives a sweet and crunchy textural experience to every bite of these squares!

CASHEW PRALINE

1. Preheat the oven to 325°F. Line a baking sheet with parchment paper.

2. Spread the cashews in an even layer on the prepared baking sheet. Toast for 5 to 8 minutes, or until golden brown. Let cool. Increase the oven temperature to 350°F.

3. In a small saucepan over medium heat, cook the sugar and water until it turns into a golden caramel liquid, taking care not to burn the sugar. This small amount cooks quickly, so keep an eye on it—it may take less than 1 minute. Pour the liquid over the nuts, doing your best to create a thin, even coating. Set aside to cool and harden.

4. Break the praline into smaller pieces and transfer them to the bowl of a food processor. Pulse until the pieces are the size of small pebbles. Transfer 1 cup of the praline (to be used in the blondie) into a small bowl. Transfer the remaining ½ cup into a separate small bowl and reserve for decorating.

CASHEW PRALINE BLONDIE

5. Spray a 13- × 9-inch baking dish with cooking spray. Line it with parchment paper.

6. In the bowl of a stand mixer fitted with the paddle attachment, cream the sugar and butter on low speed for 1 minute, or until combined. Add the eggs, egg yolks, and vanilla. Mix on low speed until combined. Scrape down the sides of the bowl. Remove the bowl from the mixer.

7. In a small bowl, mix the flour, 1 cup praline, cornstarch, salt, and baking powder. Add the dry ingredients to the wet ingredients and fold together with a spatula until just combined.

8. Pour the batter into the prepared baking dish. Use an offset spatula to spread it into an even layer. Bake for 30 to 40 minutes, or until a knife inserted in the middle comes out almost clean with moist crumbs (you don't want a clean knife for fudgy blondies). Let cool to room temperature.

BROWNED BUTTER FUDGE

9. Prepare 1 batch Browned Butter Fudge.

SALTED CARAMEL

10. Prepare ½ batch Salted Caramel, if using. Let cool to room temperature.

ASSEMBLY

11. Pour the Browned Butter Fudge onto the blondie. Using an offset spatula, spread it into an even layer. If you're having trouble spreading the fudge, warm the spatula by dipping it in a cup of hot water and drying it, then resume spreading. Continue dipping the spatula in hot water as needed. Cover the squares with plastic wrap and place in the fridge for at least 1 hour to set.

12. Transfer the squares to a cutting board by lifting the edges of the parchment paper. Pull the parchment paper away from the sides of the squares. Using a sharp chef's knife, cut into 12 equal squares. Transfer the Salted Caramel to a piping bag and cut off the tip. Drizzle half of each square with caramel, if using. Top with a sprinkle of the ½ cup reserved praline, if using.

13. Store in an airtight container in the fridge for up to 1 week. Remove from the fridge 30 minutes before serving.

BAKER'S TIP

If you're not a fan of cashews, substitute an equal amount of pecans, walnuts, or any other nut of your choice. Ashley isn't typically a fan of nuts in her blondies or brownies, but this is one of her all-time favourite party squares!

BANANA BREAD PARTY SQUARES

Makes 12 large squares

BANANA BREAD

1½ cups granulated sugar

½ cup unsalted butter, room temperature

1 cup sour cream

2 eggs

1¾ cups mashed very ripe banana (about 3 to 4 bananas)

2 teaspoons pure vanilla extract

2 cups all-purpose flour

1 teaspoon baking soda

¾ teaspoon salt

½ cup chopped walnuts (optional)

1 cup mini semi-sweet chocolate chips (optional)

BROWNED BUTTER FUDGE

1 batch (page 300)

GARNISH (OPTIONAL)

1 cup mini semi-sweet chocolate chips, more for garnish

1 cup chopped walnuts

Turn those browning bananas on your counter into something sweet and delicious. We top our Banana Bread Party Squares with flavourful Browned Butter Fudge, but you could easily skip the fudge layer and trick yourself into thinking this sweet treat is a healthy breakfast.

BANANA BREAD

1. Preheat the oven to 350°F. Spray a 13- × 9-inch baking dish with cooking spray. Line it with parchment paper.

2. In the bowl of a stand mixer fitted with the paddle attachment, cream the sugar and butter on medium speed for 2 minutes, until the mixture looks light and fluffy. Add the sour cream and beat for an additional 2 minutes. Scrape down the sides of the bowl. Reduce the speed to low. Add the eggs one at a time and beat until fully incorporated. Add the banana and vanilla. Increase the speed to medium and beat until fully incorporated.

3. Sift the flour into a medium bowl. Add the baking soda and salt. Add the dry ingredients to the wet ingredients and mix for 30 seconds on medium speed, or until fully incorporated. Scrape down the sides of the bowl. Add the walnuts and chocolate chips, if using. Mix on low speed for 30 seconds.

4. Pour the batter into the prepared baking dish. Using an offset spatula or the back of a spoon, spread it into an even layer. Bake for 30 minutes, or until a knife inserted in the middle comes out clean. Let cool.

BROWNED BUTTER FUDGE

5. Prepare 1 batch Browned Butter Fudge.

ASSEMBLY

6. Pour the Browned Butter Fudge onto the Banana Bread. Using an offset spatula, spread it into an even layer. If you're having trouble spreading the fudge, warm the spatula by dipping it in a cup of hot water and drying it, then resume spreading. Continue dipping the spatula in hot water as needed. Cover with plastic wrap and place in the fridge for at least 1 hour to set.

7. Transfer the squares to a cutting board by lifting the edges of the parchment paper. Pull the parchment paper away from the sides of the squares. Using a sharp chef's knife, cut into 12 equal squares.

8. Place 1 cup chocolate chips (if using) in a heat-resistant bowl and heat in the microwave in 30-second intervals, stirring after each interval, until melted and smooth. Transfer the chocolate to a piping bag and cut off the tip. Drizzle half of each square with chocolate. Top with the walnuts and chocolate chips, if using.

9. Store in an airtight container in the fridge for up to 1 week. Remove from the fridge 30 minutes before serving.

BAKER'S TIP

The riper your bananas are, the stronger their flavour will be. If you want to save overripe bananas so that you can make this recipe on another day, wait until the bananas brown, peel them and place them in a zip-top bag, then store in the freezer. Note that ½ cup mashed banana is equal to roughly 1 or 1½ large bananas.

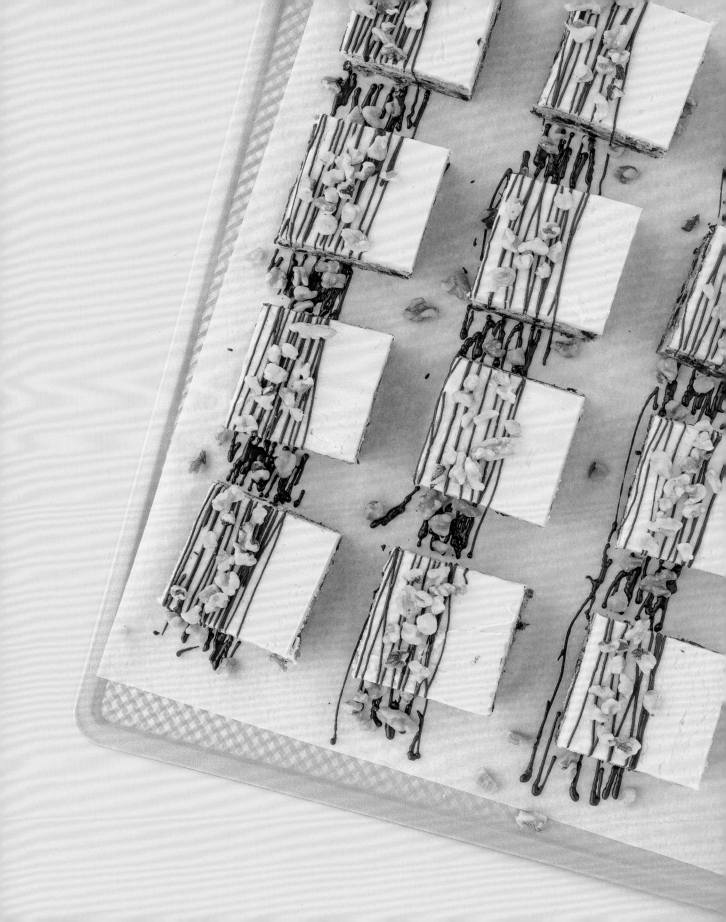

LEMON MERINGUE PARTY SQUARES

Makes 12 large squares

SHORTBREAD BASE

1 cup unsalted butter,
    room temperature
1 ¾ cups all-purpose flour
½ cup icing sugar
¼ cup cornstarch
½ teaspoon pure vanilla
    extract

LEMON CURD

2 batches (page 302)

**MERINGUE MARSHMALLOW
FLUFF**

1 batch (page 300)

Enjoy the refreshing flavour of lemon meringue pie in our easy-to-make and convenient-to-serve Lemon Meringue Party Squares. If you're going to opt for store-bought lemon juice instead of squeezing your own, use the high-quality stuff from a gourmet grocer for the best results!

SHORTBREAD BASE

1. Preheat the oven to 325°F. Spray a 13- × 9-inch baking dish with cooking spray. Line it with parchment paper.

2. In the bowl of a stand mixer fitted with the paddle attachment, cream the butter on high speed for 4 minutes, until light and fluffy. In a small bowl, combine the flour, sugar, and cornstarch. Reduce the speed of the mixer to low. Add the dry ingredients and the vanilla, beating until combined. Increase the speed to high and beat for an additional 3 minutes.

3. Transfer the shortbread to the prepared baking dish and press down firmly to create an even layer. Bake for 10 minutes. Let cool.

LEMON CURD

4. Prepare 2 batches Lemon Curd. Use immediately by pouring it over the Shortbread Base. Cover with plastic wrap and place in the fridge for at least 3 to 4 hours, or overnight, to set.

MERINGUE MARSHMALLOW FLUFF

5. Prepare 1 batch Meringue Marshmallow Fluff.

ASSEMBLY

6. Transfer the squares to a cutting board by lifting the edges of the parchment paper. Pull the parchment paper away from the sides of the squares. Using a sharp chef's knife, cut into 12 equal squares.

7. Transfer the Meringue Marshmallow Fluff to a piping bag and cut off the tip. Pipe a large dollop of fluff in the middle of each square or use a spatula to spread meringue in a single layer over the entire square, as you would on a lemon meringue pie. Using a handheld torch, toast the fluff.

8. Store in an airtight container in the fridge for up to 4 days. Remove from the fridge 30 minutes before serving.

BAKER'S TIP

Not a fan of meringue? Swap out the Meringue Marshmallow Fluff for 1 batch of our Shortbread Crumble (page 305). Toss the crumble in about ¾ cup icing sugar and sprinkle it evenly over the Lemon Curd before you put the squares in the fridge to set.

CHOCOLATE LOVER'S BROWNIE PARTY SQUARES

CHOCOLATE LOVER'S BROWNIE

1 cup + 2 tablespoons melted butter
2 tablespoons vegetable oil
2½ cups granulated sugar
4 eggs
1 egg yolk
1 tablespoon pure vanilla extract
1¼ cups all-purpose flour
1 cup cocoa powder
¼ teaspoon salt

DARK CHOCOLATE FUDGE FROSTING

1½ cups (330 g) chopped dark baking chocolate
¼ cup + 2 tablespoons whole (3.25%) milk
2 tablespoons unsalted butter, room temperature
2¾ cups icing sugar
1½ teaspoons pure vanilla extract

GARNISH

3 cups (660 g) chopped milk or dark baking chocolate
¼ cup vegetable oil

Classic. Decadent. Enticing. Mouth-watering. These are just a few of the many ways people describe the simple yet can't-get-enough-of-it flavour of these Chocolate Lover's Brownie Party Squares. Each bite will transport you to a wonderland of chocolate.

CHOCOLATE LOVER'S BROWNIE

1. Preheat the oven to 350°F. Spray a 13- × 9-inch baking dish with cooking spray. Line it with parchment paper.

2. In the bowl of a stand mixer fitted with the whisk attachment, whip the butter, oil, and sugar on medium-high speed for 1 minute. Add the eggs, egg yolk, and vanilla and continue to whip for an additional minute, or until the mixture lightens in colour.

3. Remove the bowl from the mixer. Sift the flour and cocoa powder into the bowl. Add the salt. Using a spatula, gently fold in the dry ingredients until just combined. Do not overmix.

4. Pour the batter into the prepared baking dish. Using an offset spatula or the back of a spoon, spread it into an even layer. Bake for 30 to 40 minutes or until a knife inserted in the middle comes out almost clean with moist crumbs (you don't want a clean knife for fudgy brownies). Let cool to room temperature.

DARK CHOCOLATE FUDGE FROSTING

5. In a small saucepan over medium-high heat, heat the chocolate, milk, and butter, stirring often until fully melted and combined.

6. In the bowl of a stand mixer fitted with the paddle attachment, mix the icing sugar on low speed. Slowly pour the chocolate mixture into the icing sugar. Add the vanilla. Increase the speed to high and beat for 4 minutes, until smooth. Use immediately.

ASSEMBLY

7. Pour the Dark Chocolate Fudge Frosting over the brownie. Using an offset spatula, spread it into an even layer. If you're having trouble spreading the frosting, warm the spatula by dipping it in a cup of hot water and drying it, then resume spreading. Continue dipping the spatula in hot water as needed. Cover with plastic wrap and place in the fridge for at least 1 hour to set.

8. Line a baking sheet with parchment paper.

9. Transfer the squares to a cutting board by lifting the edges of the parchment paper. Pull the parchment paper away from the sides of the squares. Using a sharp chef's knife, cut into 12 equal squares.

10. In a heat-resistant bowl, melt the chocolate in the microwave in 30-second intervals, stirring after each interval, until smooth. Add the oil and stir well to incorporate.

11. Working with 1 square at a time, dip the top of each square into the chocolate and shake gently to remove any excess. Set the square, chocolate side up, on the prepared baking sheet to harden.

12. Store in an airtight container in the fridge for up to 1 week. Remove from the fridge 30 minutes before serving.

BAKER'S TIP

For an even more chocolatey experience, fold ¾ cup chocolate chunks or chips into the brownie batter before pouring it into the dish to bake.

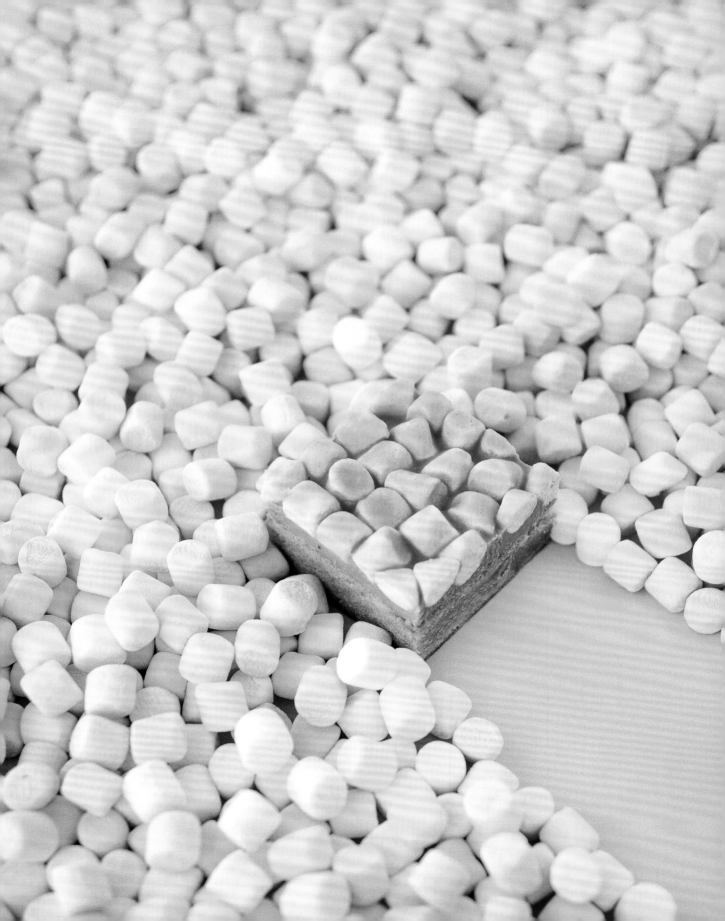

PEANUT BUTTER MARSHMALLOW PARTY SQUARES

Makes 12 large squares

BUTTERSCOTCH BLONDIE

2½ cups packed brown sugar

1½ cups melted unsalted butter

3 eggs

2 egg yolks

1 tablespoon pure vanilla extract

3¾ cups all-purpose flour

1½ teaspoons cornstarch

1½ teaspoons salt

¾ teaspoon baking powder

½ cup butterscotch chips

PEANUT BUTTER MARSHMALLOW SQUARES

1 batch (page 307, step 2)

Level-up your average Peanut Butter Marshmallow Square (PBMS) by adding a base layer of Butterscotch Blondie. One nibble of this epic creation and partygoers will find it hard to go back to a classic PBMS.

BUTTERSCOTCH BLONDIE

1. Preheat the oven to 350°F. Spray a 13- × 9-inch baking dish with cooking spray. Line it with parchment paper.

2. In the bowl of a stand mixer fitted with the paddle attachment, cream the sugar and butter on low speed for 1 minute, until combined. Add the eggs, egg yolks, and vanilla and mix until combined. Scrape down the sides of the bowl.

3. In a small bowl, mix the flour, cornstarch, salt, baking powder, and butterscotch chips. Remove the bowl from the stand mixer. Add the dry ingredients to the wet ingredients and fold together with a spatula until just combined.

4. Pour the batter into the prepared baking dish. Use an offset spatula or the back of a spoon to spread it into an even layer. Bake for 30 to 40 minutes, or until a knife inserted in the middle comes out almost clean with moist crumbs (you don't want a clean knife for fudgy blondies). Let cool to room temperature.

PEANUT BUTTER MARSHMALLOW SQUARES

5. Prepare 1 batch Peanut Butter Marshmallow Squares, following step 2 of the recipe on page 307.

ASSEMBLY

6. Pour the warm Peanut Butter Marshmallow Squares batter over the blondie. Cover with plastic wrap and place in the fridge for at least 1 hour to set.

7. Transfer the squares to a cutting board by lifting the edges of the parchment paper. Pull the parchment paper away from the sides of the squares. Using a sharp chef's knife, cut into 12 equal squares.

8. Store in an airtight container in the fridge for up to 1 week. Remove from the fridge 30 minutes before serving.

BAKER'S TIP

If you're not a fan of butterscotch, replace the butterscotch chips with an equal amount of peanut butter chips.

RED VELVET PARTY SQUARES

Take the unmistakable flavour of red velvet, combine it with a rich and fudgy brownie, top it with White Chocolate Cream Cheese Fudge Frosting and you've got one swoon-worthy dessert. We can't stop snacking on the cut edges of this one when we make it at the shop!

RED VELVET BROWNIE

1⅔ cups granulated sugar

1 cup unsalted butter, room temperature

¾ cup packed brown sugar

3 tablespoons sifted cocoa powder

3 tablespoons red liquid food colouring

4 eggs

½ cup buttermilk

1½ teaspoons pure vanilla extract

¾ teaspoon apple cider vinegar

1¾ cups all-purpose flour

¼ teaspoon salt

WHITE CHOCOLATE CREAM CHEESE FUDGE FROSTING

½ cup cream cheese, room temperature

2¼ cups icing sugar

½ teaspoon pure vanilla extract

1¼ cups (275 g) chopped white baking chocolate

2 tablespoons whole (3.25%) milk

RED VELVET BROWNIE

1. Preheat the oven to 350°F. Spray a 13- × 9-inch baking dish with cooking spray. Line it with parchment paper.

2. In the bowl of a stand mixer fitted with the paddle attachment, cream the granulated sugar, butter, and brown sugar on medium speed for 2 minutes.

3. In a small bowl, whisk together the cocoa powder and food colouring. Pour the cocoa mixture into the butter mixture and beat on medium speed for 2 minutes. Scrape down the sides of the bowl.

4. With the mixer on low speed, slowly add the eggs, one at a time, and beat until fully combined. Slowly pour in the buttermilk, vanilla, and apple cider vinegar, mixing until combined. Remove the bowl from the stand mixer and scrape down the sides of the bowl and paddle. Add the flour and salt. Using a spatula, gently fold until just combined.

5. Pour the batter into the prepared baking dish. Using an offset spatula or the back of a spoon, spread it into an even layer. Bake for 30 to 40 minutes, or until a knife inserted in the middle comes out almost clean with moist crumbs (you don't want a clean knife for fudgy brownies). Let cool to room temperature.

WHITE CHOCOLATE CREAM CHEESE FUDGE FROSTING

6. In the bowl of a stand mixer fitted with the paddle attachment, beat the cream cheese on medium-high speed for 4 to 5 minutes, scraping down the bowl after each minute. Add the sugar and vanilla and beat for an additional 2 minutes, until creamy and smooth, scraping down the bowl after each minute.

7. In a heat-resistant bowl, melt the chocolate in the microwave in 30-second intervals, stirring after each interval, until smooth.

8. With the mixer on medium-low speed, slowly add the melted chocolate and milk. Scrape down the sides of the bowl and mix on high speed for 2 to 3 minutes, until smooth and creamy. Use immediately.

ASSEMBLY

9. Pour the White Chocolate Cream Cheese Fudge Frosting over the brownie. Using an offset spatula, spread it into an even layer. If you're having trouble spreading the frosting, warm the spatula by dipping it in a cup of hot water and drying it, then resume spreading. Continue dipping the spatula in hot water as needed. Cover with plastic wrap and place in the fridge for at least 1 hour to set.

10. Transfer the squares to a cutting board by lifting the edges of the parchment paper. Pull the parchment paper away from the sides of the squares. Using a sharp chef's knife, cut into 12 equal squares.

11. Store in an airtight container in the fridge for up to 1 week. Remove from the fridge 30 minutes before serving.

BAKER'S TIP

It's important to use liquid food colouring in this recipe. To make these Red Velvet Party Squares festive for any occasion, swap out the red food colouring for blue, green (we do this in store for St. Patrick's Day!), or equal parts red and blue to make purple.

CAKES

BAKER'S NOTES

From our Kitchen to yours

xo

CAKES SERVE AS THE SHOW-STOPPING CENTREPIECE of many events and celebrations, so learning how to master the basics of baking and decorating will come in handy. This Baker's Notes section will help you resolve anything that might stump you on your cake-baking journey.

PAN SIZE

All of the cake recipes in this book are designed to work with a 6-inch round cake pan with 3-inch sides. If the sides of your pan are only 2 inches tall, the batter will overflow when baking. You can purchase 3-inch-tall pans from your local bulk food store or craft store. The diameter of the pan is important in terms of the baking time, and using a 6-inch round pan will also ensure that your cake is a little taller than most, giving it an extra wow factor. We grease our pans with vegetable shortening and a sprinkle of flour to ensure that we have no trouble getting the cake out of the pan.

BAKING TIME

Baking time for cakes in 3-inch-tall pans is usually quite a bit longer than it would be in a pan with shorter sides. If this is your first time baking a tall cake, be aware that the cakes in this book won't bake in the same way a classic sheet cake would. Start by baking for 40 to 45 minutes, but it may take close to 1 hour to bake the layers, depending on how hot your oven is. You'll know the cake is baked to completion when a butter knife inserted into the middle comes out clean, with no crumbs stuck to it. Around this time, the cake will also start to pull away from the edges of the pan. Before inserting the knife, tap the top of the cake; if it jiggles, continue baking for 5 to 10 minutes and try again. Only pierce the cake with the knife when the top is no longer jiggly to the touch or it may deflate, which will result in a misshapen cake that's not fully baked in the middle. Give your cake plenty of time to bake and remember that you can clean up while it's in the oven or use the time to prepare buttercreams and other fillings.

OVEN

If you find that you're baking a cake and it's beginning to look very dark around the edges while the middle of the cake is still jiggly when tapped, try lowering the temperature of your oven by 25°F. Every oven is different, so you may also want to try increasing or decreasing the baking time if you find that your cakes are over- or underbaking.

GIVE YOURSELF TIME

Have an event to go to in a few hours? Baking a four-layer cake for the occasion may not be the best idea! Creating a layer cake requires time to bake the cake and let it cool completely before cutting the layers, stacking them, icing the whole thing, and, finally, decorating. We recommend baking your cake the night before you want to stack and decorate it. Once the cake has cooled enough to touch (waiting until the cake has cooled completely will cause it to stick to the pan when trying to remove it), wrap each cake tightly with plastic wrap and place it in the fridge overnight. Giving the cake time to chill will allow it to set, which will make it easier to stack and decorate.

SUBSTITUTIONS

We don't recommend making substitutions in our cake recipes, but if you don't have whole (3.25%) milk on hand, you can substitute an equal amount of skim, 1%, or 2% milk. For best results, all other ingredients should be used as indicated in the recipes.

If you're putting together one of our more elaborate cakes and would prefer to use store-bought caramel, marshmallow fluff, apple pie filling, and so on, feel free! We cannot guarantee the results you'll achieve, as we prepare everything from scratch in our kitchen, but using store-bought options may save you a few steps.

SIMPLE SYRUP

Brushing each cake layer with simple syrup after it is cut is an important step to ensure that your cake stays moist throughout the assembly process. We find that our sponge cakes remain moist on their own, so you can skip the simple syrup if you like, but we believe that adding a little extra moisture to your cake layers is never a bad thing! Simple syrup is thin enough to seep into every part of your cake but thick enough that it won't make your cake soggy. Making simple syrup is easy! It's a 1:1 ratio of sugar and water, and we usually make 1 cup at a time to keep on hand.

Simple Syrup

In a medium saucepan over medium-high heat, combine 1 cup sugar and 1 cup water and bring to a boil. Stir until the sugar is dissolved and remove from the heat. Let cool to room temperature and store in an airtight container in the fridge for up to 2 weeks. See how we use simple syrup in Guide to Stacking, Crumb Coating, and Icing the Perfect Cake (below).

DECORATING

A cake from Jenna Rae Cakes is known for its designs executed with precision. Don't feel down if your first few cakes don't look exactly like the images in our book— Jenna has been decorating cakes for years, and she's learned a lot of tricks along the way. We do our best to share all of our tips and tricks in this book, but, above all, practice is key. Consider each cake you make as another opportunity to refine your skills and move one step closer to becoming a cake artist. Although the technical side of cake decorating requires discipline and focus, playing with colour palettes, sprinkles, and other garnishes is where you can let loose. We encourage creativity and want you to take these cake designs and make them your own.

TOP TIPS

- The most common errors with cakes result from undermixing and underbaking. Be sure to follow the mixing timelines in our recipes to avoid undermixing, and make sure that your knife comes out clean when inserted into the middle of a cake to avoid underbaking.

- Take care to grease your pan well with shortening and flour so that the cake slides out easily after

baking. Tap out your greased and floured pan to ensure that extra flour is discarded before adding your batter.

- Be sure to give your eggs time to whip up. If your eggs are cold, it will take longer for them to gain volume, so try to use room-temperature eggs instead.

- Give your cake adequate time to chill before pouring on any ganache or salted caramel. You'll know your cake is ready to add a warm, decorative layer when you can touch it in the fridge and your finger doesn't leave a dent or a defined mark, usually after about 30 minutes.

- Store your cake in a tall 8-inch cake box in the fridge. If the box isn't tall enough, tape the sides on an angle. No need to use plastic wrap on the opening if there is one, as the buttercream keeps the cake protected and fresh!

GUIDE TO STACKING, CRUMB COATING, AND ICING THE PERFECT CAKE

Stacking the perfect cake can be easy when you follow step-by-step directions! The tips, instructions, and images below will give you the skills necessary for your practice to yield perfection as you decorate cakes for every occasion. Follow each recipe's assembly steps to decorate your cake after completing the process below. The crumb coat is an important part of decorating a cake, as it holds in the crumbs from the cake and allows the final coating of frosting to look pristine and crumb free.

General Tips

- Make sure your cake is fully cooled and chilled before you cut it into layers. A warm or even room-temperature cake will not allow for as clean a cut, as the crumb will pull away as you slice.

- Take your time. Decorating a cake is a process to be enjoyed, not one to race through. Take time to hone your skills and your speed will increase gradually as you decorate more cakes.

- Buttercream must be used at room temperature. If you start working with buttercream that is too warm or too cold, it will make stacking and crumb coating your cake more of a challenge.

- Use a cake turntable. It will make your life so much easier.

- Use the right tools. We recommend a large offset spatula and a cake scraper with a tapered edge for smoothing exterior edges. These tools can be purchased at your local bulk food store, at a craft store, or even online.

- The diameter of your cake board should be 2 inches larger than the diameter of the cake you're making. For example, if you're making a 6-inch cake, use an 8-inch cake board. It'll be easier to handle without knicking the buttercream.

- Wipe excess buttercream from your tools regularly to help keep the edges crisp.

- Keep the cake cool while frosting it with the final coat of buttercream. If you're having a tough time getting those clean sides and edges, stick the cake back in the fridge for 10 minutes and try again!

Method

1. Using a bread knife, level each cake by trimming off any domed top that may have formed while baking. Cut each cake in half crosswise to create 4 layers. Using a silicone brush, brush 1 to 2 tablespoons Simple Syrup (see page 126) on the top of each layer.

2. Place a cake board on a cake turntable and place a small dollop of buttercream in the middle of the board. For the first layer, select a cake that has one very flat side from sitting directly in the cake pan. Place it on the cake board, cut side up. Lightly press the cake into the buttercream to make sure it sticks in place.

3. Scoop a generous amount of buttercream onto the first layer. Using an offset spatula, spread the buttercream in an even layer over the cake. Ideally, the buttercream layer should be about ½ inch thick.

4. Place a second layer of cake, with two cut sides, on top of the buttercream and lightly press down to make sure it sticks in place. Scoop a generous amount of buttercream onto the second layer. Using an offset spatula, spread the buttercream in an even layer over the cake. Ideally, the buttercream layer should be about ½ inch thick.

5. Repeat step 4 to make the third layer of cake and buttercream.

6. Place the final layer of cake on top, cut side down. This will ensure that the cake has a flat top. Lightly press the cake into the buttercream to make sure it sticks in place. Place the stacked cake in the fridge to chill for about 15 minutes, until the buttercream firms up.

7. Return the cake to the turntable. Using a bread knife, carefully trim the edges of the cake to ensure that there are no lumps or bumps and to even out the sides. Start from the top of the cake and run your knife all the way to the bottom, making small cuts around the edges. Trimming ensures that every single guest can enjoy a piece of cake that is moist and delicious, no matter how you cut the cake.

8. Use an offset spatula to cover the sides and top of the cake with a generous, even amount of buttercream. To level the top, hold the offset spatula with the tip in the middle of the cake so that the straight edge runs across the top of the cake. Apply gentle pressure and begin to move the turntable slowly. If you are right-handed, use your right hand to smooth the buttercream over the cake while moving the turntable counterclockwise with your left hand.

9. To create a crumb coat, smooth the sides of the cake. Using a cake scraper held parallel to the side of the cake, begin to move the turntable around to remove excess buttercream. Rest the cake scraper on the cake board to ensure that the edges are straight. When you complete one full turn, scrape the excess buttercream from your cake scraper into a bowl. Repeat until the cake edges are straight and smooth.

You don't have to obsess over getting smooth, sharp edges just yet—the crumb coat doesn't have to be perfect.

10. To create a defined top edge, use the cake scraper to gently pull the exterior edge of buttercream in toward the middle of the cake. Repeat this process, making your way around the entire cake until your top edge is straight and sharp. Keep in mind that this is the crumb coat stage, so don't worry if the edge isn't perfect—you can perfect it in the final buttercream coat! Return the cake to the fridge to chill. Your cake has now been crumb coated and is ready for its final decorative coat of buttercream!

11. Repeat step 8.

12. To create the final coat of buttercream, smooth the sides of the cake. Using a cake scraper held parallel to the side of the cake, begin to move the turntable around to remove excess buttercream. Rest the cake scraper on the cake board to ensure that the edges are straight. When you complete one full turn, scrape the excess buttercream from your cake scraper into a bowl. This will be the final coat of your cake, so take your time and repeat this process until the surface is smooth and straight.

13. To create a defined top edge, use the cake scraper to gently pull the exterior edge of buttercream in toward the middle of the cake. Repeat this process, making your way around the entire cake until your top edge is straight and sharp. Use light pressure when doing this, taking very small amounts of buttercream off at a time—you don't want to take off too much at the beginning or you may have to add more to achieve even, straight sides. Remember, if you're having trouble, return the cake to the fridge for 10 minutes and try again!

14. Wipe any buttercream off the cake board using a paper towel. Place the cake in the fridge to chill for about 15 minutes, or until the buttercream is firm. Now your cake is ready for any final decorative touches called for in the recipe!

VANILLA SPRINKLE CAKE

1 cup whole (3.25%) milk
¼ cup salted butter
¾ teaspoon pure vanilla
     extract
4 eggs
2 cups granulated sugar
2 cups all-purpose flour
2 teaspoons baking powder
¼ teaspoon salt
2 tablespoons long rainbow
     sprinkles, divided, more
     for garnish

**VANILLA SPRINKLE
BUTTERCREAM**

2 batches Vanilla Buttercream
     (page 296), divided
3 drops soft pink gel food
     colouring
¼ cup long rainbow sprinkles

VANILLA SPRINKLE CAKE

The cake that pleases every crowd, our signature Vanilla Sprinkle Cake is more than your standard vanilla cake. This recipe has been tweaked over and over to become the go-to cake for all those times when you are unsure of what flavour of cake to make. It's guaranteed to please the taste buds of those both young in age and young at heart.

VANILLA SPRINKLE CAKE

1. Preheat the oven to 325°F. Grease and flour two 6- × 3-inch round cake pans with shortening.

2. In a small saucepan over medium-high heat (or in a heat-resistant bowl in the microwave), heat the milk and butter until the butter is completely melted. Remove from the heat and stir in the vanilla.

3. In the bowl of a stand mixer fitted with the whisk attachment, whip the eggs on high speed for 2 minutes, or until they are light and fluffy and have doubled in size. Reduce the speed to low and slowly add the sugar. Increase the speed to high and whip for an additional minute.

4. Sift the flour, baking powder, and salt into a small bowl and stir together. With the mixer on low speed, alternate adding small amounts of the flour mixture and the milk mixture to the egg mixture, beginning and ending with the dry ingredients. Scrape the bottom of the bowl with a spatula and mix for an additional 2 to 3 minutes on medium-high speed, until the mixture looks light and fluffy.

5. Divide the batter evenly between the prepared cake pans. Sprinkle 1 tablespoon sprinkles into each pan and gently fold in using a spoon. Bake for 40 minutes, or until the edges of the cake begin to pull away from the sides of the pan and a knife inserted into the middle of the cake comes out clean. If the cake jiggles in the middle when the pan is tapped gently, continue baking before testing it with a knife. Let cool for 10 to 15 minutes in the pans. Run a knife or an offset spatula around the inside edge of the pans to release the edges of the cakes. Flip onto a wire rack and let cool to room temperature.

VANILLA SPRINKLE BUTTERCREAM

6. Prepare 2 batches Vanilla Buttercream.

7. Transfer 4 cups of the buttercream to a medium bowl. Add the food colouring and sprinkles and fold until the colour is uniform.

ASSEMBLY

8. Transfer ½ cup of the white buttercream to a piping bag fitted with a No. 2D tip.

9. Stack and crumb coat the cake using the remaining white buttercream (see instructions on pages 126 to 129).

10. Frost the cake using the pink sprinkle buttercream (see instructions on page 133, steps A to E). The sprinkles may pull along and leave indents in the buttercream. If you are having trouble creating a smooth surface, fill in the indents with buttercream and move your cake scraper very gently to smooth the buttercream without pulling any additional sprinkles. This process requires patience.

CONTINUED

11. Return the cake to the turntable. Pipe rosettes of white buttercream around the top edge of the cake to form a rosette crown (step F on page 133). Decorate the rosettes with sprinkles. Place the cake in the fridge to chill.

12. Store in a tall cake box in the fridge for up to 4 days. Once the cake has been cut, cover the cut edges with a layer of waxed paper or plastic wrap placed up against the cake. Remove from the fridge 1 hour before serving.

BAKER'S TIP

Customize this cake for the person or occasion you are celebrating by substituting the long rainbow sprinkles and the soft pink gel food colouring for equal amounts of long sprinkles and gel food colouring in your desired colour palette. Or leave out the sprinkles altogether for a classic vanilla cake.

LEMON WILDBERRY CAKE

Each flavourful bite of this Lemon Wildberry Cake is an ode to summer nights we wish would never end. Vanilla sponge cake is elevated by fresh berries and lemon zest. With Wildberry Buttercream and a drizzle of zingy Lemon Curd, you can taste the joy of summer in this beautiful dessert.

LEMON WILDBERRY CAKE

1 cup whole (3.25%) milk
¼ cup unsalted butter
¾ teaspoon pure vanilla
    extract
4 eggs
2 cups granulated sugar
2 cups + 2 tablespoons
    all-purpose flour, divided
4 tablespoons lemon zest
    (about 4 lemons)
2 teaspoons baking powder
¼ teaspoon salt
¼ cup fresh blueberries
¼ cup fresh raspberries
¼ cup hulled and chopped
    strawberries

LEMON CURD

½ batch (page 302)

WILDBERRY REDUCTION

½ batch (page 304)

VANILLA BUTTERCREAM

2 batches (page 296), divided
5 drops soft pink gel food
    colouring

WILDBERRY BUTTERCREAM

4 cups Vanilla Buttercream
1 cup Wildberry Reduction,
    strained

GARNISH (OPTIONAL)

Edible flowers

LEMON WILDBERRY CAKE

1. Preheat the oven to 325°F. Grease and flour two 6- × 3-inch round cake pans with shortening.

2. In a small saucepan over medium-high heat (or in a heat-resistant bowl in the microwave), heat the milk and butter until the butter is completely melted. Remove from the heat. Stir in the vanilla.

3. In the bowl of a stand mixer fitted with the whisk attachment, whip the eggs on high speed for 2 minutes, or until they are light and fluffy and have doubled in size. Reduce the speed to low and slowly add the sugar. Increase the speed to high and whip for an additional minute.

4. Sift 2 cups flour into a small bowl. Add the lemon zest and stir to coat the zest in the flour. Sift the baking powder and salt into the bowl and stir to combine. With the mixer on low speed, alternate adding small amounts of the flour mixture and the milk mixture to the egg mixture, beginning and ending with the dry ingredients. Scrape the bottom of the bowl with a spatula and mix for an additional 2 to 3 minutes on medium-high speed, until the mixture looks light and fluffy.

5. Remove the bowl from the stand mixer. In a small bowl, toss the blueberries, raspberries, and strawberries with 2 tablespoons flour to coat. Add the berries to the cake batter and fold in using a spatula.

6. Divide the batter evenly between the prepared cake pans. Bake for 40 minutes, or until the edges of the cake begin to pull away from the sides of the pan and a knife inserted into the middle of the cake comes out clean. If the cake jiggles in the middle when the pan is tapped gently, continue baking before testing it with a knife. Let cool for 10 to 15 minutes in the pans. Run a knife or an offset spatula around the inside edge of the pans to release the edges of the cakes. Flip onto a wire rack and let cool to room temperature.

LEMON CURD

7. Prepare ½ batch Lemon Curd. Let cool to room temperature.

WILDBERRY REDUCTION

8. Prepare ½ batch Wildberry Reduction. Let cool to room temperature.

VANILLA BUTTERCREAM

9. Prepare 2 batches Vanilla Buttercream. Place 4 cups of the buttercream in a separate bowl and reserve. This will become the Wildberry Buttercream.

10. Add the food colouring to the remaining 4 cups of buttercream in the bowl of the stand mixer and whip on high speed until the colour is uniform.

11. Transfer ½ cup of the pink buttercream to a piping bag fitted with a No. 2D tip.

CONTINUED

WILDBERRY BUTTERCREAM

12. Transfer the reserved 4 cups Vanilla Buttercream to the bowl of the stand mixer fitted with the whisk attachment.

13. Add 1 cup Wildberry Reduction to the buttercream. Whip on high speed until fully incorporated. Reserve any leftover reduction for serving.

ASSEMBLY

14. Transfer the Lemon Curd to a piping bag and cut off the tip.

15. Use the Wildberry Buttercream to stack the cake, adding a drizzle of Lemon Curd between each layer (see instructions on pages 126 to 129).

16. Crumb coat the cake with the pink buttercream (see instructions on pages 126 to 129).

17. Frost the cake using the pink buttercream (see instructions on page 137, steps A to E). To create the lined buttercream finish, press a small, clean offset spatula into the buttercream at the very bottom of the cake. Keeping the spatula exactly where it is, move the turntable in one full rotation. Move the spatula above the first line and repeat the process, creating a second scallop above the first. Clean the spatula between rotations if needed. Repeat this process until you reach the top of the cake.

18. Pipe rosettes of pink buttercream around the top edge of the cake to form a rosette crown (step F on page 137). Garnish the rosettes with edible flowers, if using.

19. Store in a tall cake box in the fridge for up to 4 days. Once the cake has been cut, cover the cut edges with a layer of waxed paper or plastic wrap placed up against the cake. Remove from the fridge 1 hour before serving.

BAKER'S TIP

We love the flavour of the mixed berries in this cake, but you can customize the berries as you wish. Try replacing the blueberries and strawberries in the cake and the reduction with an equal amount of raspberries to create a lemon raspberry cake—one of our favourites!

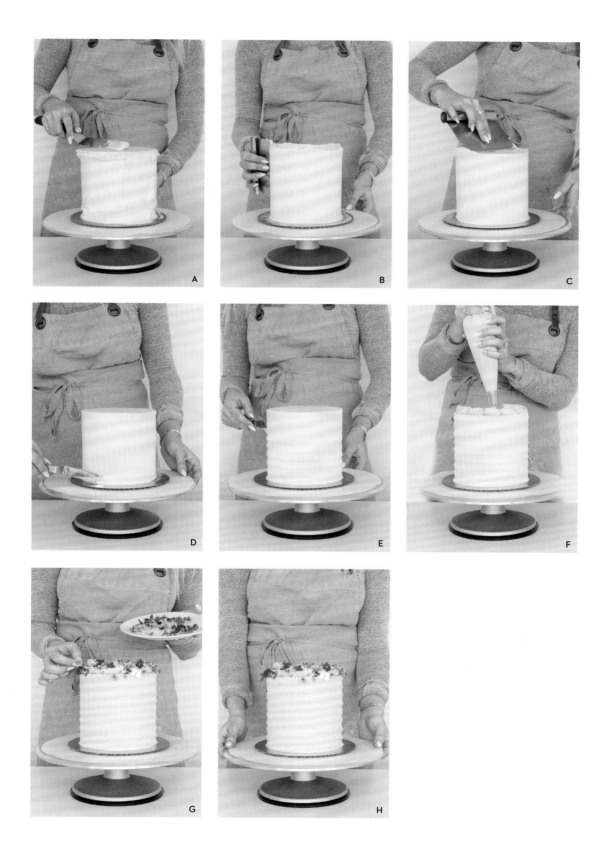

Makes one 6-inch cake with four layers; serves 8 to 10

STRAWBERRY COMPOTE

2 batches (page 303), divided

STRAWBERRY SPONGE CAKE

⅔ cup whole (3.25%) milk
¼ cup unsalted butter
¾ teaspoon pure vanilla
   extract
4 eggs
2 cups granulated sugar
2 cups all-purpose flour
2 teaspoons baking powder
¼ teaspoon salt
⅔ cup Strawberry Compote

SHORTBREAD CRUMBLE

1 batch (page 305)

STRAWBERRY BUTTERCREAM

2 batches Vanilla Buttercream
   (page 296)
1½ cups Strawberry Compote
5 drops soft pink gel food
   colouring

GARNISH

4 to 6 large strawberries,
   hulled and cut in half

STRAWBERRY SHORTCAKE

Have you ever had a traditional strawberry shortcake dessert? A buttery, flaky biscuit is topped with lightly sweetened whipped cream and fresh strawberries. We reimagined the classic dessert as a cake by marrying Strawberry Sponge Cake with whipped Strawberry Buttercream and a perfectly buttery and delicious Shortbread Crumble.

STRAWBERRY COMPOTE

1. Prepare 2 batches Strawberry Compote.

STRAWBERRY SPONGE CAKE

2. Preheat the oven to 325°F. Grease and flour two 6- × 3-inch round cake pans with shortening.

3. In a small saucepan over medium-high heat (or in a heat-resistant bowl in the microwave), heat the milk and butter until the butter is completely melted. Remove from the heat and stir in the vanilla.

4. In the bowl of a stand mixer fitted with the whisk attachment, whip the eggs on high speed for 2 minutes, or until they are light and fluffy and have doubled in size. Reduce the speed to low and slowly add the sugar. Increase the speed to high and whip for an additional minute.

5. Sift the flour, baking powder, and salt into a small bowl and stir together. With the mixer on low speed, alternate adding small amounts of the flour mixture and the milk mixture to the egg mixture, beginning and ending with the dry ingredients. Scrape the bottom of the bowl with a spatula and mix for an additional 2 to 3 minutes on medium-high speed, until the mixture looks light and fluffy. Fold in ⅔ cup Strawberry Compote.

6. Divide the batter evenly between the prepared cake pans. Bake for 40 minutes, or until the edges of the cake begin to pull away from the sides of the pan and a knife inserted into the middle of the cake comes out clean. If the cake jiggles in the middle when the pan is tapped gently, continue baking before testing it with a knife. Let cool for 10 to 15 minutes in the pans. Run a knife or an offset spatula around the inside edge of the pans to release the edges of the cakes. Flip onto a wire rack and let cool to room temperature.

SHORTBREAD CRUMBLE

7. Prepare 1 batch Shortbread Crumble, making sure to add the electric pink gel food colouring if you want to follow our design. Set aside to cool.

STRAWBERRY BUTTERCREAM

8. Prepare 2 batches Vanilla Buttercream.

9. Add 1½ cups Strawberry Compote and the food colouring to the buttercream. Whisk on high speed until combined.

CONTINUED

ASSEMBLY

10. Use about 4 cups of the Strawberry Buttercream to stack and crumb coat the cake, sprinkling ¼ cup Shortbread Crumble over the buttercream between each layer (see instructions on pages 126 to 129).

11. Frost the cake using the Strawberry Buttercream (see instructions on page 141, steps A to C), making sure to reserve about ½ cup to decorate the top of the cake.

12. To decorate, press small handfuls of Shortbread Crumble around the outside of the cake from the bottom upward until only about 1 inch of buttercream is exposed around the top of the cake (see Baker's Tip; steps D and E on page 141).

13. Transfer the reserved ½ cup Strawberry Buttercream to a piping bag and cut off the tip to create an opening about ½ inch in diameter. Pipe dollops of buttercream around the top edge of the cake to form a crown. Top each dollop with a strawberry half (steps F to H on page 141). Place the cake in the fridge to chill.

14. Store in a tall cake box in the fridge for up to 4 days. Once the cake has been cut, cover the cut edges with a layer of waxed paper or plastic wrap placed up against the cake. Remove from the fridge 1 hour before serving.

BAKER'S TIP

We recommend decorating this cake on the day you plan to serve it. The longer the uncut cake sits in the fridge, the more moisture the shortbread crumble on the exterior will collect, making it less crunchy—and we love the bit of texture that the crumble adds to this cake!

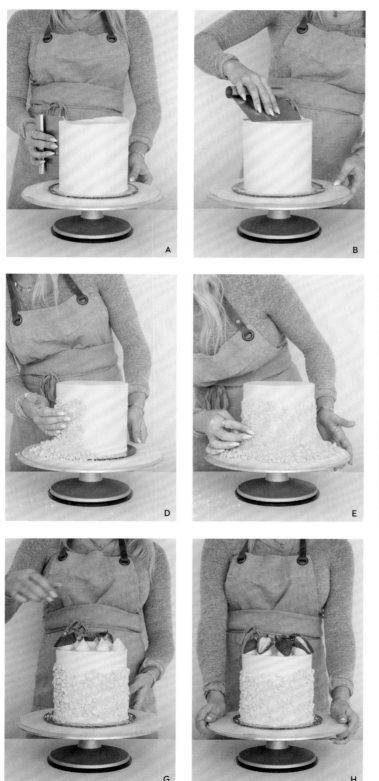

SALTED DARK CHOCOLATE ESPRESSO CAKE

Makes one 6-inch cake with four layers; serves 8 to 10

CHOCOLATE CAKE
1 batch (page 162)

CHOCOLATE ESPRESSO BUTTERCREAM
2 batches Milk Chocolate Buttercream (page 296)
3 tablespoons hot water
2 tablespoons instant espresso powder
½ teaspoon pure vanilla extract

DARK CHOCOLATE GANACHE
2 batches (page 298)

MOCHA CRUMBLE
¾ cup + 2 tablespoons all-purpose flour
½ cup granulated sugar
1 tablespoon cocoa powder, sifted
1 tablespoon instant espresso powder
¼ teaspoon pure vanilla extract
⅓ cup unsalted butter, melted

GARNISH
¾ teaspoon large flake salt, divided
2 tablespoons gold dust
1 tablespoon vodka (see Baker's Tip)
2 tablespoons instant espresso powder
1 to 2 teaspoons pure vanilla extract

If you'd openly refer to yourself as a coffee addict, the temptation of this cake will be impossible for you to resist. Four layers of chocolate sponge cake are filled with three layers of Chocolate Espresso Buttercream, creamy Dark Chocolate Ganache, crunchy Mocha Crumble, and a sprinkle of large flake sea salt to complement the rich and sweet flavours. This cake is dedicated to our favourite coffee lover: Dad.

CHOCOLATE CAKE

1. Prepare 1 batch Chocolate Cake.

CHOCOLATE ESPRESSO BUTTERCREAM

2. Prepare 2 batches Milk Chocolate Buttercream.
3. In a small bowl, stir together the hot water, espresso, and vanilla until a paste forms.
4. Add the espresso paste to the buttercream and whip on high speed until smooth.

DARK CHOCOLATE GANACHE

5. Prepare 2 batches Dark Chocolate Ganache. Let cool to room temperature.

MOCHA CRUMBLE

6. Preheat the oven to 325°F. Line a baking sheet with parchment paper.
7. In a medium bowl, combine the flour, sugar, cocoa powder, espresso, and vanilla. Add the melted butter and stir until well combined.
8. Spread the crumble in an even layer on the prepared baking sheet. Bake for 5 minutes. Remove from the oven and stir. Return to the oven and bake for an additional 4 minutes. Let cool to room temperature.

ASSEMBLY

9. Transfer the Dark Chocolate Ganache to a squeeze bottle. Heat in the microwave until a pipable consistency is achieved, about 30 seconds.
10. Use the Chocolate Espresso Buttercream to stack and crumb coat the cake (see instructions on pages 126 to 129), sprinkling ¼ cup Mocha Crumble and ¼ teaspoon sea salt and generously drizzling ganache over the buttercream between each layer.
11. Frost the cake using the Chocolate Espresso Buttercream (see instructions on page 145, steps A to C), making sure to reserve about 1½ cups for piping.
12. In a small bowl, combine the gold dust and vodka and stir until a smooth yet paintable consistency is achieved. Dip a paintbrush into the edible paint and tap the handle of the brush to splatter gold onto the side of the cake. Rotate the cake as needed and splatter the entire exterior to desired effect (step D on page 145).
13. In another small bowl, add the espresso and small amounts of vanilla until a smooth yet paintable consistency is achieved. Dip a paintbrush into the espresso mixture and tap the handle of the brush to splatter espresso onto the side of the cake. Rotate the cake as needed and splatter the entire exterior to desired effect. Place the cake in the fridge to chill for about 30 minutes.

CONTINUED

14. Pour the remaining ganache onto the cake, starting in the middle, until it covers almost the entire top of the cake. Tilt the cake to one side until the ganache spills over the edge, then tilt it in a clockwise direction so that the ganache spills over all edges of the cake, creating a drip effect (steps E and F on page 145). Place the cake in the fridge to chill for at least 30 minutes.

15. Place the cake on the turntable. Transfer the remaining Chocolate Espresso Buttercream to a piping bag and cut off the tip to create an opening about ½ inch in diameter. Holding the piping bag vertically, pipe a large dollop of buttercream in the middle of the cake. Pipe a circle of dollops around it and continue until only about ½ inch of ganache is exposed around the outside edge. Sprinkle Espresso Crumble over the ring of ganache and the buttercream (steps G and H on page 145). Place the cake in the fridge to chill.

16. Store in a tall cake box in the fridge for up to 4 days. Once the cake has been cut, cover the cut edges with a layer of waxed paper or plastic wrap placed up against the cake. Remove from the fridge 1 hour before serving.

BAKER'S TIP

1. Prefer a latte to an espresso? Try making this cake with our Vanilla Sprinkle Cake (page 130, without the sprinkles) instead of our Chocolate Cake for a softer taste. 2. We add vodka to our gold dust to make it a paintable consistency. As the paint dries, the vodka evaporates, leaving behind a beautiful gold lustre.

A

B

C

D

E

F

G

H

COTTON CANDY CAKE

COTTON CANDY CAKE

1 cup whole (3.25%) milk
¼ cup unsalted butter
¾ teaspoon pure vanilla
extract
1 tablespoon + 1 teaspoon
JRC Liquid Cotton Candy
or cotton candy flavouring
(see Baker's Tip)
4 eggs
2 cups granulated sugar
2 cups all-purpose flour
2 teaspoons baking powder
¼ teaspoon salt
2 drops soft pink gel food
colouring
2 drops sky blue gel food
colouring

**COTTON CANDY
BUTTERCREAM**

2 batches Vanilla Buttercream
(page 296)
3 tablespoons JRC Liquid
Cotton Candy or cotton
candy flavouring
3 to 4 drops soft pink gel food
colouring
3 to 4 drops sky blue gel food
colouring

GARNISH

¼ cup sprinkle mix of
your choice (we use
Sweetapolita's Wanderlust
Twinkle Sprinkle Medley)

If a cow can jump over the moon, then a unicorn can gallop through the galaxy leaving trails of glitter as it follows its nose to where this cake is being made. Both the cake and the buttercream are flavoured with cotton candy and swirled with the prettiest pastel pink and blue, often resulting in the addition of a gorgeous shade of purple.

COTTON CANDY CAKE

1. Preheat the oven to 325°F. Grease and flour two 6- × 3-inch round cake pans with shortening.

2. In a small saucepan over medium-high heat (or in a heat-resistant bowl in the microwave), heat the milk and butter until the butter is completely melted. Remove from the heat and stir in the vanilla and cotton candy flavouring.

3. In the bowl of a stand mixer fitted with the whisk attachment, whip the eggs on high speed for 2 minutes, or until they are light and fluffy and have doubled in size. Reduce the speed to low and slowly add the sugar. Increase the speed to high and whip for an additional minute.

4. Sift the flour, baking powder, and salt into a small bowl. With the mixer on low speed, alternate adding small amounts of the flour mixture and the milk mixture to the egg mixture, beginning and ending with the dry ingredients. Scrape the bottom of the bowl with a spatula and mix for an additional 2 to 3 minutes on medium-high speed, until the mixture looks light and fluffy.

5. Remove the bowl from the stand mixer and divide the batter evenly between 2 medium bowls. To one bowl, add the soft pink food colouring and use the spatula to fold in the colour until it is uniform, being careful not to overmix. To the other bowl, add the sky blue food colouring and fold until the colour is uniform, being careful not to overmix.

6. Divide the pink batter evenly between the prepared cake pans, then divide the blue batter evenly between the pans. Place the blade of a butter knife into the middle of each cake until it reaches the bottom of the pan. Swirl the batter across the diameter of each pan by making large figure-8 shapes with the knife. Bake for 40 minutes, or until the edges of the cake begin to pull away from the sides of the pan and a knife inserted into the middle of the cake comes out clean. If the cake jiggles in the middle when the pan is tapped gently, continue baking before testing it with a knife. Let cool for 10 to 15 minutes in the pans. Run a knife or an offset spatula around the inside edge of the pans to release the edges of the cakes. Flip onto a wire rack and let cool to room temperature.

COTTON CANDY BUTTERCREAM

7. Prepare 2 batches Vanilla Buttercream. Transfer 1½ cups to a medium bowl and reserve for crumb coating the cake.

8. Add the cotton candy flavouring to the buttercream in the bowl of the stand mixer and whip to combine. Transfer 1 cup to a medium bowl. Add 3 to 4 drops soft pink food colouring and use the spatula to mix until fully incorporated.

9. To the bowl of the stand mixer, add 3 to 4 drops sky blue food colouring. Whip on high speed until fully incorporated. Transfer 1 cup blue buttercream to the bowl with the pink buttercream. Reserve the pink and blue buttercream for frosting the cake. Reserve the remaining blue buttercream for stacking and decorating the cake.

CONTINUED

ASSEMBLY

10. Stack the cake using about 3 to 4 cups blue buttercream. Crumb coat the cake using the white buttercream (see instructions on pages 126 to 129).

11. Frost the cake using the pink and blue buttercream (see instructions on page 149, steps A to D). The more you pull your cake scraper across the buttercream, the more the pink and blue buttercream will mix and turn purple.

12. Transfer the remaining blue buttercream to the bowl with the leftover pink and blue buttercream that was used to frost the cake. Transfer this buttercream to a piping bag, being careful not to mix the colours together too much, and cut off the tip to create an opening about ½ inch in diameter. Pipe large dollops of buttercream around the top edge of the cake. Once the edge is complete, move inward and repeat until you reach the middle of the cake. Decorate the top of the cake with the sprinkles (steps F to H on page 149). Place the cake in the fridge to chill.

13. Store in a tall cake box in the fridge for up to 4 days. Once the cake has been cut, cover the cut edges with a layer of waxed paper or plastic wrap placed up against the cake. Remove from the fridge 1 hour before serving.

BAKER'S TIP

We tested a number of cotton candy flavourings before creating one we loved that really does taste like cotton candy. Our JRC Liquid Cotton Candy is available in our online store so that you can make a cotton candy cake that's true to what you'll find at our bakery!

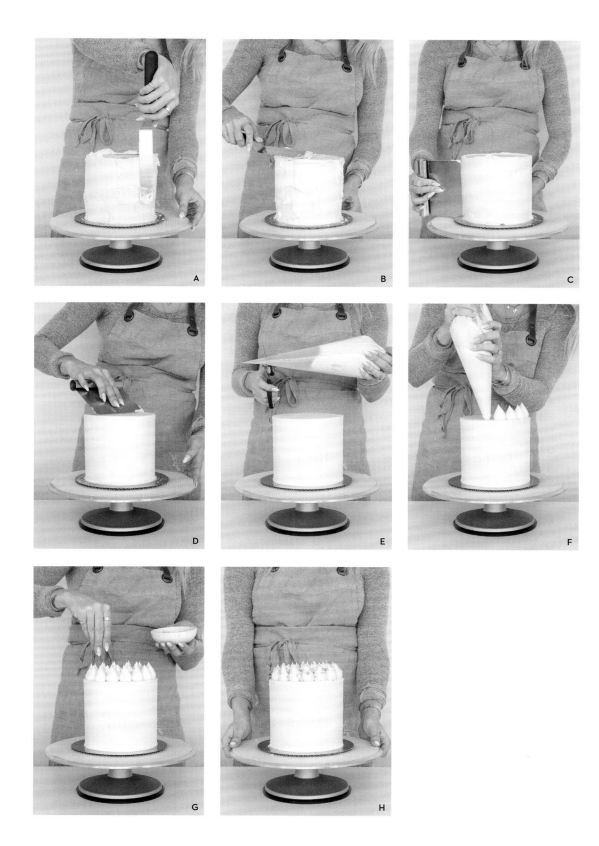

CINNAMON APPLE CRUMBLE CAKE

Makes one 6-inch cake with four layers; serves 8 to 10

CINNAMON SPICE CAKE

1 cup whole (3.25%) milk
¼ cup unsalted butter, room temperature
¾ teaspoon pure vanilla extract
4 eggs
2 cups granulated sugar
2 cups all-purpose flour
1 tablespoon cinnamon
2 teaspoons baking powder
¼ teaspoon ground nutmeg
¼ teaspoon salt

SALTED CARAMEL

1 batch (page 299), divided

SALTED CARAMEL BUTTERCREAM

2 batches Vanilla Buttercream (page 296)
1 cup Salted Caramel

SUGAR AND SPICE CRUMBLE

½ batch (page 306)

APPLE FILLING

1 batch (page 302)

WHITE CHOCOLATE GANACHE

1 batch (page 299)
4 drops soft pink gel food colouring

GARNISH (OPTIONAL)

1 Granny Smith apple
6- × ¼-inch wooden dowel

When we first introduced our Apple Crumble Cookie Sandwiches (page 33), we knew we were onto something good. We've reimagined this flavour combination across all of our offerings, from cream puffs to macarons to, finally, its very own cake! Buttery cinnamon spice crumble and thick ribbons of salted caramel are sandwiched between layers of perfectly spiced sponge cake. If you can, try using locally grown apples to support your community of farmers.

CINNAMON SPICE CAKE

1. Preheat the oven to 325°F. Grease and flour two 6- × 3-inch round cake pans with shortening.

2. In a small saucepan over medium-high heat (or in a heat-resistant bowl in the microwave), heat the milk and butter until the butter is completely melted. Remove from the heat and stir in the vanilla.

3. In the bowl of a stand mixer fitted with the whisk attachment, whip the eggs on high speed for 2 minutes, or until they are light and fluffy and have doubled in size. Reduce the speed to low and slowly add the sugar. Increase the speed to high and whip for an additional 2 minutes.

4. Sift the flour, cinnamon, baking powder, nutmeg, and salt into a small bowl and stir together. With the mixer on low speed, alternate adding small amounts of the flour mixture and the milk mixture to the egg mixture, beginning and ending with the dry ingredients. Scrape the bottom of the bowl with a spatula and mix for an additional 2 to 3 minutes on medium-high speed, until the mixture looks light and fluffy.

5. Divide the batter evenly between the prepared cake pans. Bake for 40 minutes, or until the edges of the cake begin to pull away from the sides of the pan and a knife inserted into the middle of the cake comes out clean. If the cake jiggles in the middle when the pan is tapped gently, continue baking before testing it with a knife. Let cool for 10 to 15 minutes in the pans. Run a knife or an offset spatula around the inside edge of the pans to release the edges of the cakes. Flip onto a wire rack and let cool completely.

SALTED CARAMEL

6. Prepare 1 batch Salted Caramel. Let cool to room temperature.

SALTED CARAMEL BUTTERCREAM

7. Prepare 2 batches Vanilla Buttercream.

8. Add 1 cup Salted Caramel to the buttercream. Whip on high speed for an additional 2 to 3 minutes, until fully incorporated.

SUGAR AND SPICE CRUMBLE

9. Prepare 1 batch Sugar and Spice Crumble. Let cool to room temperature.

APPLE FILLING

10. Prepare 1 batch Apple Filling. Let cool to room temperature.

CONTINUED

WHITE CHOCOLATE GANACHE

11. Prepare 1 batch White Chocolate Ganache.

12. Add the food colouring and stir until well combined.

ASSEMBLY

13. Transfer the remaining Salted Caramel to a squeeze bottle. Use the Salted Caramel Buttercream to stack and crumb coat the cake (see instructions on pages 126 to 129). To each layer, add ¼ cup Apple Filling, ¼ cup Sugar and Spice Crumble, and a drizzle of Salted Caramel, spread evenly across the buttercream.

14. Frost the cake using the Salted Caramel Buttercream (see instructions on page 153, steps A to D).

15. Line a small plate with parchment paper. Transfer the White Chocolate Ganache to a glass measuring cup with a spout. Heat the ganache in the microwave until a pourable consistency is achieved, about 30 seconds. If using the garnish, insert the dowel into the top of the apple, then dip it into the ganache until it's three-quarters covered. Let some of the excess ganache drip off before placing the apple on the prepared plate. Let cool for 15 minutes.

16. Pour the remaining ganache onto the cake, starting in the middle, until it covers almost the entire top of the cake. Tilt the cake to one side until the ganache spills over the edge, then tilt it in a clockwise direction so that the ganache spills over all edges of the cake, creating a drip effect (steps E and F on page 153).

17. Place the cake on a turntable and set the ganache-dipped apple in the middle, with the wooden dowel pointing straight up (steps G and H on page 153). Place the cake in the fridge to chill for at least 30 minutes.

18. Store in a tall cake box in the fridge for up to 4 days. Once the cake has been cut, cover the cut edges with a layer of waxed paper or plastic wrap placed up against the cake. Remove from the fridge 1 hour before serving.

BAKER'S TIP

Customize the colour of the ganache using oil-based gel food colouring to suit your guest of honour or highlight a festive occasion, or just leave it white for a more refined look.

PEANUT BUTTER MARSHMALLOW CAKE

PEANUT BUTTER CAKE

¾ cup whole (3.25%) milk

¼ cup unsalted butter

¾ teaspoon pure vanilla
  extract

4 eggs

2 cups granulated sugar

2 cups all-purpose flour

2 teaspoons baking powder

¼ teaspoon salt

¼ cup creamy peanut butter

2 tablespoons rainbow sequin
  sprinkles, divided, more
  for garnish

**PEANUT BUTTER
MARSHMALLOW SQUARES**

1 batch (page 307)

**PEANUT BUTTER PRALINE
BUTTERCREAM**

2 batches Vanilla Buttercream
  (page 296)

1 cup creamy peanut butter

2 teaspoons toffee flavouring
  (see Baker's Tip)

*When Jenna Rae Cakes first opened its doors, giant pieces of peanut butter
marshmallow squares were on the menu so that customers could indulge in their
favourite childhood treat. Creamy peanut butter and sweet butterscotch enrobe
slightly fruity multicoloured marshmallows to become irresistible. Now, we've
transformed this nostalgic flavour combination into a cake.*

PEANUT BUTTER CAKE

1. Preheat the oven to 325°F. Grease and flour two 6- × 3-inch round cake pans with shortening.

2. In a small saucepan over medium-high heat (or in a heat-resistant bowl in the microwave), heat the milk and butter until the butter is completely melted. Remove from the heat and stir in the vanilla.

3. In the bowl of a stand mixer fitted with the whisk attachment, whip the eggs on high speed for 2 minutes, or until they are light and fluffy and have doubled in size. Reduce the speed to low and slowly add the sugar. Increase the speed to high and whip for an additional minute.

4. Sift the flour, baking powder, and salt into a small bowl and stir together. With the mixer on low speed, alternate adding small amounts of the flour mixture and the milk mixture to the egg mixture, beginning and ending with the dry ingredients. Scrape the bottom of the bowl with a spatula and mix for an additional 2 to 3 minutes on medium-high speed, until the mixture looks light and fluffy. Lastly, gently fold the peanut butter into the cake batter, being careful not to deflate or overmix.

5. Divide the batter evenly between the prepared cake pans. Sprinkle 1 tablespoon sprinkles into each pan and gently fold in using a spoon. Bake for 40 minutes, or until the edges of the cake begin to pull away from the sides of the pan and a knife inserted into the middle of the cake comes out clean. If the cake jiggles in the middle when the pan is tapped gently, continue baking before testing it with a knife. Let cool for 10 to 15 minutes in the pans. Run a knife or an offset spatula around the inside edge of the pans to release the edges of the cakes. Flip onto a wire rack and let cool to room temperature.

PEANUT BUTTER MARSHMALLOW SQUARES

6. Prepare 1 batch Peanut Butter Marshmallow Squares. Cut into 1-inch squares (see Baker's Tip).

PEANUT BUTTER PRALINE BUTTERCREAM

7. Prepare 2 batches Vanilla Buttercream.

8. Add the peanut butter and toffee flavouring to the buttercream. Whip on high speed until well combined.

ASSEMBLY

9. Use the Peanut Butter Praline Buttercream to stack and crumb coat the cake (see instructions on pages 126 to 129). To each layer, add 1 Peanut Butter Marshmallow Square broken into about 6 chunks. Spread the chunks evenly across the buttercream.

10. Frost the cake using the Peanut Butter Praline Buttercream (see instructions on page 157, steps A to D), making sure to reserve about 1 cup for piping.

CONTINUED

11. Transfer the reserved buttercream to a piping bag fitted with a No. 8B tip. Press small handfuls of sprinkles into the side of the cake to cover the bottom third of it. Pipe 8 rosettes of buttercream evenly spaced around the top edge of the cake. Top each rosette with a Peanut Butter Marshmallow Square (steps E to H on page 157).

12. Store in a tall cake box in the fridge for up to 4 days. Once the cake has been cut, cover the cut edges with a layer of waxed paper or plastic wrap placed up against the cake. Remove from the fridge 1 hour before serving.

BAKER'S TIP

1. You will have leftover Peanut Butter Marshmallow Squares, but they are delicious all on their own! Indulge in leftover squares as bite-size dainties to enjoy. They look great in little paper baking cups, served on a pretty plate. 2. The toffee flavouring is a must if you want the Peanut Butter Praline Buttercream to have a rich butterscotch flavour. If you can't find toffee flavouring, praline or pralines and cream flavouring will work as a substitute. Use an equal amount.

STICKY COCONUT CAKE

Makes one 6-inch cake with
four layers; serves 8 to 10

SALTED CARAMEL

1 batch (page 299), divided

COCONUT CAKE

¾ cup whole (3.25%) milk
¼ cup unsalted butter
¾ teaspoon pure vanilla
    extract
4 eggs
2 cups granulated sugar
2 cups all-purpose flour
½ cup unsweetened shredded
    coconut
2 teaspoons baking powder
¼ teaspoon salt
¼ cup Salted Caramel, divided

**STICKY CARAMEL COCONUT
FILLING**

¼ cup unsalted butter, room
    temperature
¼ cup packed brown sugar
3 tablespoons white corn syrup
¼ cup whipping (35%) cream
1½ cups unsweetened
    shredded coconut
⅛ teaspoon salt

**SALTED CARAMEL COCONUT
BUTTERCREAM**

2 batches Vanilla Buttercream
    (page 296)
1 cup Salted Caramel
2 teaspoons coconut flavouring

GARNISH

4 cups unsweetened large
    coconut flakes (see Baker's
    Tip)

*Are the cooler months bringing you down? Are you counting the days until your
winter vacation to escape the cold and feel the warmth of sunshine on your skin
as you sip a piña colada on the beach? Kick off that countdown to paradise with
this Sticky Coconut Cake, which combines the tropical flavour of coconut with
warming salted caramel.*

SALTED CARAMEL

1. Prepare 1 batch Salted Caramel.

COCONUT CAKE

2. Preheat the oven to 325°F. Grease and flour two 6- × 3-inch round cake pans with shortening.

3. In a small saucepan over medium-high heat (or in a heat-resistant bowl in the microwave), heat the milk and butter until the butter is completely melted. Remove from the heat and stir in the vanilla.

4. In the bowl of a stand mixer fitted with the whisk attachment, whip the eggs on high speed for 2 minutes, or until they are light and fluffy and have doubled in size. Reduce the speed to low and slowly add the sugar. Increase the speed to high and whip for an additional minute.

5. Sift the flour into a small bowl. Add the coconut, baking powder, and salt and stir to combine. With the mixer on low speed, alternate adding small amounts of the flour mixture and the milk mixture to the egg mixture, beginning and ending with the dry ingredients. Scrape the bottom of the bowl with a spatula and mix for an additional 2 to 3 minutes on medium-high speed, until the mixture looks light and fluffy.

6. Divide the batter evenly between the prepared cake pans. Add 2 tablespoons Salted Caramel to each cake pan. Using a knife, swirl in the caramel. Do not combine completely; you want to have streaks of caramel in the cake. Bake for 40 minutes, or until the edges of the cake begin to pull away from the sides of the pan and a knife inserted into the middle of the cake comes out clean. If the cake jiggles in the middle when the pan is tapped gently, continue baking before testing it with a knife. Let cool for 10 to 15 minutes in the pans. Run a knife or an offset spatula around the inside edge of the pans to release the edges of the cakes. Flip onto a wire rack and let cool completely. Increase the temperature of the oven to 350°F.

STICKY CARAMEL COCONUT FILLING

7. Line a baking sheet with parchment paper.

8. In a small saucepan over medium-high heat, combine the butter, sugar, and corn syrup. Cook until the mixture begins to bubble and thicken. Slowly pour in the cream and whisk to combine. Remove from the heat, add the coconut and salt, and stir to combine.

9. Transfer the mixture to the prepared baking sheet. Bake for 5 minutes. Stir and bake for another 3 minutes until golden brown. Let cool to room temperature. Use your hands to break up any large chunks.

CONTINUED

SALTED CARAMEL COCONUT BUTTERCREAM

10. Prepare 2 batches Vanilla Buttercream.

11. Add 1 cup Salted Caramel and the coconut flavouring to the buttercream. Whip on high speed for 2 minutes, until combined.

ASSEMBLY

12. Transfer the remaining Salted Caramel to a squeeze bottle. Use the Salted Caramel Coconut Buttercream to stack and crumb coat the cake (see instructions on pages 126 to 129). To each layer, add a third of the Sticky Caramel Coconut Filling and a drizzle of Salted Caramel spread evenly across the buttercream.

13. Frost the cake using the remaining Salted Caramel Coconut Buttercream (see instructions on page 161, steps A to D).

14. Press the coconut flakes into the cake to cover the buttercream completely (steps E to H on page 161). Place the cake in the fridge to chill for at least 2 hours before serving.

15. Store in a tall cake box in the fridge for up to 4 days. Once the cake has been cut, cover the cut edges with a layer of waxed paper or plastic wrap placed up against the cake. Remove from the fridge 1 hour before serving.

BAKER'S TIP

We love using the largest coconut flakes we can find to decorate this cake! However, any size of flaked coconut will work well. Try to purchase unsweetened flakes if you can so that your cake doesn't end up being too sweet.

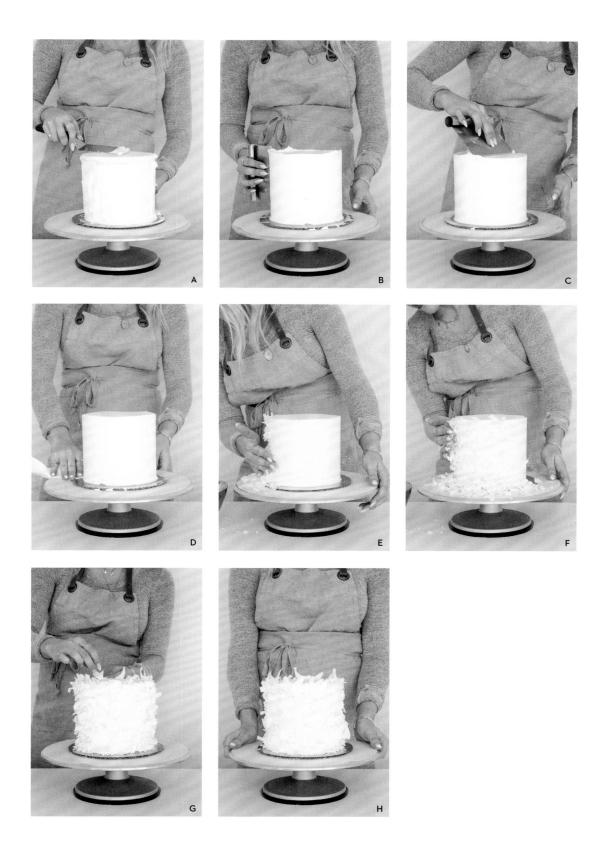

Makes one 6-inch cake with
four layers; serves 8 to 10

CHOCOLATE CAKE

½ cup unsalted butter
¾ cup (165 g) chopped
   dark baking chocolate
½ cup hot coffee
½ cup hot water
1 tablespoon pure vanilla
   extract
6 eggs
1 cup vegetable oil
¾ cup sour cream
2 cups flour
¾ cup cocoa powder, sifted
1 ¾ cups granulated sugar
1 teaspoon baking powder
¾ teaspoon baking soda
¼ teaspoon salt

**CHOCOLATE LOVER'S
BUTTERCREAM**

2 batches (page 297)

DARK CHOCOLATE GANACHE

1 batch (page 298)

**CHOCOLATE SHORTBREAD
CRUMBLE**

1 batch (page 306)

CHOCOLATE LOVER'S CAKE

Embrace chocolate in its multiple varieties and textures, all lovingly stacked into one enticing cake. Moist chocolate cake, mouth-watering chocolate buttercream, and buttery chocolate shortbread crumble hit every spot as you indulge in this cake that will have your guests begging for more.

CHOCOLATE CAKE

1. Preheat the oven to 325°F. Grease and flour two 6- × 3-inch round cake pans with shortening.

2. In a medium heat-resistant bowl, melt the butter in the microwave. Pour into the bowl of a stand mixer fitted with the whisk attachment.

3. In another medium heat-resistant bowl, melt the chocolate in the microwave in 30-second intervals, stirring well after each interval, until smooth and not hot.

4. In a measuring cup, whisk together the hot coffee, hot water, and vanilla.

5. With the mixer on low speed, slowly add the eggs to the butter, mixing until just combined. Slowly add the melted chocolate and mix until combined. Scrape down the sides of the bowl and mix for an additional 10 seconds. Add the oil and sour cream and mix until combined. Scrape down the sides of the bowl and mix for an additional 10 seconds.

6. Sift the flour and cocoa powder into a medium bowl. Add the sugar, baking powder, baking soda, and salt and stir to combine. With the mixer on low speed, add the dry ingredients to the wet ingredients in three additions, mixing until combined before adding the next addition. Slowly pour in the coffee mixture and mix on low speed, scraping down the sides of the bowl often, until combined.

7. Divide the batter evenly between the prepared cake pans. Bake for 40 minutes, or until the edges of the cake begin to pull away from the sides of the pan and a knife inserted into the middle of the cake comes out clean. If the cake jiggles in the middle when the pan is tapped gently, continue baking before testing it with a knife. Let cool for 10 to 15 minutes in the pans. Run a knife or an offset spatula around the inside edge of the pans to release the edges of the cakes. Flip onto a wire rack and let cool completely.

CHOCOLATE LOVER'S BUTTERCREAM

8. Prepare 2 batches Chocolate Lover's Buttercream.

DARK CHOCOLATE GANACHE

9. Prepare 1 batch Dark Chocolate Ganache.

CHOCOLATE SHORTBREAD CRUMBLE

10. Prepare 1 batch Chocolate Shortbread Crumble.

ASSEMBLY

11. Transfer the Dark Chocolate Ganache to a squeeze bottle. Heat in the microwave until a pipable consistency is achieved, about 30 seconds. Use the Chocolate Lover's Buttercream to stack and crumb coat the cake (see instructions on pages 126 to 129). To each layer, add ¼ cup Chocolate Shortbread Crumble and a drizzle of ganache spread evenly across the buttercream.

CONTINUED

12. Frost the cake with the remaining buttercream (see instructions on page 165, steps A to C).

13. Transfer the remaining ganache to a measuring cup with a spout. Pour it onto the cake, starting in the middle, until the ganache covers almost the entire top of the cake. Tilt the cake to one side until the ganache spills over the edge, then tilt it in a clockwise direction so that the ganache spills over all edges of the cake, creating a drip effect (steps D and E on page 165).

14. Place the cake on a turntable and use a cake scraper to pull the drips of ganache around the sides and top of the cake until the entire exterior is covered in a thin, even coating of ganache. Sprinkle ⅓ cup Chocolate Shortbread Crumble on top of the cake (steps F to H on page 165). Place the cake in the fridge to chill and allow the ganache to set, about 30 minutes.

15. Store in a tall cake box in the fridge for up to 4 days. Once the cake has been cut, cover the cut edges with a layer of waxed paper or plastic wrap placed up against the cake. Remove from the fridge 1 hour before serving.

BAKER'S TIP

To make the cake more colourful, sprinkle your favourite sprinkle mix over the Chocolate Shortbread Crumble.

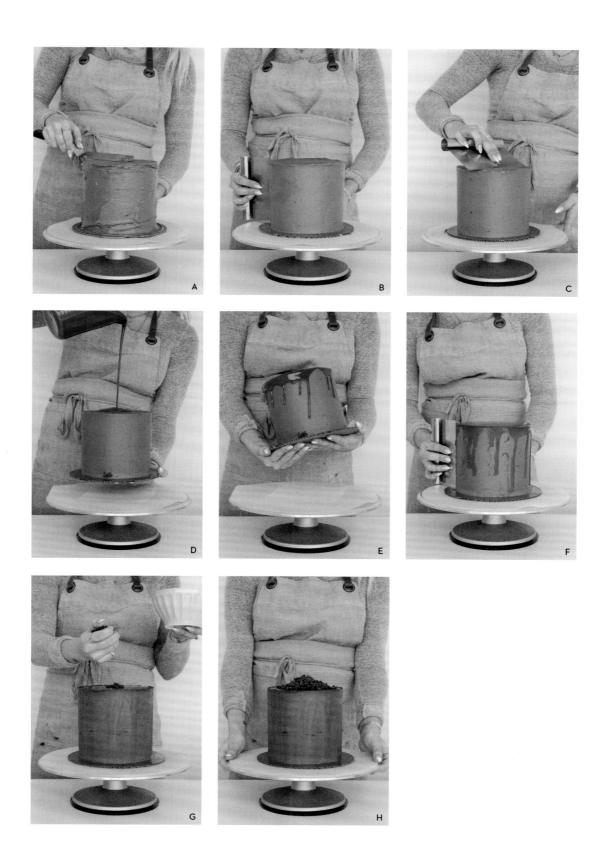

COOKIE DOUGH CAKE

*Cake and cookie dough together in one delicious dessert? Yes, please! Our
signature Cookie Dough Cake combines a classic vanilla sponge cake with
chocolate chips before it gets stacked with Vanilla Buttercream and chunks of
Cookie Dough. Each and every bite will taste like you're enjoying cake, cookies,
and a big glass of milk all at the same time. This cake's design is a true Jenna Rae
Cakes original creation, from the creamy coloured buttercream, to the ganache
drips, to the cookie dough balls atop the cake.*

COOKIE DOUGH CAKE

1. Preheat the oven to 325°F. Grease and flour two 6- × 3-inch round cake pans with shortening.
2. In a small saucepan over medium-high heat (or in a heat-resistant bowl in the microwave),
    heat the milk and butter until the butter is completely melted. Remove from the heat and stir
    in the vanilla.
3. In the bowl of a stand mixer fitted with the whisk attachment, whip the eggs on high speed
    for 2 minutes, or until they are light and fluffy and have doubled in size. Reduce the speed to
    low and slowly add the sugar. Increase the speed to high and whip for an additional minute.
4. Sift 2 cups flour, the baking powder, and salt into a small bowl. With the mixer on low speed,
    alternate adding small amounts of the flour mixture and the milk mixture to the egg mixture,
    beginning and ending with the dry ingredients. Scrape the bottom of the bowl with a spatula
    and mix for an additional 2 to 3 minutes on medium-high speed, until the mixture looks
    light and fluffy.
5. Divide the batter evenly between the prepared cake pans. Toss the chocolate chips in
    2 tablespoons flour to lightly coat them, then sprinkle ½ cup into each pan. Using a spatula,
    gently fold into the batter. Bake for 40 minutes, or until the edges of the cake begin to pull
    away from the sides of the pan and a knife inserted into the middle of the cake comes out
    clean. If the cake jiggles in the middle when the pan is tapped gently, continue baking before
    testing it with a knife. Let cool for 10 to 15 minutes in the pans. Run a knife or an offset
    spatula around the inside edge of the pans to release the edges of the cakes. Flip onto a
    wire rack and let cool to room temperature.

DARK CHOCOLATE GANACHE

6. Prepare 1 batch Dark Chocolate Ganache.

COOKIE DOUGH

7. Prepare 2 batches Cookie Dough.

VANILLA BUTTERCREAM

8. Prepare 2 batches Vanilla Buttercream.
9. Add the food colouring and whip on high speed for 1 minute until the colour is uniform.

ASSEMBLY

10. Use the Vanilla Buttercream to stack and crumb coat the cake (see instructions on
    pages 126 to 129). To each layer, add ¼ cup Cookie Dough, broken into chunks and
    spread evenly across the buttercream.

CONTINUED

11. Frost the cake with the Vanilla Buttercream (see instructions on page 169, steps A to C), reserving about 1 cup for piping.

12. Transfer the Dark Chocolate Ganache to a measuring cup with a spout. Heat in the microwave until a pourable consistency is achieved, about 30 seconds. Pour it onto the cake, starting in the middle, until the ganache covers almost the entire top of the cake. Tilt the cake to one side until the ganache spills over the edge, then tilt it in a clockwise direction so that the ganache spills over all edges of the cake, creating a drip effect (steps D and E on page 169). Place the cake in the fridge to chill for at least 30 minutes.

13. Transfer the remaining buttercream to a piping bag fitted with a No. 4B tip. Place the cake on a cake stand. Pipe 8 dollops of buttercream around the top edge of the cake (step F on page 169).

14. Scoop or roll the remaining Cookie Dough into 8 tablespoon-size balls. Press 1 ball onto each buttercream dollop (steps G and H on page 169).

15. Store in a tall cake box in the fridge for up to 4 days. Once the cake has been cut, cover the cut edges with a layer of waxed paper or plastic wrap placed up against the cake. Remove from the fridge 1 hour before serving.

BAKER'S TIP

Try substituting the mini chocolate chips with an equal amount of white chocolate chips, peanut butter chips, or a combination of both! For a total transformation, make the same substitutions in your Cookie Dough.

RED VELVET CAKE

A classic in every way, this Red Velvet Cake is filled with smooth and slightly tangy Cream Cheese Buttercream that complements the rich taste and texture of the cake. Decorated in all white with gold leaf flakes, this cake makes a stunning centrepiece for any event and really does taste as good as it looks.

RED VELVET CAKE

2¼ cups granulated sugar

¾ cup unsalted butter, room temperature

2 eggs

1 egg yolk

¼ cup red liquid food colouring

3 tablespoons cocoa powder, sifted

1 tablespoon pure vanilla extract

1½ cups buttermilk

1 tablespoon salt

3 cups all-purpose flour

4½ teaspoons cornstarch

¼ cup sour cream

1½ teaspoons baking soda

1½ teaspoons apple cider vinegar

CREAM CHEESE BUTTERCREAM

2 batches (page 297)

GARNISH

2 tablespoons edible gold leaf flakes

RED VELVET CAKE

1. Preheat the oven to 325°F. Grease and flour two 6- × 3-inch round cake pans with shortening.

2. In the bowl of a stand mixer fitted with the paddle attachment, cream the sugar and butter on high speed for 5 minutes, until the mixture looks light and fluffy. Add the eggs and egg yolk one at a time and beat for an additional minute. Scrape down the sides of the bowl and beat again for 30 seconds.

3. In a small bowl, whisk together the food colouring, cocoa powder, and vanilla until fully combined. With the mixer on low speed, slowly pour the food colouring mixture into the sugar, butter, and egg mixture, then beat on medium speed until just combined. Scrape down the sides of the bowl.

4. In a measuring cup, mix the buttermilk and salt. Sift the flour and cornstarch into a small bowl and stir together. With the mixer on low speed, alternate adding the dry ingredients and wet ingredients in four increments, scraping down the sides of the bowl between additions. Add the sour cream and mix until just combined.

5. In a small bowl, combine the baking soda and apple cider vinegar. Immediately pour into the batter and mix on medium speed until combined.

6. Divide the batter evenly between the prepared cake pans. Bake for 40 minutes, or until the edges of the cake begin to pull away from the sides of the pan and a knife inserted into the middle of the cake comes out clean. If the cake jiggles in the middle when the pan is tapped gently, continue baking before testing it with a knife. Let cool for 10 to 15 minutes in the pans. Run a knife or an offset spatula around the inside edge of the pans to release the edges of the cakes. Flip onto a wire rack and let cool to room temperature.

CREAM CHEESE BUTTERCREAM

7. Prepare 2 batches Cream Cheese Buttercream.

ASSEMBLY

8. Use the Cream Cheese Buttercream to stack, crumb coat, and frost the cake (see instructions on pages 126 to 129), reserving at least 1 cup for piping.

9. Transfer the remaining buttercream to a piping bag and cut off the tip to create an opening about ½ inch in diameter. Pipe large dollops of buttercream around the top edge of the cake, then move inward and repeat until you have covered the top of the cake completely. Sprinkle the top of the cake with the gold leaf flakes (see instructions on page 173, steps A to H). Place the cake in the fridge to chill, at least 1 hour.

10. Store in a tall cake box in the fridge for up to 4 days. Once the cake has been cut, cover the cut edges with a layer of waxed paper or plastic wrap placed up against the cake. Remove from the fridge 1 hour before serving.

BAKER'S TIP

1. This cake is perfect for Valentine's Day! You can also swap out the red liquid food colouring for an equal amount of green or blue liquid food colouring to match the decor of an event. 2. Cream Cheese Buttercream can be soft, so if you're having trouble getting a smooth finish, create a lined or textured exterior instead!

CONTINUED

GRAHAM CRACKER CAKE

¾ cup whole (3.25%) milk
3 tablespoons unsalted butter
1½ teaspoons cooking
    molasses
1½ teaspoons pure vanilla
    extract
3 eggs
1½ cups packed brown sugar
1 cup whole wheat flour
½ cup all-purpose flour
1 teaspoon cinnamon
2 teaspoons baking powder
⅛ teaspoon salt

CHOCOLATE CAKE

½ batch (page 162)

MILK CHOCOLATE GANACHE

2 batches (page 298), divided

**MILK CHOCOLATE
BUTTERCREAM**

2 batches (page 296, steps 3
    and 4), without the whipping
    cream and baking chocolate
1 cup Milk Chocolate Ganache

**MERINGUE MARSHMALLOW
FLUFF**

1 batch (page 300) or
    4 (7.5-ounce) jars store-
    bought marshmallow
    spread

**GRAHAM CRACKER
CRUMBLE**

1 batch (page 305), divided

CHOCOLATE SHARDS

1 cup (220 g) milk chocolate
    melting wafers
Edible gold leaf flakes,
    for garnish (optional)

GARNISH

Mini marshmallows, toasted
¼ cup Graham Cracker
    Crumble

S'MORES CAKE

What's your favourite part of a s'more? Is it the puffed-up, toasted, and stick-to-everything marshmallow? The warm, melted milk chocolate? Or is it the crisp graham cracker that holds it all together and adds a pleasant crunch? No matter which part of the s'more draws you in, our S'mores Cake has it all! What makes this cake extra special is the alternating layers of chocolate and graham cracker sponge cake, creating that balanced s'more flavour in every bite.

GRAHAM CRACKER CAKE

1. Preheat the oven to 325°F. Grease and flour two 6- × 3-inch round cake pans with shortening.

2. In a small saucepan over medium-high heat (or in a heat-resistant bowl in the microwave), heat the milk and butter until the butter is completely melted. Remove from the heat and stir in the molasses and vanilla.

3. In the bowl of a stand mixer fitted with the whisk attachment, whip the eggs on high speed for 2 minutes, or until they are light and fluffy and have doubled in size. Reduce the speed to low and slowly add the brown sugar. Increase the speed to high and whip for an additional minute.

4. Sift the whole wheat flour, all-purpose flour, cinnamon, baking powder, and salt into a small bowl. With the mixer on low speed, alternate adding small amounts of the flour mixture and the milk mixture to the egg mixture, beginning and ending with the dry ingredients. Scrape the bottom of the bowl with a spatula and mix for an additional 2 to 3 minutes on medium-high speed, until the mixture looks light and fluffy.

5. Divide the mixture evenly between the prepared cake pans. Bake for 40 minutes, or until the edges of the cake begin to pull away from the sides of the pan and a knife inserted into the middle of the cake comes out clean. If the cake jiggles in the middle when the pan is tapped gently, continue baking before testing it with a knife. Let cool for 10 to 15 minutes in the pans. Run a knife or an offset spatula around the inside edge of the pans to release the edges of the cakes. Flip onto a wire rack and let cool to room temperature.

CHOCOLATE CAKE

6. Prepare ½ batch Chocolate Cake.

MILK CHOCOLATE GANACHE

7. Prepare 2 batches Milk Chocolate Ganache.

MILK CHOCOLATE BUTTERCREAM

8. Prepare 2 batches Milk Chocolate Buttercream, substituting the whipping cream and baking chocolate with 1 cup Milk Chocolate Ganache. Follow steps 3 and 4 of the recipe on page 296.

MERINGUE MARSHMALLOW FLUFF

9. Prepare 1 batch Meringue Marshmallow Fluff. Let cool for a few minutes, then transfer to a piping bag and cut off the tip.

CONTINUED

GRAHAM CRACKER CRUMBLE

10. Prepare 1 batch Graham Cracker Crumble.

CHOCOLATE SHARDS

11. Line a baking sheet with parchment paper.

12. In a heat-resistant bowl, melt the chocolate wafers in the microwave in 30-second intervals, stirring after each interval, until smooth. Pour onto the prepared baking sheet. Use an offset spatula to spread the chocolate in an even layer, about ⅛ inch thick. Sprinkle with gold leaf flakes. Let set for about 10 minutes.

13. Use your hands to break the chocolate into 1- to 2-inch pieces.

ASSEMBLY

14. Use the Milk Chocolate Buttercream to stack the cake, reserving at least 1½ cups for piping and alternating between layers of Chocolate Cake and Graham Cracker Cake (see instructions on pages 126 to 129). Pipe a small ring of Meringue Marshmallow Fluff on each layer of buttercream and toast it with a handheld torch. Then sprinkle ¼ cup Graham Cracker Crumble across each layer and drizzle with Milk Chocolate Ganache. Do not trim the edges or crumb coat the cake. Place the cake in the fridge to chill.

15. Place your untrimmed cake on the turntable. Follow step 8 on page 127 to apply icing to your cake. To create a semi-naked crumb coat, smooth the sides of the cake. Using a cake scraper held parallel to the side of the cake, begin to move the turntable around to remove excess buttercream. Rest the cake scraper on the cake board to ensure that the edges are straight. When you complete one full turn, scrape the excess buttercream from your cake scraper into a bowl. Repeat until the cake edges are straight and smooth, and the cake is beginning to peek through the thin layer of buttercream. To create a defined top edge, use the cake scraper to gently pull the exterior edge of buttercream in toward the middle of the cake. Repeat this process, making your way around the entire cake until your top edge is straight and sharp (see instructions on page 177, steps A to C).

16. Spread the mini marshmallows on a baking sheet. Toast them using a handheld torch.

17. Transfer the remaining Milk Chocolate Ganache to a measuring cup with a spout. Heat in the microwave until a pourable consistency is achieved, about 30 seconds. Pour it onto the cake, starting in the middle, until the ganache covers almost the entire top of the cake. Tilt the cake to one side until the ganache spills over the edge, then tilt it in a clockwise direction so that the ganache spills over all edges of the cake, creating a drip effect (steps D and E on page 177). Place the cake in the fridge to chill for at least 30 minutes.

18. Place the cake on a turntable. Transfer the reserved Milk Chocolate Buttercream to a piping bag and cut off the tip to create an opening about ½ inch in diameter. Pipe large dollops of buttercream on the top of the cake, starting with one dollop in the middle of the cake. Pipe a circle of dollops around the first one and continue moving outward until the top of the cake is covered (step F on page 177).

19. Place the Chocolate Shards into the buttercream with spiked edges pointed up. Place the toasted marshmallows around the edges of the buttercream dollops on top of the ganache. Sprinkle with Graham Cracker Crumble (steps G and H on page 177).

20. Store in a tall cake box in the fridge for up to 4 days. Once the cake has been cut, cover the cut edges with a layer of waxed paper or plastic wrap placed up against the cake. Remove from the fridge 1 hour before serving.

BAKER'S TIP

Do you really love chocolate? Try making this cake with 4 layers of Chocolate Cake instead of 2 layers of chocolate and 2 layers of Graham Cracker Cake. and substitute the Milk Chocolate Ganache and Milk Chocolate Buttercream with equal amounts of the Dark Chocolate Ganache and Chocolate Lover's Buttercream for a super-rich treat.

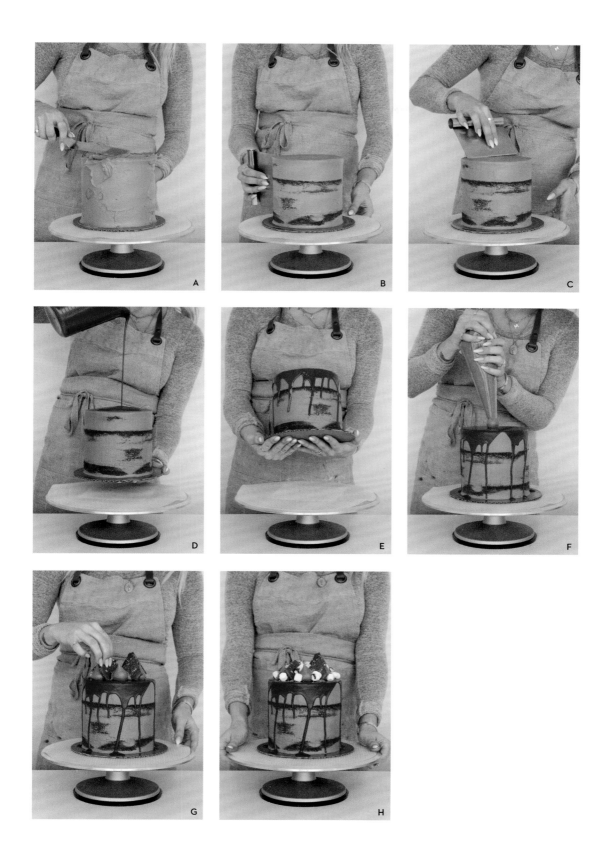

CHOCOLATE HAZELNUT CAKE

CHOCOLATE CAKE

1 batch Chocolate Cake
(page 162, steps 1 to 6)
½ cup chopped hazelnuts,
divided

**CHOCOLATE HAZELNUT
SPREAD (MAKES 2 CUPS;
SEE BAKER'S TIP)**

1 cup whole raw hazelnuts
¼ cup vegetable oil
½ teaspoon pure vanilla
extract
2 cups (440 g) chopped milk
baking chocolate
3 tablespoons icing sugar
1 tablespoon sifted cocoa
powder
½ teaspoon salt

**CHOCOLATE HAZELNUT
BUTTERCREAM**

2 batches Milk Chocolate
Buttercream (page 296)
2 cups Nutella

DARK CHOCOLATE GANACHE

1 batch (page 299)

GARNISH

2 cups chopped hazelnuts
8 hazelnut chocolates

*This simple yet stunning cake will impress your guests when you tell them you
made the Chocolate Hazelnut Spread from scratch! Insert all the "oohs," "aahs,"
and other expressions of disbelief and admiration here. Gift leftover Chocolate
Hazelnut Spread to your guests and encourage them to try baking this cake, too!
If you're in a rush, Nutella hazelnut spread works great, too.*

CHOCOLATE CAKE

1. Prepare 1 batch Chocolate Cake, following steps 1 to 6.

2. Divide the batter evenly between the prepared cake pans. Fold ¼ cup chopped hazelnuts
into each pan. Bake for 40 minutes, or until the edges of the cake begin to pull away from the
sides of the pan and a knife inserted into the middle of the cake comes out clean. If the cake
jiggles in the middle when the pan is tapped gently, continue baking before testing it with
a knife. Let cool for 10 to 15 minutes in the pans. Run a knife or an offset spatula around the
inside edge of the pans to release the edges of the cakes. Flip onto a wire rack and let cool
to room temperature.

CHOCOLATE HAZELNUT SPREAD

3. Preheat the oven to 350°F. Line a baking sheet with parchment paper.

4. Spread the whole hazelnuts evenly on the prepared baking sheet. Toast for 5 to 8 minutes,
or until the skins start to peel away from the nuts. Let cool.

5. When the hazelnuts are cool enough to handle, roll small handfuls between your hands or
a clean dish cloth to remove the skins. Place the skinned hazelnuts in the bowl of a food
processor. Mix on high speed until a sandy texture is achieved. With the food processor
running, slowly pour in the oil and vanilla and mix until combined.

6. In a heat-resistant bowl, melt the chocolate in the microwave in 30-second intervals, stirring
after each interval, until smooth. With the food processor on high speed, slowly pour in the
melted chocolate and mix until fully combined. Add the icing sugar, cocoa powder, and salt.
Mix on high speed until the mixture begins to look like a paste. Turn off the food processor,
scrape down the sides of the bowl, then mix for an additional 30 seconds.

7. Store Chocolate Hazelnut Spread in an airtight container in the fridge for up to 1 week.
It will harden when refrigerated, so be sure to microwave it in 10-second intervals until
smooth and creamy.

CHOCOLATE HAZELNUT BUTTERCREAM

8. Prepare 2 batches Milk Chocolate Buttercream.

9. Add the Nutella to the buttercream. Whip on high speed until smooth, about 2 minutes.

DARK CHOCOLATE GANACHE

10. Prepare 1 batch Dark Chocolate Ganache. Transfer the ganache to a squeeze bottle.

ASSEMBLY

11. Stack and crumb coat the cake (see instructions on pages 126 to 129). When stacking, top the
first layer with Chocolate Hazelnut Buttercream and a drizzle of ganache. Top the second
layer with Chocolate Hazelnut Spread. Top the third layer with the buttercream and a drizzle
of ganache. Use the buttercream to crumb coat the cake.

CONTINUED

12. Frost the cake using the Chocolate Hazelnut Buttercream (see instructions on page 181, steps A to C), reserving about ½ cup for piping.

13. Press small handfuls of chopped hazelnuts into the side of the cake to cover the bottom third of it (step D on page 181).

14. Pour the remaining ganache onto the cake, starting in the middle, until it covers almost the entire top of the cake. Tilt the cake to one side until the ganache spills over the edge, then tilt it in a clockwise direction so that the ganache spills over all edges of the cake, creating a drip effect. Before the chocolate sets, sprinkle the remaining hazelnuts on top of the cake and evenly space the hazelnut chocolates around the top edge of the cake to create a crown (steps E to H on page 181). Place the cake in the fridge for at least 15 minutes, to allow the ganache to set.

15. Store in a tall cake box in the fridge for up to 4 days. Once the cake has been cut, cover the cut edges with a layer of waxed paper or plastic wrap placed up against the cake. Remove from the fridge 1 hour before serving.

BAKER'S TIP

We love homemade chocolate hazelnut spread! Make a double batch and store the leftovers in a jar to spread on toast, dip berries in, or just eat with a spoon!

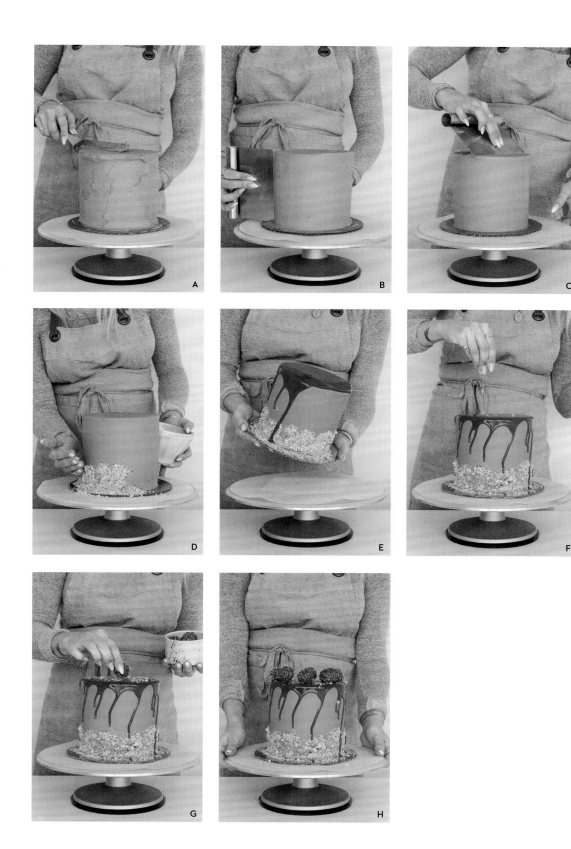

PISTACHIO WHITE CHOCOLATE CAKE

Makes one 6-inch cake with four layers; serves 8 to 10

PISTACHIO WHITE CHOCOLATE CAKE

1 cup whole (3.25%) milk
¼ cup unsalted butter
1 tablespoon + 1 teaspoon pistachio paste
¾ teaspoon pure vanilla extract
4 eggs
2 cups granulated sugar
2 cups all-purpose flour
2 teaspoons baking powder
¼ teaspoon salt
½ cup chopped pistachios, divided
½ cup mini white chocolate chips, divided

PISTACHIO BUTTERCREAM

2 batches Vanilla Buttercream (page 296)
¼ cup pistachio paste

WHITE CHOCOLATE GANACHE

1 batch White Chocolate Ganache (page 299)

PISTACHIO MACARONS

1 batch Macaron Shells (optional, page 259)

GARNISH

2 cups ground pistachios

The key to achieving the most irresistible pistachio flavour is to use Callebaut's pistachio paste—it just can't be beat. Topping this cake with homemade Pistachio Macarons makes for an exquisite display of craftsmanship. If making macarons is too intimidating, sprinkle the top of the cake with ground pistachios instead.

PISTACHIO WHITE CHOCOLATE CAKE

1. Preheat the oven to 325°F. Grease and flour two 6- × 3-inch round cake pans with shortening.

2. In a small saucepan over medium-high heat (or in a heat-resistant bowl in the microwave), heat the milk and butter until the butter is completely melted. Remove from the heat and stir in the pistachio paste and vanilla.

3. In the bowl of a stand mixer fitted with the whisk attachment, whip the eggs on high speed for 1 to 2 minutes, or until the eggs are light and fluffy and have doubled in size. Reduce the speed to low and slowly add the sugar. Increase the speed to high and whip for an additional 2 minutes.

4. Sift the flour, baking powder, and salt into a small bowl and stir together. With the mixer on low speed, alternate adding small amounts of the flour mixture and the milk mixture to the egg mixture, beginning and ending with the dry ingredients. Scrape the bottom of the bowl with a spatula and mix for an additional 2 to 3 minutes on medium-high speed, until the mixture looks light and fluffy.

5. Divide the batter evenly between the prepared cake pans. Sprinkle ¼ cup chopped pistachios and ¼ cup white chocolate chips into each pan and gently fold in using a spoon. Bake for 40 minutes, or until the edges of the cake begin to pull away from the sides of the pan and a knife inserted into the middle of the cake comes out clean. If the cake jiggles in the middle when the pan is tapped gently, continue baking before testing it with a knife. Let cool for 10 to 15 minutes in the pans. Run a knife or an offset spatula around the inside edge of the pans to release the edges of the cakes. Flip onto a wire rack and let cool completely.

PISTACHIO BUTTERCREAM

6. Prepare 2 batches Vanilla Buttercream.

7. Add the pistachio paste to the buttercream. Whip on high speed until well combined.

WHITE CHOCOLATE GANACHE

8. Prepare 1 batch White Chocolate Ganache.

PISTACHIO MACARONS

9. Prepare 1 batch Macaron Shells from our Pistachio and Goat Cheese Macarons, if using. Fill 9 shells with the Pistachio Buttercream, top them, and chill until it's time to decorate the cake. Use leftover shells to fill more macarons to serve with the cake. Extra macarons can be frozen for up to 2 months.

CONTINUED

ASSEMBLY

10. Use the Pistachio Buttercream to stack and crumb coat the cake (see instructions on pages 126 to 129). To each layer, add 1 tablespoon ground pistachios and a drizzle of White Chocolate Ganache spread evenly across the buttercream.

11. Frost the cake using the Pistachio Buttercream (see instructions on page 185, steps A to C).

12. Press small handfuls of chopped pistachios into the side of the cake to cover the bottom third of it (step D on page 185).

13. Place a toothpick halfway into the buttercream in a Pistachio Macaron, sliding it between the 2 shells. The other half of the toothpick will be inserted into the cake. Repeat with the remaining 8 macarons.

14. Line up a Pistachio Macaron with the top edge of the cake and insert the toothpick into the cake. Repeat with the remaining 8 macarons, spacing them evenly to create a macaron crown (steps F to H on page 185). Place the cake in the fridge to chill.

15. Store in a tall cake box in the fridge for up to 4 days. Once the cake has been cut, cover the cut edges with a layer of waxed paper or plastic wrap placed up against the cake. Remove from the fridge 1 hour before serving.

BAKER'S TIP

Not a fan of white chocolate? Skip it! The flavour of the cake can be 100% pistachio and it will still be 100% delicious.

PEANUT BUTTER BANANAS FOSTER CAKE

Makes one 6-inch cake with four layers; serves 8 to 10

CARAMELIZED SUGAR SHARDS

2 tablespoons water
¾ cup sugar
Edible gold leaf flakes,
    for garnish (optional)

BANANA CAKE

¾ cup whole (3.25%) milk
¼ cup unsalted butter
1 cup mashed banana
    (about 3 bananas)
¾ teaspoon pure vanilla
    extract
4 eggs
2 cups granulated sugar
2 cups all-purpose flour
2 teaspoons baking powder
¼ teaspoon salt

SALTED CARAMEL

1 batch (page 299)

PEANUT BUTTER SALTED CARAMEL BUTTERCREAM

2 batches Vanilla Buttercream
    (page 296)
1 cup creamy peanut butter
½ cup Salted Caramel

BANANAS FOSTER FILLING (MAKES 2 CUPS)

¾ cup packed brown sugar
2 tablespoons unsalted butter
¾ cup whole (3.25%) milk
4 egg yolks
1½ cups mashed very ripe
    banana (about 4 bananas)
1 teaspoon pure vanilla extract

GARNISH

¾ cup chopped peanuts
1 cup candied banana slices

We love bananas foster! If you're unfamiliar with this dessert, it's made up of caramelized bananas served with a scoop of vanilla ice cream. Sounds good, right? This cake brings bananas foster to life in a new way . . . with the sneaky yet outstanding addition of peanut butter. With its banana sponge cake and salted caramel touches, you will not be able to resist this flavour combo!

CARAMELIZED SUGAR SHARDS

1. Line a baking sheet with parchment paper or a Silpat mat.

2. Pour the water into a medium saucepan. Cover the surface with the sugar and do not stir. Cook over medium-low heat until the sugar starts to dissolve. Increase the heat to medium-high and cook until the sugar turns a dark golden brown, about 4 minutes.

3. Pour the caramelized sugar onto the prepared baking sheet. Sprinkle with the gold leaf flakes, if using. Let harden.

4. Using a sharp knife, break the candy into shards about 2 inches long. Use immediately or store in an airtight container at room temperature for up to 2 days.

BANANA CAKE

5. Preheat the oven to 325°F. Grease and flour two 6- × 3-inch round cake pans with shortening.

6. In a small saucepan over medium-high heat (or in a heat-resistant bowl in the microwave), heat the milk and butter until the butter is completely melted. Remove from the heat and stir in the banana and vanilla.

7. In the bowl of a stand mixer fitted with the whisk attachment, whip the eggs on high speed for 2 minutes, or until they are light and fluffy and have doubled in size. Reduce the speed to low and slowly add the sugar. Increase the speed to high and whip for an additional 2 minutes.

8. Sift the flour, baking powder, and salt into a small bowl and stir together. With the mixer on low speed, alternate adding small amounts of the flour mixture and the milk mixture to the egg mixture, beginning and ending with the dry ingredients. Scrape the bottom of the bowl with a spatula and mix for an additional 2 to 3 minutes on medium-high speed, until the mixture looks light and fluffy.

9. Divide the batter evenly between the prepared cake pans. Bake for 40 minutes, or until the edges of the cake begin to pull away from the sides of the pan and a knife inserted into the middle of the cake comes out clean. If the cake jiggles in the middle when the pan is tapped gently, continue baking before testing it with a knife. Let cool for 10 to 15 minutes in the pans. Run a knife or an offset spatula around the inside edge of the pans to release the edges of the cakes. Flip onto a wire rack and let cool completely.

SALTED CARAMEL

10. Prepare 1 batch Salted Caramel.

PEANUT BUTTER SALTED CARAMEL BUTTERCREAM

11. Prepare 2 batches Vanilla Buttercream.

12. Add the peanut butter and ½ cup Salted Caramel to the buttercream. Whip on high speed until well combined.

CONTINUED

BANANAS FOSTER FILLING

13. In a small saucepan over medium heat, cook the brown sugar and butter until the mixture is bubbling and caramelized, about 3 to 5 minutes. Slowly pour in the milk and stir with a wooden spoon or heat-safe spatula until fully combined.

14. Place the egg yolks in a small bowl. Slowly pour the caramelized mixture into the yolks in a slow and steady stream while whisking constantly to temper the yolks. Return the mixture to the saucepan and cook on low heat, stirring constantly, until the mixture thickens, about 2 to 3 minutes. Remove from the heat, add the banana and vanilla, and stir until well incorporated. Transfer to a medium bowl and cover with plastic wrap placed directly on the surface of the mixture to prevent a skin forming. Let cool to room temperature.

ASSEMBLY

15. Use the Peanut Butter Salted Caramel Buttercream to stack and crumb coat the cake (see instructions on pages 126 to 129). To each layer, add ¼ cup Bananas Foster Filling, a drizzle of Salted Caramel, and a sprinkle of chopped peanuts (¾ cup total) spread evenly across the buttercream.

16. Frost the cake with the Peanut Butter Salted Caramel Buttercream (see instructions on page 189, steps A to C).

17. In a heat-resistant bowl, heat the remaining Salted Caramel in the microwave until warm to the touch. Pour it onto the cake, starting in the middle, until it covers almost the entire top of the cake. Tilt the cake to one side until the caramel spills over the edge, then tilt it in a clockwise direction so that the caramel spills over all edges of the cake, creating a drip effect (steps D and E on page 189). Place the cake in the fridge to chill for at least 15 minutes.

18. Return the cake to the turntable and alternate topping the cake with a crown of candied bananas and Caramelized Sugar Shards (steps F to H on page 189). Place the cake in the fridge to chill.

19. Store in a tall cake box in the fridge for up to 4 days. Once the cake has been cut, cover the cut edges with a layer of waxed paper or plastic wrap placed up against the cake. Remove from the fridge 1 hour before serving.

BAKER'S TIP

Looking for a more traditional bananas foster taste? Replace the Peanut Butter Salted Caramel Buttercream with Salted Caramel Buttercream (page 151) and omit the chopped peanuts between each layer of cake. Serve with a scoop of vanilla ice cream.

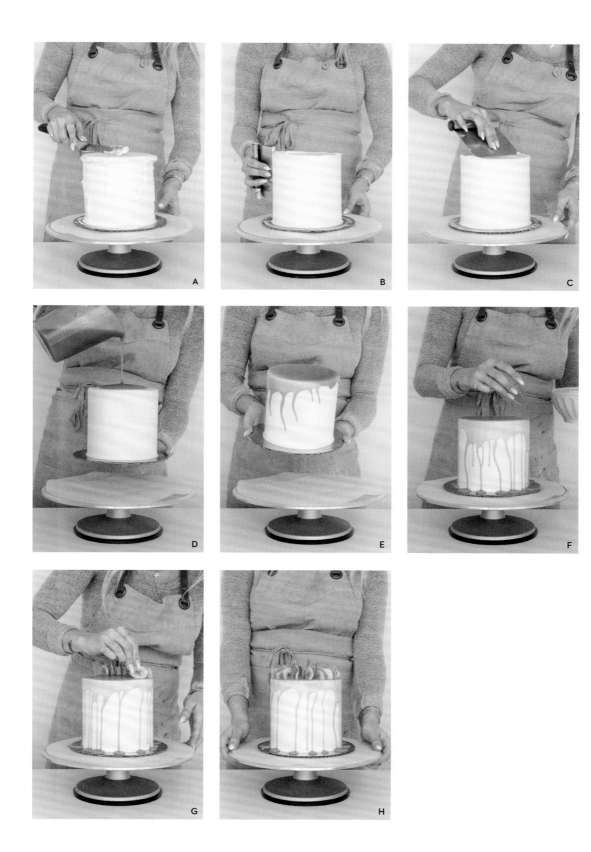

CARROT CAKE WITH SPICED CANDIED WALNUTS

Makes one 6-inch cake with
four layers; serves 8 to 10

CARROT SPONGE CAKE

1 cup milk

¼ cup unsalted butter

¾ teaspoon pure vanilla
extract

4 eggs

2 cups granulated sugar

2 cups flour

2 teaspoons baking powder

1 tablespoon cinnamon

¼ teaspoon ground nutmeg

¼ teaspoon salt

3 cups grated carrot

CREAM CHEESE BUTTERCREAM

2 batches (page 297)

3 drops peach gel food
colouring

SPICED CANDIED WALNUTS

1 batch (page 307)

GARNISH

2 tablespoons edible gold
leaf flakes

Although we enjoy a good carrot cake any time of the year, this cake is usually requested most often around Easter. Delicately spiced and perfectly moist, our carrot cake is just as good as your old favourite.

CARROT SPONGE CAKE

1. Preheat the oven to 325°F. Grease and flour two 6- × 3-inch round cake pans.

2. In a small saucepan over medium-high heat (or in a heat-resistant bowl in the microwave), heat the milk and butter until the butter is completely melted. Remove from the heat and stir in the vanilla.

3. In the bowl of a stand mixer fitted with the whisk attachment, whip the eggs on high speed for 2 minutes, or until they are light and fluffy and have doubled in size. Reduce the speed to low and slowly add the sugar. Increase the speed to high and whip for an additional minute.

4. Sift the flour, baking powder, cinnamon, nutmeg, and salt into a small bowl and stir together. With the mixer on low speed, alternate adding small amounts of the flour mixture and the milk mixture to the egg mixture, beginning and ending with the dry ingredients. Scrape the bottom of the bowl with a spatula and mix for an additional 2 to 3 minutes on medium-high speed, until the mixture looks light and fluffy. Remove the bowl from the stand mixer and fold in the carrot using the spatula.

5. Divide the batter evenly between the prepared cake pans. Bake for 40 minutes, or until the edges of the cake begin to pull away from the sides of the pan and a knife inserted into the middle of the cake comes out clean. If the cake jiggles in the middle when the pan is tapped gently, continue baking before testing it with a knife. Let cool for 10 to 15 minutes in the pans. Run a knife or an offset spatula around the inside edge of the pans to release the edges of the cakes. Flip onto a wire rack and let cool to room temperature.

CREAM CHEESE BUTTERCREAM

6. Prepare 2 batches Cream Cheese Buttercream.

7. Add the food colouring to the buttercream. Whip on high speed until combined.

SPICED CANDIED WALNUTS

8. Prepare 1 batch Spiced Candied Walnuts.

ASSEMBLY

9. Use the Cream Cheese Buttercream to stack and crumb coat the cake (see instructions on pages 126 to 129). To each layer, add ½ cup Spiced Candied Walnuts spread evenly across the buttercream.

10. Frost the cake using the Cream Cheese Buttercream (see instructions on page 193, steps A to D), reserving at least ½ cup for piping. To finish the final layer of frosting, hold a small offset spatula vertically and make small left-to-right movements with your wrist to slightly rough up the buttercream. Keep the spatula on the cake and move the turntable around until the entire cake is finished with a rustic coat of buttercream.

11. Transfer the remaining buttercream to a piping bag and cut off the tip to create an opening about ½ inch in diameter. Pipe large dollops of buttercream around the top edge of the cake. Once the outside edge is complete, move inward and repeat until you reach the middle of the cake (step E on page 193).

CONTINUED

12. Sprinkle the remaining Spiced Candied Walnuts on top of the cake. Using a paint brush, garnish the top of the cake with gold leaf flakes (steps F to H on page 193). Place the cake in the fridge to chill.

13. Store in a tall cake box in the fridge for up to 4 days. Once the cake has been cut, cover the cut edges with a layer of waxed paper or plastic wrap placed up against the cake. Remove from the fridge 1 hour before serving.

BAKER'S TIP

Not a fan of walnuts? Swap out the walnut pieces in the Spiced Candied Walnuts for pecan pieces! If you really love nuts, feel free to add raw nuts to the cake as well. Simply fold about 1 cup chopped raw nuts into the cake batter before pouring it into the pans.

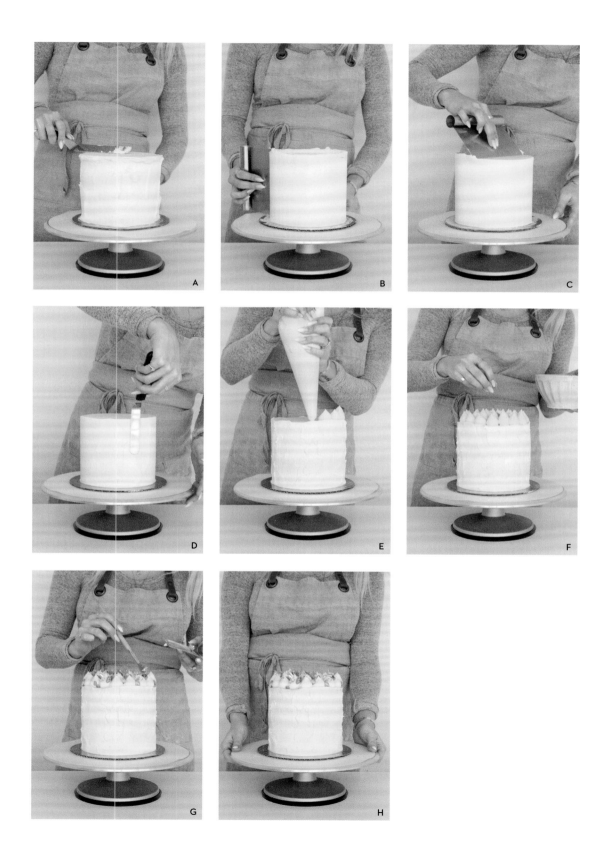

CREAM PUFFS

BAKER'S
NOTES

From our Kitchen to yours
xo

IF YOU'VE EVER CONSIDERED making cream puffs at home from scratch, you've probably read the comments sections of recipes where things went horribly wrong for a home baker who simply wanted to create something new and fun. We want you to be successful in all of your cream puff adventures, so we have put our hearts into providing directions, tips, and tricks that will help make you successful. The crispy outer shell, the light and slightly sweet whipped cream filling, and the prettiest little toppings make cream puffs treats that are hard to resist, and we want yours to be perfect every time. Pay close attention to our detailed directions and fear not! We are here to help and will walk you through every step.

MAKING THE DOUGH

Making the dough for a cream puff, called pâte à choux (or choux), is different from making most doughs because it's mixed and cooked over heat. We recommend cutting the butter into small chunks so that they melt quickly. This will prevent you from boiling the water for an extended period while waiting for the butter to melt. When it comes time to add the flour, make sure to stir it in completely and to continuously fold and stir the mixture until no lumps remain. When it's ready, the ball of dough should be slightly yellow and shiny, and a skin should form at the bottom of the pan.

PIPING THE DOUGH

The way you pipe the pâte à choux onto your parchment-lined baking sheet can drastically affect how it bakes. We suggest using a No. 2A tip to pipe the choux. This is the smallest tip we recommend. It will create a large, solid mass as well as a nice large, open pocket on the inside that you can fill easily. If you don't have a large tip, or can't find one at the store, it would be better to cut a large opening in a piping bag than to use a smaller tip you have on hand.

When piping the pâte à choux, be sure to make each dollop the same size, 1½ inches in diameter. Use our Pâte à Choux Piping Template (page 309) to keep your cream puffs the same size. Different-size dollops will

need a different amount of time in the oven. Try to pipe one tray with dollops that are the same size, then the next tray can be a different size, if desired.

CRAQUELIN

Have you ever wondered what the secret to round, evenly baked pâte à choux is? The answer is craquelin! A disc of craquelin placed on top of the choux before baking helps the top bake evenly and round, making it easier to dip into poured fondant. We like to add flavour and colour to our craquelin as well.

FILLING THE PASTRY

Finding a No. 230 tip for filling the cream puffs can sometimes be difficult. If you're having a hard time finding the right tip, you can fill the cream puffs like this instead:

1. Using a paring knife, cut a small slit into the bottom of each puff once they have cooled completely.
2. Cut off the tip of a piping bag to make a small hole.
3. Press the piping bag into each slit you cut and fill the puff.

BAKING

We recommend baking the pâte à choux for 25 to 30 minutes at 350°F. It's important that you do not open your oven before the 25-minute mark, as doing so will release any steam that has built up in the oven and may cause your choux to collapse. That steam is needed to help the choux rise. Make sure the choux looks puffed up and golden brown on top before you take it out of the oven. When you think the pastry is ready, open the oven quickly and remove one piece. Let cool slightly (about 30 seconds), then break it open to see if it's still wet inside. If it is, allow the choux to bake for an additional minute or two.

TROUBLESHOOTING

Cream puffs can be challenging for the home baker and seasoned baker alike. With so many steps and so many parts of getting the recipe right based on knowing what the dough should look and feel like, it can be intimidating to attempt these treats at home. Our basic troubleshooting guide follows. When things don't go as planned, these tips will help you correct any issues you may have encountered.

Choux Isn't Rising

If the pâte à choux isn't rising in the oven, it could be because the batter is too wet. First, try placing a cake pan filled with water in the oven alongside the choux to create more steam to help the batter rise. If this doesn't work, it probably means that your batter is too wet from adding too many eggs and you'll need to start over. It won't suffice to add more flour to stiffen it up.

Choux Is Browning Too Much

If the choux is getting quite dark in the oven but the middle still hasn't risen, try turning down the heat to 300°F. If that doesn't do the trick, try placing a cake pan filled with water in the oven alongside the choux to create more steam to help the batter rise without continuing to brown.

Choux Collapsed

If the choux looks great in the oven but then begins to collapse when cooling, it may not be baked all the way through. The next time you make a batch, bake it for longer and try testing one piece of choux before removing the whole batch from the oven.

Choux Is Dry and Crumbly

If your choux comes out of the oven dry and crumbly, your batter may have been too dry. When adding the eggs, you want the batter to look nice and shiny and have a ribbon consistency. If the batter doesn't look shiny and is too stiff to reach the ribbon stage, try whisking an egg in a separate bowl and adding it 1 teaspoon at a time until the batter reaches the right consistency. Dry and crumbly choux also means you may have overbaked the pastry. Try reducing the baking time.

PLAIN PUFFS

Pâte à choux can be a little intimidating the first few times you make it. Rest assured that even if your first few batches don't turn out perfectly, you will master these delicious French pastries.

CRAQUELIN (MAKES 2½ CUPS, OR ABOUT 30 LARGE ROUNDS; SEE BAKER'S TIP)

½ cup unsalted butter, room temperature
¾ cup granulated sugar
¾ cup + 2 tablespoons all-purpose flour
3 to 4 drops gel food colouring of your choice (optional)
1 teaspoon flavouring of your choice (optional)

PÂTE À CHOUX

½ cup water
¼ cup unsalted butter, cubed and at room temperature
¼ teaspoon salt
⅔ cup all-purpose flour
2 to 3 eggs

CRAQUELIN

1. In the bowl of a stand mixer fitted with the paddle attachment, cream the butter and sugar on high speed until the mixture looks light and fluffy, about 2 minutes. Scrape down the sides of the bowl and add the flour. Beat on low speed until incorporated. Increase the speed to medium-high and beat for 1 to 2 minutes until fully combined and a thick dough forms. Add the food colouring and flavouring (if using) and beat on medium-high speed until combined.

2. Cut a piece of parchment paper to the size of a baking sheet and place it on a clean work surface. Transfer the dough to the paper. Cut another sheet of parchment paper to roughly the same size and place it on top of the dough. Using a rolling pin, roll out the craquelin to a thickness of ⅛ inch.

3. Remove the top layer of paper and use a 2¾-inch round cookie cutter to cut circles of craquelin. Cut the circles as close together as possible to maximize the yield (see Baker's Tip and photo H).

4. Store the craquelin in an airtight container, layered between pieces of parchment paper, in the fridge for up to 1 week. If you want to make the craquelin well in advance, transfer the dough circles to a baking sheet lined with parchment paper, then wrap the baking sheet in plastic wrap and store in the freezer for up to 1 month.

PÂTE À CHOUX

5. Preheat the oven to 350°F. Line 2 baking sheets with the Pâte à Choux Piping Template (page 309). Place a layer of parchment paper on top. Fit a piping bag with a No. 2A tip.

6. In a medium saucepan over medium-high heat, bring the water, butter, and salt to a boil (see photo A). Using a heat-resistant spatula or a wooden spoon, stir in the flour and continuously fold and stir the mixture until the choux is slightly yellow, shiny, and begins to form a ball (see photos B and C). You'll know it's ready when a skin begins to form on the bottom of the saucepan and a metal spoon inserted into the dough ball stands up straight.

7. Transfer the choux to the bowl of a stand mixer fitted with the paddle attachment and mix on medium-low speed until the bowl is warm to the touch, about 4 minutes. Add 2 eggs, one at a time, while the mixer is running (see photo D). The dough is ready when it is shiny and keeps its shape while still looking nice and smooth after you turn off the mixer and remove the paddle (see photo E). It should fall from a spoon, but only after a few seconds. If the choux doesn't look shiny and is still stiff, whisk the third egg in a small bowl and add it little by little. If the mixture becomes too runny, you'll need to start the recipe over again.

8. Scoop the choux into the prepared piping bag (see photo F). Pipe dollops of choux onto the prepared baking sheets following the template. To pipe the choux, hold the piping bag 1 inch above the parchment paper. Apply pressure until a dollop of choux reaches the edges of the template. Release pressure to stop the flow and swirl your wrist as you pull the piping bag away (see photo G).

9. Top each dollop of choux with a circle of craquelin. Bake for 25 to 30 minutes, or until the choux have puffed up and are golden brown on top. Do not open the oven before the 25-minute mark to ensure that the choux puff up nice and big! If you take them out too early, they will deflate. Let cool to room temperature on the baking sheets. The puffs are now ready to be filled.

10. Store unfilled puffs in an airtight container at room temperature for up to 1 day. You can freeze unfilled puffs in an airtight container for up to 1 month.

BAKER'S TIP

1. We use this Craquelin recipe as the base for our flavoured and coloured craquelin. Refer to each flavoured recipe and follow the directions carefully. 2. You can re-roll any leftover Craquelin trimmings by mixing them together by hand and rolling out again, as many times as needed.

PLAIN CHOCOLATE PUFFS

Makes 24 cream puffs

**CHOCOLATE CRAQUELIN
(MAKES 2¼ CUPS, OR
ABOUT 30 LARGE ROUNDS)**

½ cup unsalted butter,
    room temperature
¾ cup granulated sugar
¾ cup + 1 tablespoon
    all-purpose flour
1 tablespoon cocoa powder

CHOCOLATE PÂTE À CHOUX

½ cup water
¼ cup unsalted butter, cubed
    and at room temperature
¼ teaspoon salt
⅔ cup all-purpose flour
1 teaspoon sifted cocoa powder
2 to 3 eggs

Use this recipe as your base if you want an extra-chocolatey cream puff! Not only do they taste amazing, but they're gorgeous when topped with our Chocolate Craquelin.

CHOCOLATE CRAQUELIN

1. In the bowl of a stand mixer fitted with the paddle attachment, cream the butter and sugar on high speed until the mixture looks light and fluffy, about 2 minutes. Scrape down the sides of the bowl. With the mixer on low speed, add the flour and cocoa powder and beat until incorporated. Increase the speed to medium-high and beat until fully combined and a thick dough forms.

2. Cut a piece of parchment paper to the size of a baking sheet and place it on a clean work surface. Transfer the dough to the paper. Cut another sheet of parchment paper to roughly the same size and place it on top of the dough. Using a rolling pin, roll out the craquelin to a thickness of ⅛ inch.

3. Remove the top layer of paper and use a 2¾-inch round cookie cutter to cut circles of craquelin. Cut the circles as close together as possible to maximize the yield.

4. Store the craquelin in an airtight container, layered between pieces of parchment paper, in the fridge for up to 1 week. If you want to make the craquelin well in advance, transfer the dough circles to a baking sheet lined with parchment paper, then wrap the baking sheet in plastic wrap and store in the freezer for up to 1 month.

CHOCOLATE PÂTE À CHOUX

5. Preheat the oven to 350°F. Line 2 baking sheets with the Pâte à Choux Piping Template (page 309). Place a layer of parchment paper on top. Fit a piping bag with a No. 2A tip.

6. In a medium saucepan over medium-high heat, bring the water, butter, and salt to a boil. Using a heat-resistant spatula or a wooden spoon, stir in the flour and cocoa powder and continuously fold and stir the mixture until the choux is shiny and begins to form a ball. You'll know it's ready when a skin begins to form on the bottom of the saucepan and a metal spoon inserted into the dough ball stands up straight.

7. Transfer the choux to the bowl of a stand mixer fitted with the paddle attachment and mix on medium-low speed until the bowl is warm to the touch, about 4 minutes. Add 2 eggs, one at a time, while the mixer is running. The dough is ready when it is shiny and keeps its shape while still looking nice and smooth after you turn off the mixer and remove the paddle. It should fall from a spoon, but only after a few seconds. If the choux doesn't look shiny and is still stiff, whisk the third egg in a small bowl and add it little by little. If the mixture becomes too runny, you'll need to start the recipe over again.

8. Scoop the choux into the prepared piping bag. Pipe dollops of choux onto the prepared baking sheet following the template. To pipe the choux, hold the piping bag 1 inch above the parchment paper. Apply pressure until a dollop of choux reaches the edges of the template. Release pressure to stop the flow and swirl your wrist as you pull the piping bag away.

9. Top each dollop of choux with a circle of Chocolate Craquelin, or your choice of craquelin. Bake for 25 to 30 minutes, or until the choux have puffed up and are golden brown on top. Do not open the oven before the 25-minute mark to ensure that the choux puff up nice and big! If you take them out too early, they will deflate. Let cool to room temperature on the baking sheet. The puffs are now ready to be filled.

10. Store unfilled puffs in an airtight container at room temperature for up to 1 day. You can freeze unfilled puffs in an airtight container for up to 1 month.

1 cup (220 g) chopped white
  baking chocolate
4 cups icing sugar
¼ cup white corn syrup
¼ cup water
¾ teaspoon pure vanilla
  extract
2 to 3 drops gel food colouring
  of your choice (optional)

POURED FONDANT

*Poured fondant (also known as soft fondant) is different from the traditional
fondant you use to decorate cakes. We've seen people buy regular fondant from
the store and try heating it to use as poured fondant. Unfortunately, that method
doesn't work very well. We suggest making your own instead. Poured fondant can
also be purchased from most cake decorating stores if you're short on time.*

1. In a heat-resistant bowl, heat the white chocolate in the microwave in 20-second intervals,
    stirring after each interval, until smooth.

2. In the bowl of a stand mixer fitted with the paddle attachment, mix the icing sugar, corn
    syrup, water, vanilla, and food colouring (if using) until combined. Add the white chocolate
    and mix until smooth, scraping down the sides of the bowl as needed.

3. Store in an airtight container at room temperature for up to 1 week. Before using, transfer the
    fondant to a heat-resistant container and warm it in the microwave in 20- to 30-second
    intervals, stirring after each interval, until melted and smooth.

BAKER'S TIP

To smooth out any lumps and bumps after dipping your cream puff into the poured fondant,
simply wet your finger and press along any imperfections before the fondant dries.

VANILLA SPRINKLE CREAM PUFFS

Makes 24 cream puffs

PLAIN PUFFS

1 batch (page 200)

VANILLA BEAN WHIPPED CREAM

4 cups whipping (35%) cream
¼ cup icing sugar
¼ cup skim milk powder
1 tablespoon vanilla bean paste

VANILLA BEAN POURED FONDANT

1 batch Poured Fondant (page 204)
1 tablespoon vanilla bean paste (see Baker's Tip)

GARNISH

2 cups long rainbow sprinkles

Is there anything more heavenly than this Vanilla Sprinkle Cream Puff? It's light and airy, and the flavour isn't too overpowering. With its garnish of sprinkles, it will make any moment a celebration.

PLAIN CREAM PUFFS

1. Prepare 1 batch Plain Puffs.

VANILLA BEAN WHIPPED CREAM

2. In the bowl of a stand mixer fitted with the whisk attachment, whip the cream, icing sugar, skim milk powder, and vanilla bean paste on medium-high speed until the mixture looks light and fluffy and stiff peaks form, about 2 minutes. Be careful not to overwhip.

VANILLA BEAN POURED FONDANT

3. Prepare 1 batch Poured Fondant, adding the vanilla bean paste to the bowl of the stand mixer before mixing in step 2.

ASSEMBLY

4. Line a baking sheet with parchment paper.

5. Transfer the Vanilla Bean Whipped Cream to a piping bag fitted with a No. 230 tip. Puncture the bottom of a puff with the piping tip and insert it halfway. Squeeze the piping bag to fill the puff. You'll know it's full when filling begins to spill out of the hole and the puff feels heavy. Place the filled cream puff on the prepared baking sheet. Repeat with the remaining puffs.

6. Place the sprinkles in a shallow medium bowl. Heat the Vanilla Bean Poured Fondant in the microwave in 30-second intervals, stirring after each interval, until melted and smooth. Carefully dip a cream puff into the fondant until the craquelin is nearly covered. Hold the cream puff over the bowl and gently shake until no more fondant drips off. Immediately roll the cream puff in the sprinkles. Return it to the prepared baking sheet. Repeat with the remaining cream puffs.

7. Store in an airtight container in the fridge until time to serve. Serve cream puffs on the day they are made for maximum freshness and deliciousness.

BAKER'S TIP

1. If you don't have vanilla bean paste to use in the Vanilla Bean Poured Fondant, substitute 1 tablespoon pure vanilla extract and the seeds of 1 vanilla bean. **2.** Coordinate these cream puffs with the theme of your event by replacing the rainbow sprinkles with sprinkles in a solid colour of your choice!

RASPBERRY CHEESECAKE CREAM PUFFS

RASPBERRY CRAQUELIN

1 batch Craquelin (page 200, steps 1 to 4)

1 tablespoon freeze-dried raspberries

2 drops soft pink gel food colouring

PÂTE À CHOUX

1 batch (page 200, steps 5 to 8)

RASPBERRY WHITE CHOCOLATE (FOR DECORATION; OPTIONAL)

2 cups (440 g) pink chocolate melting wafers

¼ cup freeze-dried raspberries (see Baker's Tip)

Edible gold leaf flakes (optional)

RASPBERRY CHEESECAKE FILLING

1¼ cups cream cheese, room temperature

¾ cup granulated sugar

Pinch of salt

2 eggs

2 tablespoons whole (3.25%) milk

½ teaspoon pure vanilla extract

1 batch Raspberry Reduction (page 303)

RASPBERRY CHEESECAKE WHIPPED CREAM

2 cups whipping (35%) cream

2 tablespoons icing sugar

2 tablespoons skim milk powder

2 cups Raspberry Cheesecake Filling

Fruity and delicious, these cream puffs combine the decadence of a raspberry cheesecake with the lightness of whipped cream. Topped with a colourful piece of chocolate, these puffs are party ready. The Raspberry Cheesecake Whipped Cream is a labour of love, but the result is worth the extra steps to create this decadent, rich filling.

RASPBERRY CRAQUELIN

1. Prepare 1 batch Craquelin, following steps 1 to 4, adding the freeze-dried raspberries with the food colouring when called for in step 1.

PÂTE À CHOUX

2. Prepare 1 batch Pâte à Choux, following steps 5 to 8.

3. Top each dollop of choux with a circle of Raspberry Craquelin. Bake for 25 to 30 minutes, or until the choux have puffed up and are golden brown on top. Do not open the oven before the 25-minute mark to ensure that the choux puff up nice and big! Let cool to room temperature on the baking sheets.

RASPBERRY WHITE CHOCOLATE

4. Line a baking sheet with parchment paper.

5. In a large heat-resistant bowl, melt the chocolate wafers in the microwave in 30-second intervals, stirring after each interval, until smooth.

6. Pour the chocolate onto the prepared baking sheet. Using an offset spatula, spread it in an even layer, about ⅛ inch thick. Sprinkle the raspberries and gold leaf flakes (if using) overtop. Set aside for 20 minutes to harden.

RASPBERRY CHEESECAKE FILLING

7. Preheat the oven to 300°F. Line a 13- × 9-inch baking dish with parchment paper.

8. In the bowl of a stand mixer fitted with the whisk attachment, whip the cream cheese on medium-high speed for 3 to 4 minutes, until smooth, stopping to scrape down the sides of the bowl every 30 to 45 seconds. Add the sugar and salt and whip on medium speed until fully incorporated, about 2 minutes. Scrape down the sides of the bowl.

9. In a small bowl, whisk together the eggs, milk, and vanilla. With the mixer on low speed, slowly pour the egg mixture into the cream cheese mixture and whip until combined. Scrape down the sides of the bowl. Add the Raspberry Reduction and whip on medium-high speed until fully combined. Scrape down the sides of the bowl and whip for an additional 30 seconds.

10. Pour the batter into the prepared baking dish. Bake for 20 to 25 minutes, or until the centre of the cheesecake has a firm jiggle. Let cool in the dish for 5 minutes before placing it in the fridge to cool to room temperature.

11. Transfer to a food processor and purée until smooth and creamy.

CONTINUED

RASPBERRY CHEESECAKE WHIPPED CREAM

12. In the bowl of a stand mixer fitted with the whisk attachment, whip the cream, icing sugar, and skim milk powder on medium-high speed until the mixture looks light and fluffy and stiff peaks form, about 2 minutes. Be careful not to overwhip.

13. Pour the Raspberry Cheesecake Filling into the whipped cream and carefully fold together using a spatula. Be gentle as you fold to prevent the whipped cream from deflating.

ASSEMBLY

14. Line a baking sheet with parchment paper.

15. Transfer half of the Raspberry Cheesecake Whipped Cream to a piping bag fitted with a No. 230 tip. Puncture the bottom of a puff with the piping tip and insert it halfway. Squeeze the piping bag to fill the puff. You'll know it's full when filling begins to spill out of the hole and the puff feels heavy. Place the filled cream puff on the prepared baking sheet. Repeat with the remaining puffs.

16. Using your hands, break the Raspberry White Chocolate into shards about 1 to 2 inches long. Transfer the remaining Raspberry Cheesecake Whipped Cream to a piping bag fitted with a No. 8B tip. Pipe a generous dollop of whipped cream on each cream puff. Top each dollop with a chocolate shard.

17. Store in an airtight container in the fridge until time to serve. Serve cream puffs on the day they are made for maximum freshness and deliciousness.

BAKER'S TIP

It can be tricky to find freeze-dried raspberries in some grocery stores. We recommend ordering them online.

MOCHA CREAM PUFFS

CHOCOLATE ESPRESSO CRAQUELIN

½ cup unsalted butter, room temperature
¾ cup granulated sugar
2 teaspoons espresso powder
1 teaspoon hot water
¾ cup all-purpose flour
2 tablespoons cocoa powder

CHOCOLATE PÂTE À CHOUX

1 batch (page 203, steps 5 to 8)

CHOCOLATE SHARDS

2 cups (440 g) milk chocolate melting wafers
1 tablespoon edible gold leaf flakes, for garnish
¼ cup instant coffee, for garnish

MOCHA MOUSSE

¾ cup + 1½ cups whipping (35%) cream, divided
3 tablespoons instant coffee
2 egg yolks
2 tablespoons granulated sugar
1¾ cups (385 g) chopped milk baking chocolate

We could literally eat the filling of this cream puff with a spoon. It's thick and creamy and reminds us of a coffee dessert that our mom used to make on hot summer days when we were younger.

CHOCOLATE ESPRESSO CRAQUELIN

1. In the bowl of a stand mixer fitted with the paddle attachment, cream the butter and sugar on high speed until the mixture looks light and fluffy, about 2 minutes. Scrape down the sides of the bowl.

2. In a small bowl, stir together the espresso and hot water. Pour into the butter and sugar mixture and beat on medium speed until combined. Scrape down the sides of the bowl. Reduce the speed to low, add the flour and cocoa powder, and beat until incorporated. Beat on high speed until fully combined and a thick dough forms.

3. Cut a piece of parchment paper to the size of a baking sheet and place it on a clean work surface. Transfer the dough to the paper. Cut another sheet of parchment paper to roughly the same size and place it on top of the dough. Using a rolling pin, roll out the craquelin to a thickness of ⅛ inch.

4. Remove the top layer of paper and use a 2¾-inch round cookie cutter to cut circles of craquelin. Cut the circles as close together as possible to maximize the yield.

5. Store the craquelin in an airtight container, layered between pieces of parchment paper, in the fridge for up to 1 week. If you want to make the craquelin well in advance, transfer the dough circles to a baking sheet lined with parchment paper, then wrap the baking sheet in plastic wrap and store in the freezer for up to 1 month.

CHOCOLATE PÂTE À CHOUX

6. Prepare 1 batch Chocolate Pâte à Choux, following steps 5 to 8.

7. Top each dollop of choux with a circle of Chocolate Espresso Craquelin. Bake for 25 to 30 minutes, or until the choux have puffed up and are golden brown on top. Do not open the oven before the 25-minute mark to ensure that the choux puffs up nice and big! If you take them out too early, they will deflate. Let cool to room temperature on the baking sheets.

CHOCOLATE SHARDS

8. Line a baking sheet with parchment paper.

9. In a large heat-resistant bowl, melt the chocolate in the microwave in 30-second intervals, stirring well after each interval, until smooth but not hot.

10. Pour the chocolate onto the prepared baking sheet. Using an offset spatula, spread it in an even layer, about ⅛ inch thick. Sprinkle with the gold leaf flakes and instant coffee. Set aside to harden.

11. Break the chocolate into shards about 2 to 3 inches long.

MOCHA MOUSSE

12. In a small saucepan over medium-high heat, combine ¾ cup cream and the instant coffee until the coffee has dissolved and the mixture is just about to boil.

CONTINUED

13. In a medium bowl, whisk together the egg yolks and sugar. Slowly whisk the cream mixture into the egg mixture, tempering the egg yolks, to make custard. Return the custard to the saucepan and cook on low heat, stirring continuously, until a thermometer inserted in the mixture reaches 165°F. Remove from the heat.

14. In a medium heat-resistant bowl, melt the chocolate in the microwave in 30-second intervals, stirring between each interval, until smooth. Pour into the saucepan with the custard, stir, and let the mixture cool to 110°F.

15. In the bowl of a stand mixer fitted with the whisk attachment, whip the remaining 1½ cups cream on high speed until light and fluffy and soft peaks form, about 2 minutes.

16. Using a spatula, gently fold the whipped cream into the custard until fully incorporated. Use immediately.

ASSEMBLY

17. Line a baking sheet with parchment paper.

18. Transfer most of the Mocha Mousse to a piping bag fitted with a No. 230 tip, reserving about ¼ cup. Puncture the bottom of a puff with the piping tip and insert it halfway. Squeeze the piping bag to fill the puff. You'll know it's full when filling begins to spill out of the hole and the puff feels heavy. Place the filled cream puff on the prepared baking sheet. Repeat with the remaining puffs.

19. Transfer the reserved Mocha Mousse to a piping bag fitted with a No. 8B tip. Pipe a generous dollop of mousse on each cream puff. Top each dollop with a Chocolate Shard.

20. Store in an airtight container in the fridge until time to serve. Serve cream puffs on the day they are made for maximum freshness and deliciousness.

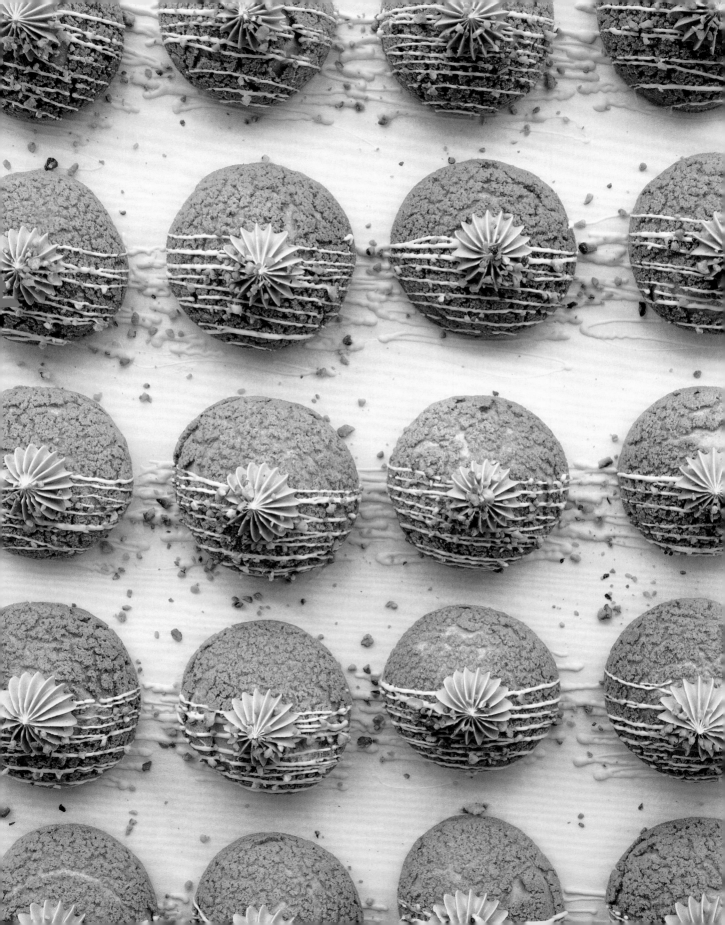

PISTACHIO WHITE CHOCOLATE CREAM PUFFS

Makes 24 cream puffs

GREEN CRAQUELIN

1 batch Craquelin (page 200, steps 1 to 4)

1 to 3 drops avocado green gel food colouring

PÂTE À CHOUX

1 batch (page 200, steps 5 to 8)

PISTACHIO PASTRY CREAM

1 cup (220 g) chopped white baking chocolate

½ cup pistachio paste

¼ cup unsalted butter, room temperature

12 egg yolks

½ cup granulated sugar

½ cup cornstarch

2 teaspoons pure vanilla extract

4½ cups whole (3.25%) milk

GARNISH

1 cup (220 g) chopped white baking chocolate

¼ cup ground pistachios

These pastel beauties are filled with a heavenly Pistachio Pastry Cream that's rich and decadent. Pistachio is a classic flavour in the pastry world, which makes these the perfect pastry to pair with afternoon tea.

GREEN CRAQUELIN

1. Prepare 1 batch Craquelin, following steps 1 to 4, adding the food colouring when called for in step 1.

PÂTE À CHOUX

2. Prepare 1 batch Pâte à Choux, following steps 5 to 8.

3. Top each dollop of choux with a circle of Green Craquelin. Bake for 25 to 30 minutes, or until the choux have puffed up and are golden brown on top. Do not open the oven before the 25-minute mark to ensure that the choux puffs up nice and big! If you take them out too early, they will deflate. Let cool to room temperature on the baking sheets.

PISTACHIO PASTRY CREAM

4. Add the chocolate, pistachio paste, and butter to a large bowl. Do not stir and set aside.

5. In a medium bowl, whisk together the egg yolks, sugar, cornstarch, and vanilla.

6. In a small saucepan over medium-high heat, heat the milk until it begins to steam and small bubbles form on the surface. Slowly pour the milk into the sugar mixture, whisking constantly to temper the egg yolks. Whisk until fully combined.

7. Return the mixture to the saucepan and cook over low heat, whisking constantly to prevent burning and to ensure a smooth and creamy consistency. Continue whisking until the mixture thickens and a thick ribbon of pastry cream drips from the whisk when lifted out of the saucepan. Remove from the heat and pour over chopped baking chocolate, butter, and pistachio paste. Let sit for 1 minute and whisk to combine. Let cool to room temperature.

8. Transfer the mixture to a shallow medium dish and cover with plastic wrap placed directly on the surface of the mixture to prevent a skin forming. Store in an airtight container in the fridge for up to 1 week.

ASSEMBLY

9. Line a baking sheet with parchment paper.

10. Transfer the Pistachio Pastry Cream to a piping bag fitted with a No. 230 tip. Puncture the bottom of a puff with the piping tip and insert it halfway. Squeeze the piping bag to fill the puff. You'll know it's full when filling begins to spill out of the hole and the puff feels heavy. Place the filled cream puff on the prepared baking sheet. Repeat with the remaining puffs.

11. Heat the white chocolate for garnish in the microwave in 30-second intervals, stirring after each interval, until melted and smooth. Transfer to a piping bag and cut off the tip to create a small opening. Drizzle in a zigzag pattern over half of each cream puff. Sprinkle the ground pistachios over the white chocolate drizzle.

12. Store in an airtight container in the fridge until time to serve. Serve cream puffs on the day they are made for maximum freshness and deliciousness.

BAKER'S TIP

We love the personality that the Green Craquelin gives these puffs! Try adding gel food colouring to the craquelin you make in other recipes for a colourful experience.

PAVLOVA CREAM PUFFS

Ashley's all-time favourite dessert is pavlova, so it's no surprise that this is her favourite cream puff. Wildberry Whipped Cream fills each puff before it's rolled in crisp meringue shards for the perfect finishing touch.

Makes 24 cream puffs

PINK MERINGUE

1 batch Mini Meringues
(page 289, steps 1 to 4)
3 drops soft pink gel food
colouring

PLAIN PUFFS

1 batch (page 200)

WILDBERRY WHIPPED CREAM

3 cups whipping (35%) cream
3 tablespoons icing sugar
3 tablespoons skim milk
powder
2 teaspoons vanilla bean paste
1 batch Wildberry Reduction
(page 304)

PINK POURED FONDANT

1 batch Poured Fondant
(page 204)
3 drops soft pink gel food
colouring

PINK MERINGUE

1. Prepare 1 batch Mini Meringues, following steps 1 to 4.

2. Add the food colouring and whip on medium-high speed for 20 seconds until fully incorporated.

3. Divide the mixture evenly between the prepared baking sheets. Using an offset spatula, spread it in a thin, even layer. Bake for 2 hours. Let cool to room temperature. Break into small pieces, about ⅛ inch wide, and store in an airtight container at room temperature for up to 2 weeks.

PLAIN CREAM PUFFS

4. Prepare 1 batch Plain Puffs.

WILDBERRY WHIPPED CREAM

5. In the bowl of a stand mixer fitted with the whisk attachment, whip the cream, icing sugar, skim milk powder, and vanilla bean paste on medium-high speed until the mixture looks light and fluffy and medium peaks form, about 2 minutes. Be careful not to overwhip. Add 1 cup Wildberry Reduction and whip to stiff peaks.

PINK POURED FONDANT

6. Prepare 1 batch Poured Fondant, adding the food colouring in step 2.

ASSEMBLY

7. Line a baking sheet with parchment paper.

8. Transfer the Wildberry Whipped Cream to a piping bag fitted with a No. 230 tip. Puncture the bottom of a puff with the piping tip and insert it halfway. Squeeze the piping bag to fill the puff. You'll know it's full when filling begins to spill out of the hole and the puff feels heavy. Place the filled cream puff on the prepared baking sheet. Repeat with the remaining puffs.

9. Place the Pink Meringue pieces in a medium bowl. Heat the Pink Poured Fondant in the microwave in 30-second intervals, stirring after each interval, until melted and smooth. Carefully dip a cream puff into the fondant until the craquelin is nearly covered. Hold the cream puff over the bowl and gently shake until no more fondant drips off. Immediately roll the cream puff in the meringue pieces. Return it to the prepared baking sheet. Repeat with the remaining cream puffs.

10. Store in an airtight container in the fridge until time to serve. Serve cream puffs on the day they are made for maximum freshness and deliciousness.

BAKER'S TIP

Substitute the Wildberry Reduction in the whipped cream with Raspberry Reduction (page 303) or strawberry reduction, depending on the season.

CHOCOLATE LOVER'S CREAM PUFFS

Makes 24 cream puffs

PLAIN CHOCOLATE PUFFS

1 batch (page 203)

DARK CHOCOLATE PASTRY CREAM

4½ cups whole (3.25%) milk
1 cup (220 g) chopped dark baking chocolate
¾ cup granulated sugar
12 egg yolks
½ cup cornstarch
1 tablespoon pure vanilla extract
¼ cup unsalted butter

GARNISH

3 cups (660 g) chopped milk or dark baking chocolate
¼ cup vegetable oil
Edible gold leaf flakes

Who doesn't love a good makeover? In this recipe, we gave every element of our regular cream puff a chocolate intervention. The choux is chocolate, the craquelin is chocolate, the filling is Dark Chocolate Pastry Cream, and we've skipped the usual fondant topping in favour of chocolate. This is the makeover of the season.

CHOCOLATE CREAM PUFFS

1. Prepare 1 batch Plain Chocolate Puffs.

DARK CHOCOLATE PASTRY CREAM

2. In a small saucepan over medium-high heat, heat the milk until it begins to steam and small bubbles form on the surface.

3. In a medium heat-resistant bowl, melt the chocolate in the microwave in 30-second intervals, stirring between each interval, until smooth.

4. In a medium bowl, whisk together the sugar, egg yolks, cornstarch, and vanilla.

5. Slowly pour the milk into the sugar mixture, whisking constantly to temper the egg yolks, until combined. Return the mixture to the saucepan and cook over low heat, whisking constantly to prevent burning and to ensure a smooth and creamy consistency. Continue whisking until the mixture thickens and a thick ribbon of pastry cream drips from the whisk when lifted out of the saucepan. Remove from the heat and whisk in the melted chocolate and butter until fully combined. Let cool to room temperature.

6. Transfer the mixture to a shallow medium dish and cover with plastic wrap placed directly on the surface of the mixture to prevent a skin forming. Store in an airtight container in the fridge for up to 1 week.

ASSEMBLY

7. Line a baking sheet with parchment paper.

8. Transfer the Dark Chocolate Pastry Cream to a piping bag fitted with a No. 230 tip. Puncture the bottom of a puff with the piping tip and insert it halfway. Squeeze the piping bag to fill the puff. You'll know it's full once filling begins to spill out of the hole and the puff feels heavy. Place the filled cream puff on the prepared baking sheet. Repeat with the remaining puffs.

8. In a small yet deep heat-resistant bowl, melt the chocolate in the microwave in 30-second intervals, stirring after each interval, until smooth. Add the oil and stir well to incorporate. Carefully dip a cream puff into the chocolate until the craquelin is nearly covered. Hold the cream puff over the bowl and gently shake until no more chocolate drips off. Return it to the prepared baking sheet and immediately garnish with gold leaf flakes. Repeat with the remaining cream puffs.

9. Store in an airtight container in the fridge until time to serve. Serve cream puffs on the day they are made for maximum freshness and deliciousness.

BAKER'S TIP

To add even more chocolate to these Chocolate Lover's Cream Puffs, substitute the sprinkle of gold leaf flakes for a sprinkle of mini chocolate chips.

COTTON CANDY CREAM PUFFS

Makes 24 cream puffs

PLAIN PUFFS

1 batch (page 200)

COTTON CANDY WHIPPED CREAM

4 cups whipping (35%) cream
¼ cup icing sugar
¼ cup skim milk powder
2 to 3 teaspoons JRC Liquid
   Cotton Candy or cotton
   candy flavouring
2 drops soft pink gel food
   colouring

POURED FONDANT

1 batch Poured Fondant
   (page 204), divided
   (see Baker's Tip)
2 drops soft pink gel food
   colouring
2 drops sky blue gel food
   colouring

GARNISH

½ cup sprinkle mix of your
   choice (see Baker's Tip)

Hop onto a dandelion fluff and float away into cotton candy clouds of pink and blue. These light, fluffy, and sweet Cotton Candy Cream Puffs will help you sail away with their dreamy taste and an even more ethereal look.

PLAIN CREAM PUFFS

1. Prepare 1 batch Plain Puffs.

COTTON CANDY WHIPPED CREAM

2. In a stand mixer fitted with the whisk attachment, whip the cream, icing sugar, skim milk powder, cotton candy flavouring, and food colouring until the mixture looks light and fluffy and stiff peaks form, about 2 minutes. Be careful not to overwhip.

POURED FONDANT

3. Prepare 1 batch Poured Fondant.

4. Divide the fondant evenly between 2 small bowls. To one bowl, add the soft pink food colouring and stir until the colour is uniform. To the other bowl, add the sky blue food colouring and stir until the colour is uniform.

ASSEMBLY

5. Line a baking sheet with parchment paper. Place the sprinkle mix in a small bowl.

6. Transfer the Cotton Candy Whipped Cream to a piping bag fitted with a No. 230 tip. Puncture the bottom of a puff with the piping tip and insert it halfway. Squeeze the piping bag to fill the puff. You'll know it's full when filling begins to spill out of the hole and the puff feels heavy. Place the filled cream puff on the prepared baking sheet. Repeat with the remaining puffs.

7. Heat the pink fondant and the blue fondant in the microwave in 30-second intervals, stirring after each interval, until melted and smooth. Transfer 1 cup of each colour to a single heat-resistant bowl. Using a knife, gently swirl the two colours together. Carefully dip a cream puff into the fondant until the craquelin is nearly covered. Hold the puff over the bowl and gently shake until no more fondant drips off. Return it to the baking sheet and immediately garnish with the sprinkle mix. Repeat with the remaining cream puffs.

8. Store in an airtight container in the fridge until time to serve. Serve cream puffs on the day they are made for maximum freshness and deliciousness.

BAKER'S TIP

1. If you want to save some time, use a store-bought variety of poured fondant—just make sure that it's poured fondant and not regular fondant! **2.** Poured fondant dries quickly. Premake your sprinkle mix for quick and easy sprinkling. If your fondant gets too hard to dip, simply heat it in the microwave in 15-second intervals, stirring after each interval, until it loosens up again.

EVERYTHING BAGEL CREAM PUFFS

Makes 24 cream puffs

EVERYTHING BAGEL CRAQUELIN

½ cup unsalted butter, room temperature
¾ cup granulated sugar
¾ cup + 2 tablespoons all-purpose flour
½ teaspoon dried chives
½ teaspoon dried onion flakes
¼ teaspoon minced garlic
¼ teaspoon poppy seeds
¼ teaspoon white sesame seeds
¼ teaspoon black sesame seeds

CHIVE ONION PÂTE À CHOUX

½ cup water
¼ cup unsalted butter, room temperature
¼ teaspoon salt
⅔ cup all-purpose flour
1 teaspoon dried chives
1 teaspoon dried onion flakes
2 to 3 eggs

HERB AND GARLIC CREAM CHEESE FILLING

3 cups plain cream cheese, room temperature
¼ cup + 2 tablespoons whipping (35%) cream
1½ teaspoons chopped fresh parsley
1 teaspoon minced garlic
¾ teaspoon chopped fresh chives, more for garnish
Pinch of salt

Since pâte à choux is not very sweet on its own, you can get creative and fill your puffs with all kinds of savoury fillings. One of our go-to morning snacks is a toasted everything bagel with cream cheese, so we created a savoury cream puff that embodies those classic flavours. We had to include this recipe in the book because it's one of our most requested cream puff flavours, and one of our personal favourites!

EVERYTHING BAGEL CRAQUELIN

1. In the bowl of a stand mixer fitted with the paddle attachment, cream the butter and sugar on high speed until the mixture looks light and fluffy, about 2 minutes. Scrape down the sides of the bowl and add the flour. Beat on low speed until incorporated. Add the chives, onion flakes, garlic, poppy seeds, white sesame seeds, and black sesame seeds. Increase the speed to medium-high and beat until fully combined and a thick dough forms.

2. Cut a piece of parchment paper to the size of a baking sheet and place it on a clean work surface. Transfer the dough to the paper. Cut another sheet of parchment paper to roughly the same size and place it on top of the dough. Using a rolling pin, roll out the craquelin to a thickness of ⅛ inch.

3. Remove the top layer of paper and use a 2¾-inch round cookie cutter to cut circles of craquelin. Cut the circles as close together as possible to maximize the yield.

4. Store the craquelin in an airtight container, layered between pieces of parchment paper, in the fridge for up to 1 week. If you want to make the craquelin well in advance, transfer the dough circles to a baking sheet lined with parchment paper, then wrap the baking sheet in plastic wrap and store in the freezer for up to 1 month.

CHIVE ONION PÂTE À CHOUX

5. Preheat the oven to 350°F. Line 2 baking sheets with the Pâte à Choux Piping Template (page 309). Place a layer of parchment paper on top. Fit a piping bag with a No. 2A tip.

6. In a medium saucepan over medium-high heat, bring the water, butter, and salt to a boil. Using a heat-resistant spatula or a wooden spoon, stir in the flour, chives, and onion flakes and continuously fold and stir the mixture until the choux is slightly yellow, shiny, and begins to form a ball. You'll know it's ready when a skin begins to form on the bottom of the saucepan and a metal spoon inserted into the dough stands up straight.

7. Transfer the choux to the bowl of a stand mixer fitted with the paddle attachment and mix on medium-low speed until the bowl is warm to the touch, about 4 minutes. Add 2 eggs, one at a time, while the mixer is running. The dough is ready when it is shiny and keeps its shape while still looking nice and smooth after you turn off the mixer and remove the paddle. It should fall from a spoon, but only after a few seconds. If the choux doesn't look shiny and is still stiff, whisk the third egg in a small bowl and add it little by little. If the mixture becomes too runny, you'll need to start the recipe over again.

8. Scoop the choux into the prepared piping bag. Pipe dollops of choux onto the prepared baking sheets following the template. To pipe the choux, hold the piping bag 1 inch above the parchment paper. Apply pressure until a dollop of choux reaches the edges of the template. Release pressure to stop the flow and swirl your wrist as you pull the piping bag away.

CONTINUED

9. Top each dollop of choux with a circle of Everything Bagel Craquelin. Bake for 25 to 30 minutes, or until the choux have puffed up and are golden brown on top. Do not open the oven before the 25-minute mark to ensure that the choux puff up nice and big! If you take them out too early, they will deflate. Let cool to room temperature on the baking sheets.

10. Store in an airtight container at room temperature for up to 1 day. You can freeze unfilled puffs in an airtight container for up to 1 month.

HERB AND GARLIC CREAM CHEESE FILLING

11. In a stand mixer fitted with the whisk attachment, whip the cream cheese on high speed for 2 minutes, scraping down the sides of the bowl every 30 seconds, until smooth. Reduce the speed to medium, slowly pour in the cream, and mix until combined. Scrape down the sides of the bowl. Mix for an additional 30 seconds to 1 minute on high speed, or until the mixture is creamy and smooth. Scrape down the sides of the bowl. Add the parsley, garlic, chives, and salt and mix on medium speed until the spices are evenly distributed.

ASSEMBLY

12. Line a baking sheet with parchment paper. Transfer ½ cup Herb and Garlic Cream Cheese Filling to a piping bag fitted with a No. 8B tip and set aside for decorating.

13. Transfer the remaining filling to a piping bag fitted with a No. 230 tip. Puncture the bottom of a puff with the piping tip and insert it halfway. Squeeze the piping bag to fill the puff. You'll know it's full when filling begins to spill out of the hole and the puff feels heavy. Place the filled cream puff on the prepared baking sheet. Repeat with the remaining puffs.

14. Using the piping bag fitted with the No. 8B tip, pipe a generous dollop of filling on each cream puff. Garnish with fresh chives.

15. Store in an airtight container in the fridge until time to serve. Serve cream puffs on the day they are made for maximum freshness and deliciousness.

BAKER'S TIP

Are there other spices you love? Feel free to add your favourite spices to the Herb and Garlic Cream Cheese Filling. We both love spicy food, so we add hot pepper flakes to ours to kick up the heat.

LEMON MERINGUE CREAM PUFFS

Makes 24 cream puffs

YELLOW CRAQUELIN

1 batch Craquelin (page 200,
   steps 1 to 4)
2 drops lemon yellow gel
   food colouring

PÂTE À CHOUX

1 batch (page 200, steps 5 to 8)

LEMON WHIPPED CREAM

3 cups whipping (35%) cream
3 tablespoons icing sugar
3 tablespoons skim milk
   powder
Zest of 2 lemons
1 batch Lemon Curd
   (page 302), chilled

MERINGUE MARSHMALLOW FLUFF

1 batch (page 300) or
   4 (7.5-ounce) jars store-
   bought marshmallow
   spread

Dipping these cream puffs into our freshly whipped Meringue Marshmallow Fluff and torching them to a slight, oven-kissed golden brown makes them hard to resist!

CRAQUELIN

1. Prepare 1 batch Craquelin, following steps 1 to 4, adding the food colouring when called for in step 1.

PÂTE À CHOUX

2. Prepare 1 batch Pâte à Choux, following steps 5 to 8.
3. Top each dollop of choux with a circle of Yellow Craquelin. Bake for 25 to 30 minutes, or until the choux have puffed up and are golden brown on top. Do not open the oven before the 25-minute mark to ensure that the choux puffs up nice and big! If you take them out too early, they will deflate. Let cool to room temperature on the baking sheets.

LEMON WHIPPED CREAM

4. In a stand mixer fitted with the whisk attachment, whip the cream, icing sugar, skim milk powder, and lemon zest on medium-high speed, until the mixture looks light and fluffy and medium peaks form, about 2 minutes. Be careful not to overwhip. Gently fold in the Lemon Curd until just combined.

MERINGUE MARSHMALLOW FLUFF

5. Prepare 1 batch Meringue Marshmallow Fluff.

ASSEMBLY

6. Set out a clean baking sheet but do not line it with parchment paper.
7. Transfer the Lemon Whipped Cream to a piping bag fitted with a No. 230 tip. Puncture the bottom of a puff with the piping tip and insert it halfway. Squeeze the piping bag to fill the puff. You'll know it's full when filling begins to spill out of the hole and the puff feels heavy. Place the filled cream puff on the baking sheet. Repeat with the remaining puffs.
8. Carefully dip a cream puff into the Meringue Marshmallow Fluff until the craquelin is nearly covered. Be careful when you pull the cream puff out of the fluff, as it will be very sticky. Return the cream puff to the baking sheet. Using a handheld torch, toast the fluff on top of the cream puff. Repeat with the remaining cream puffs.
9. Store in an airtight container in the fridge until time to serve. Serve cream puffs on the day they are made for maximum freshness and deliciousness.

BAKER'S TIP

Not a fan of meringue? Skip it and serve the yellow puffs plain—Lemon Cream Puffs are amazing in the summer months!

EARL GREY CREAM PUFFS

Makes 24 cream puffs

PLAIN PUFFS

1 batch (page 200)

EARL GREY PASTRY CREAM

5 cups whole (3.25%) milk
¼ cup loose leaf Earl Grey tea,
    more for garnish
12 egg yolks
1 cup granulated sugar
¾ cup cornstarch
1 teaspoon vanilla bean paste
¼ cup unsalted butter, room
    temperature

**POWDER BLUE POURED
FONDANT**

1 batch Poured Fondant
    (page 204)
1 very small drop sky blue gel
    food colouring
1 very small drop royal purple
    gel food colouring

GARNISH

Edible gold leaf flakes

A delectable teatime treat, our Earl Grey Cream Puffs incorporate both tea and pastry! Purchase some loose leaf Earl Grey tea from your favourite local shop to garnish each puff as we did. It's naturally beautiful and fragrant.

PLAIN CREAM PUFFS

1. Prepare 1 batch Plain Puffs.

EARL GREY PASTRY CREAM

2. In a small saucepan over medium heat, bring the milk and tea to a boil. Reduce the heat to low and simmer for 10 minutes. Using a fine-mesh sieve, strain out the tea leaves. Return the milk to the saucepan and heat until it begins to steam and small bubbles form on the surface.

3. In a medium bowl, whisk together the egg yolks, sugar, cornstarch, and vanilla bean paste. Slowly pour the milk into the sugar mixture, whisking constantly to temper the egg yolks until fully combined. Return the mixture to the saucepan and cook on low heat, whisking constantly to prevent burning and to ensure a smooth and creamy consistency. Continue whisking until the mixture thickens and a thick ribbon of pastry cream drips from the whisk when lifted out of the saucepan. Remove from the heat and whisk in the butter until melted and combined.

4. Transfer the mixture to a shallow medium dish and cover with plastic wrap placed directly on the surface of the mixture to prevent a skin forming. Store in an airtight container in the fridge for up to 1 week.

POWDER BLUE POURED FONDANT

5. Prepare 1 batch Poured Fondant, adding the food colouring in step 2. To ensure that you don't add too much food colouring, place 1 drop of each colour on a piece of parchment paper and use a toothpick to add colour to the fondant.

ASSEMBLY

6. Line a baking sheet with parchment paper.

7. Transfer the Earl Grey Pastry Cream to a piping bag fitted with a No. 230 tip. Puncture the bottom of a puff with the piping tip and insert it halfway. Squeeze the piping bag to fill the puff. You'll know it's full once filling begins to spill out of the hole and the puff feels heavy. Place the filled cream puff on the prepared baking sheet. Repeat with the remaining puffs.

8. In a deep heat-resistant bowl, heat the Powder Blue Poured Fondant in the microwave in 30-second intervals, stirring after each interval, until smooth. Carefully dip a cream puff into the fondant until the craquelin is nearly covered. Hold the cream puff over the bowl and gently shake until no more fondant drips off. Return it to the prepared baking sheet and immediately sprinkle with gold leaf flakes and loose leaf tea. Repeat with the remaining cream puffs.

9. Store in an airtight container in the fridge until time to serve. Serve cream puffs on the day they are made for maximum freshness and deliciousness.

BAKER'S TIP

This recipe will work with any of your favourite teas! Just swap out the loose leaf Earl Grey tea with an equal amount of your favourite blend for an aromatic treat. We love to use chai when the colder weather hits in the fall.

MACARONS

BAKER'S NOTES

From our Kitchen to yours

xo

AH, MACARONS. They're our best sellers and for good reason—they're colourful, versatile, crisp but chewy, and beautiful. We make thousands upon thousands each week, and we get so many questions about our method and how we've perfected them. The first time Jenna made macarons, they turned out perfectly, and she wondered what all the fuss was about. The second, third, and fourth times, however, were total flops. Our best advice? Practice makes perfect!

When you make macarons, there are a few things to keep in mind:

DO NOT GIVE UP! Try, try, and try again. Every time you make macarons, you'll learn something new. Be patient with yourself and your macarons. You'll nail them in time, and it will all be worth it.

DO YOUR RESEARCH. If something doesn't work out and your macarons look a certain, funny way, research what could have happened and adjust for that next time.

HAVE FUN! Baking should be a fun experience. If making macarons is shifting from fun to dreadful, take a break and try again later.

SET YOURSELF UP FOR SUCCESS

Making macarons can feel like a long process when you have to wait for a skin to form on the shells, bake the shells, allow them to cool, then fill them, but the process of making the batter for the shells moves quite quickly.

To prevent yourself from making a mistake, measure out all ingredients before getting started. Have them ready in individual bowls and bring the egg whites to room temperature. With the ingredients ready to go, you'll be able to follow the recipe with ease.

CONTROL YOUR SURROUNDINGS

If it's really hot and humid on the day you decide to make macarons, we'd suggest you wait for a different day or turn up your air conditioning. When the seasons change, we adjust our macaron recipe. If it's raining,

we adjust the recipe. If it's hot, we adjust the recipe. We recommend you make macarons in a space where you can control the temperature and humidity. Macarons form their skin best in a slightly cool place that has low humidity. If possible, run a dehumidifier in your kitchen while you prepare macarons, and if you find it is warm, run a fan for air circulation. Be careful that the fan doesn't blow directly on the macarons. This may make the outer skin form faster, but it also encourages the macarons to dry out faster and can cause lopsided shells. The shells are ready to go into the oven when the skin has formed yet they still look a little glossy on top.

MACARONAGE: HOW TO PROPERLY MIX MACARON BATTER

The "macaronage" process (the process of mixing the batter) is the most important part of the entire macaron recipe. At this stage, if you overmix or undermix the batter, you won't get the desired results. When folding your meringue and almond mixture together, take care not to stir. Instead, press the mixture against the sides of the bowl while you fold to remove air bubbles. As soon as the batter starts to look homogeneous, you can start testing its consistency. Using your spatula, lift up the batter and watch how it drops back into the bowl. It shouldn't "plop"; rather, it should flow slowly from the spatula with a lava-like consistency. You can also let the batter rest for 25 seconds; if it settles and the surface smooths out, you'll know the batter has been mixed enough. As soon as you see this, do not mix any further. If the batter is very soft and runny and doesn't hold its shape when flowing from the spatula, you've gone too far. Every batter is different due to humidity, weather, and other external factors, so you have to use your judgment to gauge when to stop mixing. Practice makes perfect! You'll know that you've reached the perfect consistency when you pipe the macarons into circles that don't spread too much and the batter is thick enough to have slightly domed edges but not so thick that the "points" from piping do not flatten out after 25 seconds of rest, or after a few hard taps on the table.

TESTING FOR DONENESS

Knowing when it's time to take macaron shells out of the oven is an important piece of the macaron puzzle. We have a couple of ways to test for doneness, depending on whether you use parchment paper or a Silpat mat to line your baking sheet.

Parchment Paper

Macaron shells are ready when you can easily lift one off the parchment paper. The bottom of the shell will be a solid layer, without any soft bubbles, and will be starting to brown slightly. If you can't lift a shell off the paper, or if part of the bottom still looks wet, you'll need to bake the shells a little longer.

Silpat Mat

Perform what we call "the wiggle test" to determine if macaron shells should come out of the oven. Open the oven and pull out the baking sheet halfway. Gently touch the top of a shell with a finger. It should be firm to the touch, and your finger shouldn't make a dent. Next, use a thumb and pointer finger to gently grasp the top of the macaron around the edge. You should be able to gently wiggle the top of the shell while the foot remains intact. Your fingers should not crush into it. If you dent the shell with your fingers, it requires additional baking time.

OUR FAVOURITE TIPS AND TRICKS

Everyone at Jenna Rae Cakes has some favourite tips and tricks for making macarons. It's the little things that make a big difference, and each baker has a few things they like to do to keep the macaron baking process running smoothly. Here are a few tips and tricks we implement in the kitchen to speed things along.

- While macarons are forming their skin, clean up the kitchen and start preparing any fillings. Depending on the humidity and temperature in your kitchen, forming a skin can take anywhere from 30 to 90 minutes.

- Prepare the egg whites first. If you're cracking whole eggs and separating the egg yolks from the egg whites, be careful not to break a yolk. If absolutely any egg yolk mixes with the egg whites, remove it completely or start cracking the eggs all over again. Egg yolks contain fat, and any fat in the egg whites (including from a greasy mixing bowl!) will yield a meringue that does not whip up. If you start by preparing the egg whites, you'll be able to take as much time as you need to make sure everything is just right.

- Get a digital thermometer. We love using a digital thermometer because we can set it to a temperature and it will notify us when that temperature is reached. This is extremely handy for macarons!

- Use a scale to measure ingredients. You'll notice that we provide ingredient measurements in grams in this chapter. We always use a scale to weigh our ingredients for the most accurate recipe every single time. With macarons, accuracy is especially important. A kitchen scale is easy to find at any home store and is relatively affordable ($10 to $20). Once you start using one, you'll realize it comes in handy for a lot of recipes!

- We find that finished macarons taste best after sitting in the fridge overnight—after the flavours have melded together.

TROUBLESHOOTING

We often hear from other bakers on Instagram, who ask for guidance based on the experiences we've had in our own kitchen. These troubleshooting tips will help you adjust your macarons if things don't quite work out the first time around.

- If the feet of your macarons expanded outward instead of upward, the batter was likely overmixed.

- Macaron shells can come out hollow for a few different reasons. The shells may have been underbaked (see Testing for Doneness, page 234), you may have overwhipped or underwhipped your meringue, or you may not have mixed your batter enough (see Macaronage, page 233).

- If the tops of the shells look splotchy, it may be because they are still wet. Your kitchen may be too humid for a skin to form properly, or the shells may be underbaked.

- Overbaking shells may make them hard and cause them to shatter. Try reducing the baking time on your next attempt. If you're still having issues, it's possible that the sugar in the batter has overheated. Reduce the oven temperature and use a digital thermometer placed inside your oven to make sure it's not hotter than it appears to be.

- If the shells rise unevenly during baking, there are a couple of possible culprits. It's possible that an even skin did not form before baking. An uneven skin can result from resting in a place with uneven airflow. Make sure there isn't a draft that blows on one area of the macarons and not the other. Another possibility is that your oven fan is too strong, if you are using a convection oven. The oven fan can blow the shells slightly off, causing an uneven rise.

- Macaron shells that look like they're exploding on top are often caused by too thin of a skin forming before baking. If you touch the top of an uncooked shell and batter transfers to your fingers, the shell needs to sit longer to form a skin. With a properly formed skin, no batter will transfer to your finger and the indent from your finger will begin to spring back.

- If you pipe the batter onto a baking sheet and it spreads so much that the macarons begin running into each other, the batter may have been overmixed. You can also try piping the batter to a smaller size to accommodate for the spread.

- Toppings that are either too big or too fine—especially toppings like salt and sugar that melt—may cause shells to crack on top during baking.

- If the feet of your shells are small because they didn't rise enough during baking, try tapping the macarons less after piping the batter.

- If your macarons aren't smooth on top and your batter leaves a tail, try tapping the macarons more to see if the tail dissipates. If that doesn't seem to help, your batter may be too thick or undermixed.

- If your shells turn quite brown on top during baking, try turning your oven temperature down by 25°F and baking your shells for an extra 2 to 5 minutes.

Makes 48 macaron shells,
or 24 macarons

1¼ cups (140 g) almond flour
1 cup + 2 tablespoons (140 g)
    icing sugar
⅓ cup (110 g) egg whites, room
    temperature, divided (about
    4 eggs)
½ cup + 2 tablespoons (140 g)
    granulated sugar
2 tablespoons + 1 teaspoon
    (35 g) water
Gel food colouring (optional)
Garnishes, such as sprinkles,
    chopped pistachios, brown
    sugar, and so on (optional)

MACARON SHELLS

We're so happy to share our tried-and-true macaron shell recipe, which will be the base for all of the macaron recipes in this book. We use the Italian method for making macarons because we love the resulting texture—a crisp outer shell and a chewy centre. You'll notice that this recipe mentions when to add food colouring but doesn't specify a colour. Each of the recipes for distinct flavours of macaron that follow will indicate the amount of food colouring needed. You'll also notice that this recipe includes weight measurements in grams. Why? Because every single gram matters. Follow it to a T for optimal results!

Before you start this recipe, make sure to have all ingredients measured out and equipment ready to go. Once you start heating the sugar, you will need to move quickly. We also recommend carefully reading over the entire Baker's Notes section of this chapter (page 233). Every detail is important when it comes to making macarons, and you'll want to set yourself up for success with each attempt.

1. Preheat the oven to 300°F. Line 4 baking sheets with the Macaron Shells Piping Template (page 308). Place a layer of parchment paper on top.

2. In a medium bowl, sift together the almond flour and icing sugar.

3. Place half of the egg whites in the bowl of a stand mixer fitted with the whisk attachment. Because it's important to be precise when making macarons, we recommend using a kitchen scale to measure exactly half the amount (55 g) before transferring the egg whites to the bowl. Whip on high speed until soft peaks form, about 1 minute.

4. In a small saucepan over medium-high heat, bring the granulated sugar and water to a boil. Attach a candy thermometer to the saucepan and continue boiling over medium-high heat until the mixture reaches 235°F (see Baker's Tip).

5. With the mixer on low speed, slowly pour the hot sugar mixture into the whipped egg whites along the side of the bowl, taking care not to pour it directly on the whisk. Once all of the syrup is added, increase the speed to medium-high and whisk until the meringue mixture is glossy and stiff peaks form, about 4 to 5 minutes. Turn off the mixer. Scrape as much meringue as possible off the whisk into the bowl and transfer the meringue to a clean bowl.

6. Fit the stand mixer with the paddle attachment and return the bowl to the stand. (There's no need to wash it!) Pour the remaining egg whites into the bowl and add the sugar and flour mixture. Add the food colouring, if using. Beat the mixture on low speed until the dry ingredients are fully incorporated and the colour is uniform.

BAKER'S TIP

To avoid an inaccurate reading when working with a candy thermometer, be sure it does not touch the bottom of the saucepan. The thermometer should be submerged in the syrup, hovering above the bottom of the saucepan.

7. Add about one-quarter of the meringue to the bowl and beat on low speed until just combined. Scrape as much batter as possible off the paddle and into the bowl. Scrape down the sides of the bowl, being careful not to overmix the batter. Using a spatula, gently fold in the remaining meringue, taking care not to collapse the meringue, until no streaks of meringue remain. You want to fold the batter until it achieves the consistency of molten lava (see Macaronage, page 233).

8. Transfer the batter to a piping bag fitted with a No. 12 tip. Holding the bag vertically just above the baking sheet, pipe the batter onto the template, making sure that each dollop of dough is the same size.

9. Gently tap the baking sheet on a counter or table a few times to eliminate any air bubbles from the batter and help it spread. Garnish as desired and set aside to allow a skin to form (30 to 90 minutes). Touch the batter gently with a finger to determine if a skin has formed. If the batter doesn't stick to your finger and the impression left by your finger bounces back, the batter is oven ready.

10. Bake for 12 to 15 minutes, or until the macaron shells form feet, they are starting to brown slightly, and a shell can be removed easily from the parchment paper. If you can't lift a shell easily off the paper, or if part of the bottom still looks wet, continue baking. Let cool to room temperature before filling.

11. Fill the shells as directed by the recipe.

12. Store between layers of parchment paper in an airtight container in the fridge for up to 6 days or in the freezer for up to 1 month.

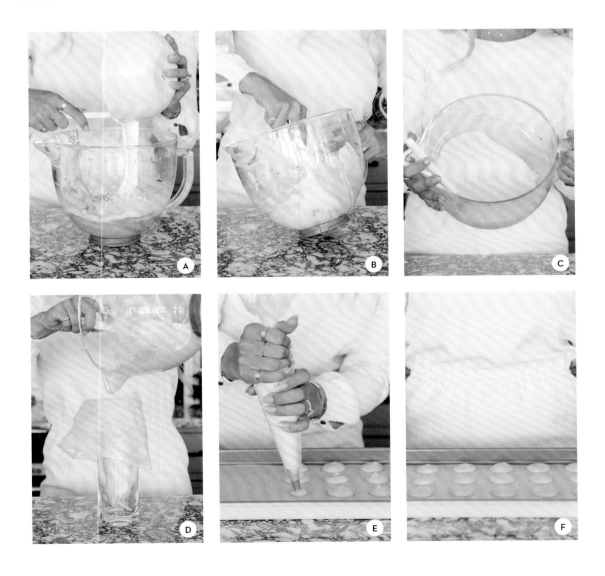

MACARON SHELLS

1 batch Macaron Shells
(page 236)

2 to 4 drops ivory gel food
colouring

¼ cup small, round black
sprinkles, for garnish

COOKIE DOUGH

½ batch (page 301)

COOKIE DOUGH MACARONS

Whip it real good! The secret to our Cookie Dough Macarons is our cookie dough filling that has been whipped until it's nice and light and fluffy!

MACARON SHELLS

1. Prepare 1 batch Macaron Shells, adding the food colouring and garnishing with the sprinkles when called for.

COOKIE DOUGH

2. Prepare ½ batch Cookie Dough.

ASSEMBLY

3. Transfer the Cookie Dough to a piping bag fitted with a No. 1A tip.

4. Arrange the Macaron Shells in rows, paired with shells of similar size. Flip over half of the shells. Holding the piping bag about ½ inch above the flipped shells, pipe a dollop of Cookie Dough onto each with an even pressure. Leave a thin ring of shell exposed around the exterior edge. Place the remaining shells, right side up, on top of the filling and press down gently to help them stick. The Cookie Dough will spread slightly to the edges of the shells.

5. Place finished macarons in the fridge to chill for easier handling. Store macarons in an airtight container in the fridge for up to 6 days or in the freezer for up to 1 month.

BAKER'S TIP

The longer the Cookie Dough sits, the stiffer it will become. Try making the Cookie Dough right before using it for easy piping.

BIRTHDAY CAKE BATTER MACARONS

Makes 24 macarons

MACARON SHELLS

¼ cup long rainbow sprinkles, for garnish

¼ cup small, round rainbow sprinkles, for garnish

1 batch Macaron Shells (page 236)

4 to 6 drops hot pink gel food colouring (see Baker's Tip)

BIRTHDAY CAKE BATTER FILLING

¼ cup unsalted butter, room temperature

⅓ cup granulated sugar

½ teaspoon pure vanilla extract

¼ cup whole (3.25%) milk

¼ teaspoon JRC Liquid Cake Batter or cake batter flavouring (see Baker's Tip)

1 to 2 drops pink gel food colouring (optional)

1 cup all-purpose flour, heat treated (see Flour, page 7)

1 tablespoon milk powder

Pinch of salt

Birthday Cake Batter Macarons are topped with what we lovingly call "party mix" sprinkles! A combination of long rainbow sprinkles and small, round rainbow sprinkles make these macarons party perfection.

MACARON SHELLS

1. In a small bowl, mix together the long rainbow sprinkles and the small, round rainbow sprinkles.

2. Prepare 1 batch Macaron Shells, adding the food colouring and garnishing with the sprinkle mixture when called for.

BIRTHDAY CAKE BATTER FILLING

3. In a stand mixer fitted with the paddle attachment, cream the butter and sugar on high speed until the mixture looks light and fluffy, about 2 minutes. Add the vanilla, milk, flavouring, and food colouring, if using. Mix on medium speed for 30 seconds until well combined. Scrape down the sides of the bowl and add the flour, milk powder, and salt. Mix on medium-high speed for 1 minute. If needed, add more food colouring, 1 drop at a time, until the colour of the filling matches that of the shells.

ASSEMBLY

4. Transfer the Birthday Cake Batter Filling to a piping bag fitted with a No. 1A tip.

5. Arrange the Macaron Shells in rows, paired with shells of similar size. Flip over half of the shells. Holding the piping bag about ½ inch above the flipped shells, pipe a dollop of filling onto each with an even pressure. Leave a thin ring of shell exposed around the exterior edge. Place the remaining shells, right side up, on top of the filling and press down gently to help them stick. The filling will spread slightly to the edges of the shells.

6. Place finished macarons in the fridge to chill for easier handling. Store macarons in an airtight container in the fridge for up to 6 days or in the freezer for up to 1 month.

BAKER'S TIP

1. We make our Birthday Cake Batter Macarons pink, but the colour can be adjusted to suit the theme of your party or event. 2. Our JRC Liquid Cake Batter flavouring gives these macarons the lick-the-spatula taste you crave when you think about cake batter.

ASSORTED MACARONS

JENNA Rae CAKES

CUSTOM CAKES AND SWEET TREATS

580 ACADEMY ROAD / THE FORKS

JENNARAECAKES.COM

BLUEBERRY PANCAKE MACARONS

Makes 24 macarons

MACARON SHELLS

1 batch Macaron Shells
  (page 236)
2 drops electric purple gel
  food colouring
2 drops royal blue gel food
  colouring

PANCAKE BATTER FILLING

¼ cup unsalted butter,
  room temperature
⅓ cup granulated sugar
½ teaspoon pure vanilla
  extract
¼ cup whole (3.25%) milk
1 tablespoon maple syrup
2 drops ivory gel food
  colouring (optional)
1 cup all-purpose flour,
  heat treated and sifted
  (see Flour, page 7)
1 tablespoon milk powder
Pinch of salt
35 fresh blueberries

If a lazy Saturday or Sunday morning had a dedicated breakfast food, it would be pancakes. We bring the taste of relaxing weekends to life with these Blueberry Pancake Macarons. They are a hit for Father's Day or a classy brunch—and mimosas are encouraged!

MACARON SHELLS

1. Prepare 1 batch Macaron Shells, but instead of adding the food colouring in step 6, prepare the batter through step 7 and stop mixing it a bit early. In this case, it is okay to undermix the batter. Divide it evenly between 2 medium bowls. To one bowl, add the electric purple food colouring and gently fold with a spatula to combine. To the other bowl, add the royal blue food colouring and gently fold with a spatula to combine. Transfer the purple batter to the bowl with the blue batter. Gently fold the batter with a spatula two to three times to make a swirl.

2. Continue with steps 8 to 10 of the Macaron Shells recipe.

PANCAKE BATTER FILLING

3. In a stand mixer fitted with the paddle attachment, cream the butter and sugar on high speed until the mixture looks light and fluffy, about 2 minutes. Add the vanilla, milk, maple syrup, and food colouring and mix on medium speed for 30 seconds until well combined. Scrape down the sides of the bowl and add the flour, milk powder, and salt. Mix on medium-high speed for 1 minute.

ASSEMBLY

4. Transfer the Pancake Batter Filling to a piping bag fitted with a No. 12 tip.

5. Arrange the Macaron Shells in rows, paired with shells of similar size. Flip over half of the shells. Holding the piping bag about ½ inch above the flipped shells, pipe a ring of filling onto each with an even pressure, leaving a "hole" in the middle of each ring and a thin ring of shell exposed around the exterior edge.

6. Drop a blueberry into the middle of each filling ring. If your blueberries are small, add more than one to fill the hole. Place the remaining shells, right side up, on top of the filling and press down gently to help them stick. The filling will spread slightly to the edges of the shells.

7. Place finished macarons in the fridge to chill for easier handling. Store macarons in an airtight container in the fridge for up to 6 days or in the freezer for up to 1 month.

BAKER'S TIP

Not a fruit lover? Nix the blueberries and double up on the Pancake Batter Filling to create Pancake Batter Macarons! Substitute the 2 drops electric purple gel food colouring and 2 drops royal blue gel food colouring in the Macaron Shells with 4 drops ivory gel food colouring.

SOUR PEACH CANDY MACARONS

Makes 24 macarons

MACARON SHELLS

1 batch Macaron Shells
(page 236)
3 drops peach gel food
colouring

SOUR PEACH BUTTERCREAM

½ batch Vanilla Buttercream
(page 296)
1 teaspoon peach flavouring,
more to taste
½ teaspoon powdered
citric acid, more to taste
(see Baker's Tip)
3 drops peach gel food
colouring

GARNISH

¼ cup vodka (see Baker's Tip)
1 cup granulated sugar
1 tablespoon powdered citric
acid (see Baker's Tip)

Do you remember five-cent candies? Sour peach candies are the ones we always stocked our bags with when we were kids. Translating this popular candy into a macaron flavour led to our very first theme day—five-cent candy day—where we transformed countless childhood treats, including sour cherry and sour watermelon candies into nostalgic and irresistible baked goods. If peach isn't your favourite sour candy flavour, try substituting the peach flavouring with an equal amount of cherry or watermelon flavouring.

MACARON SHELLS

1. Prepare 1 batch Macaron Shells, adding the food colouring when called for.

SOUR PEACH BUTTERCREAM

2. Prepare ½ batch Vanilla Buttercream.

3. Add the flavouring, citric acid, and food colouring and whip until combined. Taste the buttercream and add more flavouring and/or citric acid, if desired. If needed, add more food colouring, 1 drop at a time, until the colour of the filling matches that of the shells. Whip to combine.

ASSEMBLY

4. Pour the vodka into a small dish. In a shallow small dish, combine the sugar and citric acid to make sour sugar. Dip a fan paintbrush into the vodka and paint the tops of 2 to 3 shells. Place them in the sour sugar mixture, vodka side down. Gently shake the bowl to coat the shells in sour sugar. Return the shells to the baking sheet, sour sugar side up. Repeat until all shells are covered in sour sugar.

5. Transfer the Sour Peach Buttercream to a piping bag fitted with a No. 1A tip.

6. Arrange the Macaron Shells in rows, paired with shells of similar size. Flip over half of the shells. Holding the piping bag about ½ inch above the flipped shells, pipe a dollop of buttercream onto each with an even pressure. Leave a thin ring of shell exposed around the exterior edge. Place the remaining macaron shells, right side up, on top of the buttercream and press down gently to help them stick. The buttercream will spread slightly to the edges of the shells.

7. Place finished macarons in the fridge to chill for easier handling. Store macarons in an airtight container in the fridge for up to 6 days or in the freezer for up to 1 month.

BAKER'S TIP

1. A little citric acid can go a long way! It's best to start with a small amount and increase it if needed. 2. We use vodka to adhere the sour sugar because it doesn't soften the shells, and evaporates while it dries, leaving behind the sour sugar.

BROWNIE BATTER MACARONS

MACARON SHELLS

1 batch Macaron Shells
   (page 236)
4 to 6 drops fuchsia gel
   food colouring

BROWNIE BATTER

1 batch (page 301)

GARNISH

3 cups (660 g) chopped
   dark baking chocolate
¼ cup vegetable oil

These Brownie Batter Macarons will put any prepackaged bite-size brownie you've purchased to shame. This two-bite treat explodes with whipped brownie batter flavour, and if that's not enough, we finish them off by dipping them in dark chocolate. Don't even try to resist!

MACARON SHELLS

1. Prepare 1 batch Macaron Shells, adding the food colouring when called for.

BROWNIE BATTER

2. Prepare 1 batch Brownie Batter.

ASSEMBLY

3. Transfer the Brownie Batter to a piping bag fitted with a No. 1A tip.

4. Arrange the Macaron Shells in rows, paired with shells of similar size. Flip over half of the shells. Holding the piping bag about ½ inch above the shells, pipe a dollop of Brownie Batter onto each with an even pressure. Leave a thin ring of shell exposed around the exterior edge. Place the remaining shells, right side up, on top of the filling and press down gently to help them stick. The Brownie Batter will spread slightly to the edges of the shells. Place macarons in an airtight container in the fridge for at least 30 minutes for easier handling.

5. Line a baking sheet with parchment paper. In a medium heat-resistant bowl, melt the chocolate in the microwave in 30-second intervals, stirring after each interval, until smooth. Add the oil and mix until well combined.

6. Remove the macarons from the fridge (see Baker's Tip). Dip a macaron in the chocolate until it is half covered. Hold it above the bowl and gently shake off any excess chocolate. Place it on the prepared baking sheet. Repeat with the remaining macarons. Place the baking sheet in the fridge for at least 30 minutes to allow the chocolate to harden.

7. Store macarons in an airtight container in the fridge for up to 6 days or in the freezer for up to 1 month.

BAKER'S TIP

Dipping the macarons in hot coating chocolate can soften the Brownie Batter and cause the shells to slide. Make sure that your macarons are well chilled before dipping them in hot chocolate. You'll know they're ready to be dipped when you cannot easily slide the top shell off of the bottom shell.

EARL GREY CRÈME BRÛLÉE MACARONS

Makes 24 macarons

MACARON SHELLS

1 batch Macaron Shells
    (page 236)
3 drops violet gel food
    colouring
¼ drop black gel food
    colouring
½ cup brown sugar, sifted,
    for garnish

EARL GREY CRÈME BRÛLÉE FILLING

5 egg yolks
½ cup packed brown sugar
1½ cups whipping (35%) cream
¼ cup loose leaf Earl Grey tea

This recipe combines two exceptional flavours in one phenomenal macaron. We started making Earl Grey and Crème Brûlée macarons separately, then decided to combine them after trying an unforgettable crème brûlée at a fine dining restaurant. One bite of these macarons will whisk you away to a five-star restaurant where exceptional flavours meet the impeccable execution of a refined dessert. Take pride in the fact that you made it yourself!

MACARON SHELLS

1. Prepare 1 batch Macaron Shells, adding the food colouring and garnishing with the brown sugar when called for.

EARL GREY CRÈME BRÛLÉE FILLING

2. Preheat the oven to 350°F. Set out a shallow large baking dish or cake pan.

3. In a medium bowl, whisk together the egg yolks and brown sugar.

4. In a small saucepan over medium-high heat, heat the cream and tea until the mixture begins to bubble. Turn off the heat and let steep for 10 minutes. Using a fine-mesh sieve, strain the mixture. Return the cream to the saucepan and bring it to a simmer over medium-high heat. Remove from the heat.

5. Pour the cream into the egg yolk and sugar mixture, whisking constantly to temper the egg yolks. Return the mixture to the saucepan and cook over medium heat, whisking constantly, until it thickens, about 5 to 6 minutes.

6. Pour the mixture into an 8- × 4-inch loaf pan. Bake for 20 to 25 minutes, or until the top of the filling is bubbling and dark brown.

7. Immediately transfer the filling to a food processor. Blend on high speed until creamy and smooth (see Baker's Tip). Transfer to a shallow dish, cover with plastic wrap placed directly on the surface to prevent a skin forming, and place in the fridge to set, about 1 hour.

ASSEMBLY

8. Transfer the Earl Grey Crème Brûlée Filling to a piping bag fitted with a No. 1A tip.

9. Arrange the Macaron Shells in rows, paired with shells of similar size. Flip over half of the shells. Holding the piping bag about ½ inch above the flipped shells, pipe a dollop of filling onto each with an even pressure. Leave a thin ring of shell exposed around the exterior edge. Place the remaining shells, right side up, on top of the filling and press down gently to help them stick. The filling will spread slightly to the edges of the shells.

10. Using a handheld torch, toast each side of the macaron until the brown sugar begins to bubble and the shells begin to turn golden brown.

11. Place finished macarons in the fridge to chill for easier handling. Store macarons in an airtight container in the fridge for up to 2 days or in the freezer for up to 1 month.

BAKER'S TIP

When you start to blend the Earl Grey Crème Brûlée Filling in the food processor, it may seem as if it's not going to come together. Trust us, it will! Just keep blending until it's silky and smooth.

LEMON MERINGUE MACARONS

MACARON SHELLS

1 batch Macaron Shells
(page 236)

4 to 6 drops bright yellow
gel food colouring

¼ cup small, round white
sprinkles, for garnish

**MERINGUE MARSHMALLOW
FLUFF**

½ batch (page 300; see Baker's
Tip) or 2 (7.5-ounce) jars
store-bought marshmallow
spread

LEMON CURD

½ batch (page 302)

Toasting the meringue in these Lemon Meringue Macarons brings to mind the taste of a homemade lemon meringue pie fresh from grandma's oven. Alongside the bright, lip-puckering flavour of the lemon curd filling, each bite is a powerful flavour experience.

MACARON SHELLS

1. Prepare 1 batch Macaron Shells, adding the food colouring and garnishing with the sprinkles when called for.

MERINGUE MARSHMALLOW FLUFF

2. Prepare ½ batch Meringue Marshmallow Fluff.

LEMON CURD FILLING

3. Prepare ½ batch Lemon Curd.

ASSEMBLY

4. Transfer the Meringue Marshmallow Fluff to a piping bag fitted with a No. 12 tip.

5. Arrange the Macaron Shells in rows, paired with shells of similar size. Flip over half of the shells. Holding the piping bag about ½ inch above the flipped shells, pipe a ring of meringue onto each with an even pressure, leaving a "hole" in the middle of each ring and a thin ring of shell exposed around the exterior edge. Using a handheld torch, gently toast the meringue.

6. Transfer the Lemon Curd to a piping bag fitted with a No. 12 tip.

7. Pipe a dollop of curd into the middle of each meringue ring. Place the remaining shells, right side up, on top of the filling and press down gently to help them stick. The meringue will spread slightly to the edges of the shells.

8. Place finished macarons in the fridge to chill for easier handling. Store macarons in an airtight container in the fridge for up to 6 days or in the freezer for up to 1 month.

BAKER'S TIP

For best results, make the Meringue Marshmallow Fluff on the day you plan to use it so that it remains stiff and easy to pipe.

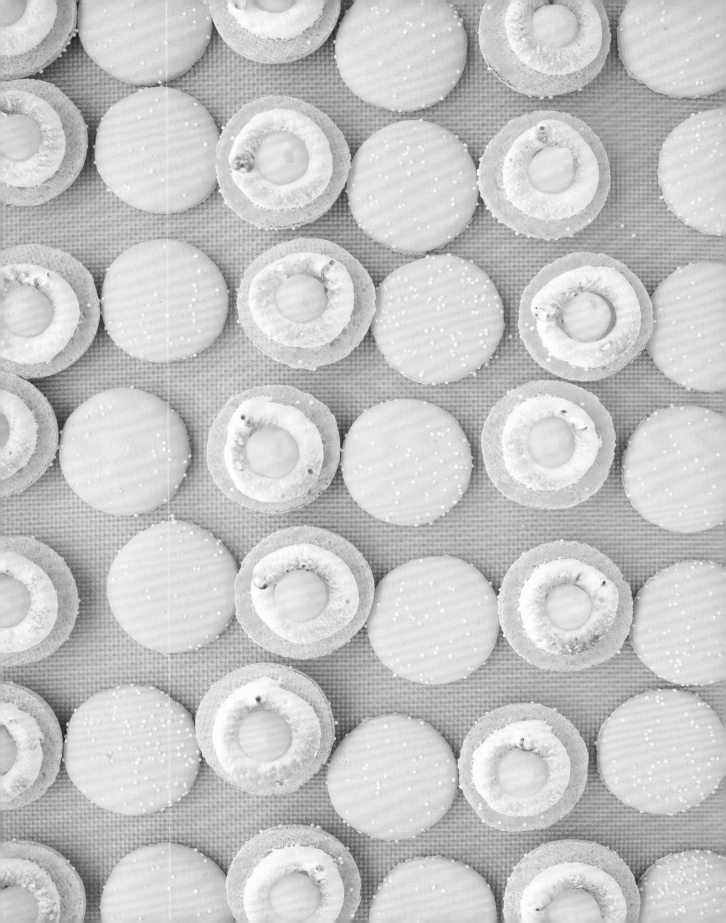

S'MORES MACARONS

MACARON SHELLS

1 batch Macaron Shells
(page 236)

4 to 6 drops electric purple
gel food colouring

2 tablespoons small, round
white sprinkles, for garnish

2 tablespoons long chocolate
sprinkles, for garnish

**GRAHAM CRACKER
CRUMBLE**

½ batch (page 305)

**MERINGUE MARSHMALLOW
FLUFF**

½ batch (page 300) or
2 (7.5-ounce) jars store-
bought marshmallow
spread

**MILK CHOCOLATE
BUTTERCREAM**

½ batch (page 296)

Turning this campfire favourite into a macaron seemed wild when we did it. It was a flavour that was extremely unusual compared to those being offered by other bakeries, but we have never let dessert norms keep us from expanding our flavour selection. Once S'mores Macarons hit the pastry case and became a customer favourite, they sparked endless creativity in our kitchen.

MACARON SHELLS

1. Prepare 1 batch Macaron Shells, adding the food colouring and garnishing with the sprinkles when called for.

GRAHAM CRACKER CRUMBLE

2. Prepare ½ batch Graham Cracker Crumble.

MERINGUE MARSHMALLOW FLUFF

3. Prepare ½ batch Meringue Marshmallow Fluff.

MILK CHOCOLATE BUTTERCREAM

4. Prepare ½ batch Milk Chocolate Buttercream.

ASSEMBLY

5. Transfer the Milk Chocolate Buttercream to a piping bag fitted with a No. 12 tip.

6. Arrange the Macaron Shells in rows, paired with shells of similar size. Flip over half of the shells. Holding the piping bag about ½ inch above the flipped shells, pipe a ring of buttercream onto each with an even pressure, leaving a "hole" in the middle of each ring and a thin ring of shell exposed around the exterior edge.

7. Transfer the Meringue Marshmallow Fluff to a piping bag fitted with a No. 12 tip.

8. Pipe a dollop of meringue into the middle of each buttercream ring. Using a handheld torch, gently toast the meringue (see Baker's Tip). Sprinkle a small amount of Graham Cracker Crumble on top. Place the remaining shells, right side up, on top of the filling and press down gently to help them stick. The buttercream will spread slightly to the edges of the shells.

9. Place finished macarons in the fridge to chill for easier handling. Store macarons in an airtight container in the fridge for up to 6 days or in the freezer for up to 1 month.

BAKER'S TIP

Using a handheld torch will ensure precision when toasting the Meringue Marshmallow Fluff, which will prevent the Milk Chocolate Buttercream from melting. Pick one up at a craft store and use it for all of your small projects.

COTTON CANDY MACARONS

Makes 24 macarons

MACARON SHELLS

1 batch Macaron Shells
   (page 236)
2 drops sky blue gel food
   colouring
2 drops soft pink gel food
   colouring
2 drops regal purple gel
   food colouring
¼ cup sprinkle mix of your
   choice, for garnish

**COTTON CANDY
BUTTERCREAM**

½ batch Vanilla Buttercream
   (page 296)
2 teaspoons JRC Liquid Cotton
   Candy or cotton candy
   flavouring
3 drops regal purple gel
   food colouring

Mirror, mirror, on the wall, which is the most magical macaron of all? Cotton Candy Macarons, of course! With enchanting colours, fairy-like sprinkles, and a sweet flavour, the entire makeup of these macarons is magic. You'll be the enchantress that makes wishes come true when you bring these whimsical Instagram favourites to a party.

MACARON SHELLS

1. Prepare 1 batch Macaron Shells, but instead of adding the food colouring in step 6, prepare the batter through step 7 and stop mixing it a bit early. In this case, it is okay to undermix the batter. Transfer ½ cup of the batter to a small bowl, then divide the remaining batter evenly between 2 medium bowls. To one medium bowl, add the sky blue food colouring and gently fold with a spatula to combine. To the other medium bowl, add the soft pink food colouring and gently fold with a spatula to combine. To the small bowl, add the regal purple food colouring and gently fold with a spatula to combine. Pour the blue batter into one side of a clean medium bowl. Pour the pink batter into the other side of the bowl. Pour the purple batter in a line where the pink and blue batters meet. Gently fold with a spatula two to three times to make a swirl.

2. Continue with steps 8 to 10 of the Macaron Shells recipe, garnishing with the sprinkle mix when called for.

COTTON CANDY BUTTERCREAM

3. Prepare ½ batch Vanilla Buttercream.

4. Add the cotton candy flavouring and the food colouring to the buttercream. Whip on medium speed until fully incorporated.

ASSEMBLY

5. Transfer the Cotton Candy Buttercream to a piping bag fitted with a No. 1A tip.

6. Arrange the Macaron Shells in rows, paired with shells of a similar size. Flip over half of the shells. Holding the piping bag about ½ inch above the flipped shells, pipe a dollop of buttercream onto each with an even pressure. Leave a thin ring of shell exposed around the exterior edge. Place the remaining shells, right side up, on top of the buttercream and press down gently to help them stick. The buttercream will spread slightly to the edges of the shells.

7. Place finished macarons in the fridge to chill for easier handling. Store macarons in an airtight container in the fridge for up to 6 days or in the freezer for up to 1 month.

BAKER'S TIP

You can choose to omit the regal purple gel food colouring from the macaron batter and use only the sky blue and soft pink. Simply divide the batter between 2 bowls instead of among 3 before adding the food colouring. The swirl won't have as much depth, but it will still be pretty!

SALTED CARAMEL MACARONS

Makes 24 macarons

MACARON SHELLS

1 batch Macaron Shells
   (page 236)
½ cup coarse sea salt, for
   garnish (see Baker's Tip)

SALTED CARAMEL

1 batch (page 299), divided

**SALTED CARAMEL
BUTTERCREAM**

½ batch Vanilla Buttercream
   (page 296)
½ cup Salted Caramel

The macaron that started it all, Jenna can clearly remember making and selling our first Salted Caramel Macarons. Although we've improved our recipe since then, it's still a cult favourite and will have a spot on our menu forever. The centres of these macarons ooze with our liquid Salted Caramel, encircled by a ring of Salted Caramel Buttercream, and the shells are topped with coarse sea salt.

MACARON SHELLS

1. Prepare 1 batch Macaron Shells, garnishing with the coarse sea salt when called for.

SALTED CARAMEL FILLING

2. Prepare 1 batch Salted Caramel. Let cool to room temperature.

SALTED CARAMEL BUTTERCREAM

3. Prepare ½ batch Vanilla Buttercream.

4. Add ½ cup Salted Caramel to the buttercream. Whip on medium speed until incorporated.

ASSEMBLY

5. Transfer the Salted Caramel Buttercream to a piping bag fitted with a No. 12 tip. Transfer the remaining Salted Caramel to a squeeze bottle.

6. Arrange the Macaron Shells in rows, paired with shells of a similar size. Flip over half of the shells. Holding the piping bag about ½ inch above the flipped shells, pipe a ring of buttercream onto each with an even pressure, leaving a "hole" in the middle of each ring and a thin ring of shell exposed around the exterior edge.

7. Squeeze Salted Caramel into the middle of each buttercream ring. Place the remaining shells, right side up, on top of the filling and press down gently to help them stick. The buttercream will spread slightly to the edges of the shells.

8. Place finished macarons in the fridge to chill for easier handling. Store macarons in an airtight container in the fridge for up to 6 days or in the freezer for up to 1 month.

BAKER'S TIP

Be careful when choosing salt to sprinkle on top of the Macaron Shells. Fine grains of salt will cause the shells to bubble and crack on top during baking, and extra-large rocks of salt will sink into the shells as they bake.

PISTACHIO AND GOAT CHEESE MACARONS

Makes 24 macarons

MACARON SHELLS

1 batch Macaron Shells
(page 236)

4 drops avocado gel food
colouring

¼ cup ground pistachios, for
garnish (see Baker's Tip)

**PISTACHIO AND GOAT
CHEESE FILLING**

2 cups goat cheese, room
temperature

¼ cup pure liquid honey

2 tablespoons pistachio paste

The best parts of a cheese board are infused into one mouth-watering macaron in this recipe. Our Pistachio and Goat Cheese Macarons flawlessly combine creamy goat cheese and sticky, sweet honey with bold pistachio flavour. Those who prefer savoury to sweet won't be able to get their fill of these macarons.

MACARON SHELLS

1. Prepare 1 batch Macaron Shells, adding the food colouring and garnishing with the pistachios when called for.

PISTACHIO AND GOAT CHEESE FILLING

2. In a stand mixer fitted with the paddle attachment, add the goat cheese, honey, and pistachio paste and whip on medium speed until smooth.

ASSEMBLY

3. Transfer the Pistachio and Goat Cheese Filling to a piping bag fitted with a No. 1A tip.

4. Arrange the Macaron Shells in rows, paired with shells of a similar size. Flip over half of the shells. Holding the piping bag about ½ inch above the flipped shells, pipe a dollop of filling onto each with an even pressure. Leave a thin ring of shell exposed around the exterior edge. Place the remaining shells, right side up, on top of the filling and press down gently to help them stick. The filling will spread slightly to the edges of the shells.

5. Place finished macarons in the fridge to chill for easier handling. Store macarons in an airtight container in the fridge for up to 2 days or in the freezer for up to 1 month.

BAKER'S TIP

For best results, grind the pistachios you plan to use as garnish in a food processor. Transfer the ground pistachios to a fine-mesh sieve to strain out the pistachio dust so that you're left with only larger chunks of nut. Sprinkling extremely fine particles of pistachio dust or large chunks of nut onto your macarons can cause the shells to crack during baking.

SALTED DARK CHOCOLATE ESPRESSO MACARONS

Makes 24 macarons

MACARON SHELLS

1 batch Macaron Shells
(page 236)
5 drops golden brown gel
food colouring
¼ cup coarse sea salt, for
garnish (see Baker's Tip)
2 tablespoons coarse instant
espresso, for garnish

SALTED ESPRESSO GANACHE

1¼ cups whipping (35%) cream
1 tablespoon instant espresso
powder
¼ teaspoon salt
1½ cups (330 g) chopped
dark baking chocolate

Rich, creamy ganache bursts with coffee flavour while a touch of salt cuts the sweetness of these delectable macarons. Salted dark chocolate espresso is a signature flavour at Jenna Rae Cakes, and you'll always find some baked good with this flavour in our pastry cabinet. Fill your home with the irresistible aroma of chocolate espresso as you indulge in these treats.

MACARON SHELLS

1. Prepare 1 batch Macaron Shells, adding the food colouring and garnishing with the salt and instant espresso when called for.

SALTED ESPRESSO GANACHE

2. In a medium saucepan over medium-high heat, heat the cream, espresso, and salt until the espresso has dissolved, the mixture begins to steam, and small bubbles form on the surface.

3. Place the chocolate in a medium heat-resistant bowl. Pour the hot mixture over the chocolate and let sit for 30 seconds. Whisk until the chocolate is melted and the mixture is creamy and smooth. Let stand at room temperature for at least 1 hour.

ASSEMBLY

4. Transfer the Salted Espresso Ganache to a piping bag fitted with a No. 1A tip (see Baker's Tip).

5. Arrange the Macaron Shells in rows, paired with shells of similar size. Flip over half of the shells. Holding the piping bag about ½ inch above the flipped shells, pipe a dollop of ganache onto each with an even pressure. Leave a thin ring of shell exposed around the exterior edge. Place the remaining shells, right side up, on top of the ganache and press down gently to help them stick. The ganache will spread slightly to the edges of the shells.

6. Place finished macarons in the fridge to chill for easier handling. Store macarons in an airtight container in the fridge for up to 6 days or in the freezer for up to 1 month.

BAKER'S TIP

1. Be careful when choosing salt to sprinkle on top of the Macaron Shells. Fine grains of salt will cause the shells to bubble and crack on top during baking, and extra-large rocks of salt will sink into the shells as they bake. 2. Piping ganache can be a little tricky. You want the ganache to be warm enough to pipe but not so warm that it spills everywhere. Room temperature ganache pipes the best, and if you find it getting a little stiff, pop the piping bag into the microwave for 10 seconds.

RASPBERRY ROSE MACARONS

If you enjoy floral and fruity flavours, you'll love indulging in our Raspberry Rose Macarons. The delicate taste of rose softens the tartness of the raspberries to create a perfect balance that will keep you coming back for more.

MACARON SHELLS

1 batch Macaron Shells
  (page 236)
3 drops dusty rose gel food
  colouring
¼ cup dried rose petals,
  chopped, for garnish

RASPBERRY ROSE FILLING

½ batch Raspberry Reduction
  (page 303)
½ batch Vanilla Buttercream
  (page 296)
1 teaspoon rose flavouring
  (see Baker's Tip)

MACARON SHELLS

1. Prepare 1 batch Macaron Shells, adding the food colouring and garnishing with the rose petals when called for.

RASPBERRY ROSE FILLING

2. Prepare ½ batch Raspberry Reduction.

3. Prepare ½ batch Vanilla Buttercream.

4. In the bowl of a stand mixer fitted with the whisk attachment, whip the Vanilla Buttercream, Raspberry Reduction, and rose flavouring on high speed for 1 to 2 minutes, until well combined.

ASSEMBLY

5. Transfer the Raspberry Rose Filling to a piping bag fitted with a No. 12 tip.

6. Arrange the Macaron Shells in rows, paired with shells of a similar size. Flip over half of the shells. Holding the piping bag about ½ inch above the flipped shells, pipe a dollop of filling onto each with an even pressure. Leave a thin ring of shell exposed around the exterior edge. Place the remaining shells, right side up, on top of the filling and press down gently to help them stick. The filling will spread slightly to the edges of the shells.

7. Place finished macarons in the fridge to chill for easier handling. Store macarons in an airtight container in the fridge for up to 6 days or in the freezer for up to 1 month.

BAKER'S TIP

Rose water and rose flavouring are quite different. Rose flavouring has a more concentrated flavour, which means you need only a small amount to achieve a prominent taste. Rose water is much less concentrated and is also a thinner liquid. You would need to add much more of it to give the filling a noticeable rose flavour, which means you would run the risk of adding so much liquid that the buttercream starts to thin out. Try your best to find and use rose flavouring.

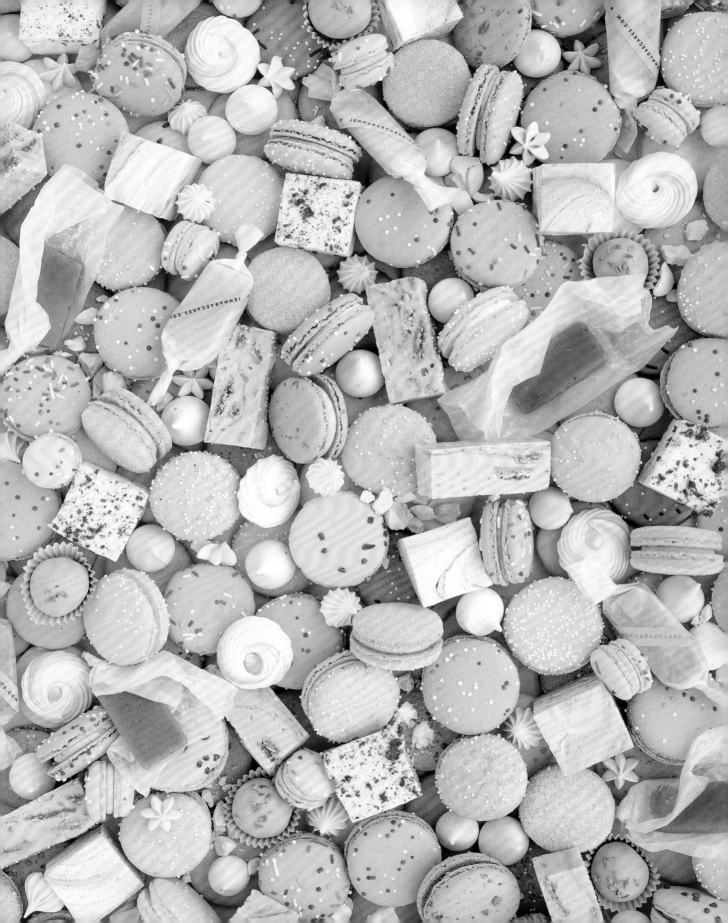

CANDIES & CONFECTIONS

BAKER'S
NOTES

From our
Kitchen to yours
xo

POPCORN, CARAMELS, AND MARSHMALLOWS, OH MY!

We like to make as much as we can from scratch, and that often means whipping up marshmallows (pages 273 and 274) for our Cotton Candy Hot Chocolate (page 277) or creating Peanut Caramel Nougat Bites (page 282) to top cupcakes or stuff inside cookie sandwiches. We know what you're thinking: *Make marshmallows from scratch? Seems like a stretch!* Let us be the first to tell you that you can do it! With a couple of essential tools and tips, you'll be off to the races.

Candy Thermometer

It is crucial to have a quality candy thermometer when making so many of the recipes you'll find in this section. When you heat syrup to different temperatures, you cook different amounts of water out of it. As the temperature of the syrup climbs, the remaining sugar and water will yield different consistencies, which lend themselves to different kinds of candies and confections. Nougat and marshmallows should be cooked to lower temperatures than lollipops, which is why marshmallows are soft and lollipops are hard. Be sure that the thermometer does not make contact with the bottom of the saucepan, where the heat from the stovetop will affect the reading.

Give Yourself Time

Marshmallows need time to set, truffles need time to set and harden between coats of chocolate, and meringues need to sit in an oven overnight! If you're looking for a quick recipe, head to the Party Squares section and try one of those instead. Making candy and confections often requires a little extra attention. Be sure you have time and remove distractions to focus on the task at hand, and you'll wonder why you didn't make your own candy sooner!

Tempering

Tempering chocolate is an important step in making truffles or any specialty dipped chocolates. When tempering chocolate, you bring it through a series of temperatures in a controlled way, and the result is chocolate that hardens with a gorgeous, professional-looking, shiny appearance. It is firm and breaks with a snap while also melting in your mouth. If chocolate is not tempered correctly, the cocoa butter in it will crystalize unevenly, resulting in chocolate that looks dull or streaky, and it often won't hold its shape. It will have a texture that is almost chewy, may take a long time to dry, and will spoil more quickly. To make sure your chocolate is perfectly tempered every time, follow these steps:

1. Place two-thirds of the chocolate you are using in a large metal bowl. Set up a double boiler: fill a medium saucepan halfway with water, place it on the stovetop, then set the large metal bowl over the saucepan, taking care that the bowl doesn't make direct contact with the water. Place a candy thermometer in the chocolate, removing it only to stir the chocolate.

2. Heat the chocolate over medium heat until it reaches the following temperatures: for dark chocolate, the temperature should reach but not exceed 120°F. For milk or white chocolate, the temperature should reach but not exceed 105°F.

3. When the chocolate has fully melted and comes to temperature, remove the bowl from the saucepan and wipe the bottom to get rid of any condensation, taking care to not allow any of the steam from the hot water to come into contact with the chocolate. Keep the saucepan over the heat.

4. Add the remaining third of the chocolate to the bowl in small amounts, allowing each addition to melt before adding more. Continue adding chocolate and stirring until the chocolate reaches 82°F.

5. Return the bowl to sit over the saucepan and heat over medium heat, stirring often. For dark chocolate, heat to a temperature between 88°F and 91°F. For milk and white chocolate, heat to a temperature between 85°F and 87°F. Once the chocolate reaches temperature, remove the bowl from the heat.

6. Spread a small amount of chocolate onto a piece of wax paper. If the chocolate looks dull or streaky and doesn't appear to harden, you'll need to begin tempering the chocolate again at step 2, adding more chocolate to bring the temperature down when you reach step 4. If the chocolate has a glossy, shiny finish and dries quickly, you have tempered it successfully, and you can use it to coat your truffles or dipped chocolates.

7. Once the chocolate has been tempered, it must be used before it cools and hardens. If the chocolate cools to 84°F to 86°F and is still liquid, it can be reheated to a liquid consistency for dipping. If the chocolate has solidified, you will need to reheat it to the temperatures indicated in step 5, then test it to see if the temper has held.

If you do not want to try tempering chocolate, you can use melting wafers instead. Simply place the chocolate in a heat-resistant bowl and melt it in a microwave oven in 30-second intervals, stirring after each interval, until smooth. Melting wafers won't create the same luxurious taste or texture, but they will work.

2½ cups granulated sugar
2 cups whipping (35%) cream
¾ cup white corn syrup
1 tablespoon pure vanilla extract
½ cup unsalted butter, room temperature, cut into 1-inch cubes
½ teaspoon fleur de sel, for garnish

CHEWY SALTED CARAMELS

Our sweet and salty caramels won't last in your candy dish for long! In this recipe, a chewy caramel is topped with fleur de sel that will keep people coming back for more.

1. Spray a 13- × 9-inch baking dish generously with cooking spray. Line it with parchment paper and spray again with cooking spray.

2. In a large saucepan over medium-high heat, cook the sugar, cream, corn syrup, and vanilla until a candy thermometer reads 245°F. Do not stir.

3. Add the butter and stir until melted. Continue to cook the caramel until the temperature reaches 245°F again.

4. Pour the mixture into the prepared baking dish. Let stand for 5 minutes before sprinkling with the fleur de sel. Let stand at room temperature for 2 to 4 hours, until set completely.

5. Transfer the caramel to a cutting board by lifting the edges of the parchment paper. Pull the parchment paper away from the sides of the caramel. Using a sharp chef's knife, cut into 24 pieces, each about 3 × 1½ inches. Wrap individual pieces in wax paper to turn them into a festive gift or treat to serve guests, if desired.

6. Store in an airtight container in the fridge for up to 2 weeks.

BAKER'S TIP

Dip these caramels in chocolate for an extra indulgent treat. Follow steps 10 and 11 in Peanut Caramel Nougat Bites (page 282).

Makes 48 (1½-inch square) marshmallows

1 cup water, divided
4 tablespoons unflavoured gelatin powder
2 cups granulated sugar
½ cup light corn syrup
½ teaspoon salt
2 tablespoons pure vanilla extract
2 teaspoons cornstarch
1 cup icing sugar

VANILLA MARSHMALLOWS

Impress the crowd huddled around the bonfire when you bring out a styled tray of homemade marshmallows that roast to golden brown, toasty perfection. These marshmallows are great when toasted over a fire, but you can also add them as a topping to your hot chocolate.

1. Spray a 13- × 9-inch baking dish with cooking spray.
2. To the bowl of a stand mixer fitted with the whisk attachment, add ½ cup water and sprinkle in the gelatin powder. Do not stir. Set aside and let the gelatin bloom, about 5 minutes.
3. In a small saucepan over high heat, combine the granulated sugar, corn syrup, remaining ½ cup water, and salt. Bring to a rolling boil and let boil for 1 minute.
4. Whip the gelatin and water on low speed for 30 seconds. Increase the speed to medium and slowly pour the sugar mixture into the bowl, taking care not to pour it directly on the whisk attachment. Increase the speed to high and whip for 8 to 10 minutes, until the mixture has tripled in size and looks thick and shiny. Turn off the mixer, add the vanilla, then whip on medium speed for 30 seconds, until incorporated.
5. Immediately pour the mixture into the prepared baking dish. Spray an offset spatula with cooking spray so that it doesn't stick to the mixture and quickly spread it in an even layer. Spray the top of the mixture lightly with cooking spray. Cover and let stand at room temperature for at least 8 hours, or overnight, to set. Even if you're in a hurry, let set for at least 4 hours.
6. Flip the marshmallow onto a textured plastic cutting board (not a smooth or wooden cutting board or it will stick!). With a wet towel on hand to wipe the knife between cuts, cut the marshmallow into 1½-inch squares.
7. In a small bowl, sift together the cornstarch and icing sugar and whisk to combine. Lightly toss each marshmallow in the mixture to coat, then toss it gently in your hands to remove any excess coating.
8. Store in an airtight container at room temperature for up to 1 week.

BAKER'S TIP

We cut our marshmallows quite small to top all kinds of baked goods in our shop, but feel free to cut yours as large as you like! Jumbo marshmallows in hot chocolate are a special treat.

RASPBERRY CHAMPAGNE MARSHMALLOWS

Makes 48 (1½-inch square) marshmallows

1 cup water, divided
4 tablespoons unflavoured gelatin powder
2 cups granulated sugar
½ cup light corn syrup
½ teaspoon salt
½ cup Champagne (or Prosecco)
2 tablespoons pure vanilla extract
2 drops soft pink gel food colouring
¾ cup freeze-dried raspberries, divided
2 teaspoons cornstarch
1 cup icing sugar

A sweet treat for a bridal shower or adult birthday party, our Raspberry Champagne Marshmallows are a more sophisticated take on a classic treat. Serve these marshmallows on a vintage tray styled with fresh flowers for a bridal shower, or stack two or three in a champagne glass with a raspberry placed on the rim for a show-stopping feature on a dessert table.

1. Spray a 13- × 9-inch baking dish with vegetable cooking spray and set aside.

2. To the bowl of a stand mixer fitted with the whisk attachment, add ½ cup water and sprinkle in the gelatin powder. Do not stir. Set aside and allow the gelatin to bloom, about 5 minutes.

3. In a small saucepan over high heat, combine the granulated sugar, corn syrup, remaining ½ cup water, and salt. Bring to a rolling boil and let boil for 1 minute.

4. Whip the gelatin and water on low speed for 30 seconds. Increase the speed to medium and slowly pour the sugar mixture into the bowl, taking care not to pour it directly on the whisk attachment. Increase the speed to high and whip for 10 minutes, until the mixture has tripled in size and looks thick and shiny. Turn off the mixer and add the Champagne, vanilla, food colouring, and ½ cup freeze-dried raspberries. Whip on medium speed for 30 seconds, until incorporated.

5. Immediately pour the mixture into the prepared baking dish. Spray an offset spatula with cooking spray so that it doesn't stick to the mixture and quickly spread it in an even layer. Sprinkle with the remaining ¼ cup freeze-dried raspberries. Spray the top of the mixture lightly with cooking spray. Cover and let stand at room temperature for at least 8 hours, or overnight, to set. Even if you're in a hurry, let set for at least 4 hours.

6. Flip the marshmallow onto a textured plastic cutting board (not a smooth or wooden cutting board or it will stick!). With a wet towel on hand to wipe the knife between cuts, cut the marshmallow into 1½-inch squares.

7. In a small bowl, sift together the cornstarch and icing sugar. Lightly toss each marshmallow in the mixture to coat, then toss it gently in your hands to remove any excess coating.

8. Store in an airtight container at room temperature for up to 1 week.

BAKER'S TIP

Strawberry Rosé is another delicious summery flavour combo you can try! Substitute the freeze-dried raspberries with an equal amount of freeze-dried strawberries and the Champagne with an equal amount of your favourite rosé wine for a perfect patio-inspired treat!

COTTON CANDY HOT CHOCOLATE

Serves 5

COTTON CANDY MARSHMALLOWS

½ cup water, divided

2 tablespoons unflavoured gelatin powder

1 cup granulated sugar

¼ cup white corn syrup

¼ teaspoon salt

1½ teaspoons pure vanilla extract

1½ teaspoons JRC Liquid Cotton Candy or cotton candy flavouring

2 drops soft pink gel food colouring

2 drops sky blue gel food colouring

COTTON CANDY HOT CHOCOLATE

3½ cups (770 g) chopped white baking chocolate

4 cups dairy or non-dairy milk of choice

1 teaspoon pure vanilla extract

1½ teaspoons JRC Liquid Cotton Candy or cotton candy flavouring (see Baker's Tip)

1 drop soft pink gel food colouring

Sprinkles of your choice, for garnish (optional)

Cotton Candy Hot Chocolate is an Instagram-worthy take on a winter classic. Tinted a soft shade of pink and topped with Cotton Candy Marshmallows, this inventive hot chocolate will please family and friends at a holiday gathering or after a chilly afternoon spent playing outdoors.

COTTON CANDY MARSHMALLOWS

1. Spray a 9-inch square baking dish with cooking spray.

2. To the bowl of a stand mixer fitted with the whisk attachment, add ¼ cup water and sprinkle in the gelatin powder. Do not stir. Set aside and allow the gelatin to bloom, about 5 minutes.

3. In a small saucepan over high heat, combine the sugar, corn syrup, remaining ¼ cup water, and salt. Bring to a rolling boil and let boil for 1 minute.

4. Whip the gelatin and water on low speed for 30 seconds. Increase the speed to medium and slowly pour the sugar mixture into the bowl, taking care not to pour it directly on the whisk attachment. Increase the speed to high and whip for 10 minutes, until the mixture has tripled in size and looks thick and shiny. Turn off the mixer, add the vanilla and cotton candy flavouring, then whip on medium speed for 30 seconds, until incorporated.

5. Remove the bowl from the mixer, making sure to scrape off any mixture stuck to the whisk attachment. Add the soft pink and sky blue food colourings to different areas of the mixture. Spray an offset spatula with cooking spray so that it doesn't stick to the mixture and gently fold in the colour to create a swirl, being sure to reach all the way around the sides and to the bottom of the mixing bowl. Do not overmix or the marshmallow will begin to break down and won't be as light and fluffy.

6. Immediately pour the marshmallow into the prepared baking dish. Spray the offset spatula with cooking spray again and quickly spread the mixture in an even layer. Spray the top of the mixture lightly with cooking spray. Cover and let stand at room temperature for at least 8 hours, or overnight, to set. Even if you're in a hurry, let set for at least 4 hours.

7. Flip the marshmallow onto a textured plastic cutting board (not a smooth or wooden cutting board or it will stick). With a wet towel on hand to wipe the knife between cuts, cut the marshmallow into jumbo 3-inch squares.

8. Store the marshmallows in an airtight container at room temperature for up to 1 week.

COTTON CANDY HOT CHOCOLATE

9. In a heat-resistant bowl, melt the white chocolate in the microwave in 30-second intervals, stirring after each interval, until smooth.

10. In a medium saucepan over medium-low heat, bring the milk to a simmer. Remove from the heat and add the melted chocolate, vanilla, cotton candy flavouring, and soft pink food colouring. Whisk together until combined.

11. Divide the hot chocolate evenly among 5 mugs. Add a Cotton Candy Marshmallow to each and garnish with the sprinkles, if using. Serve immediately.

12. Store the hot chocolate in an airtight container in the fridge for up to 1 week.

BAKER'S TIP

To make this hot chocolate festive for the winter months, try substituting the cotton candy flavouring with ¼ teaspoon peppermint extract.

CARAMEL PECAN POPCORN

10 cups popped popcorn
1 cup packed brown sugar
½ cup clear corn syrup
½ cup unsalted butter,
 room temperature
½ teaspoon salt
1 teaspoon pure vanilla extract
½ teaspoon baking soda
½ cup pecan halves (see
 Baker's Tip)
½ cup chopped dark, milk, or
 white chocolate melting
 wafers, for garnish

We love making this popcorn for birthday parties and movie nights at home. It has a hard caramel coating and is filled with toasted pecans and drizzled with chocolate for an extra-delectable treat! Feel free to leave out the pecans if you prefer a nut-free option.

1. Preheat the oven to 250°F. Spray a baking sheet generously with cooking spray. Line a second baking sheet with parchment paper.

2. Pour the popcorn onto the greased baking sheet. Remove and discard any kernels that did not pop.

3. In a medium saucepan over medium heat, bring the sugar, corn syrup, butter, and salt to a boil, stirring constantly with a heat-safe spatula. Let boil for 5 minutes, continuing to stir. Remove from the heat, stir in the vanilla and baking soda, and immediately pour the mixture evenly over the popcorn. Using a spatula, stir the popcorn to coat evenly.

4. Bake for 45 minutes, removing the pan from the oven every 15 minutes to stir the popcorn. Let cool to room temperature, and increase the oven temperature to 350°F. Break the popcorn into bite-size pieces on the baking sheet.

5. Arrange the pecans in an even layer on the lined baking sheet. Bake for 5 minutes, then let cool.

6. In a heat-resistant bowl, melt the chocolate wafers in the microwave in 30-second intervals, stirring after each interval, until smooth. Transfer the chocolate to a piping bag and cut off the tip. Drizzle evenly over the popcorn, sprinkle with the toasted pecans, and let cool to room temperature.

7. Store in an airtight container at room temperature for up to 1 week. Make sure not to leave it in a sunny area or the chocolate will melt!

BAKER'S TIP

1. Ten cups of popcorn may seem like a lot, but it goes quickly! This recipe serves about four people, so if you want to make enough for only one or two, cut the recipe in half. 2. Not a fan of pecans? No problem! Simply replace them with an equal amount of the nut of your choice or remove the nuts altogether for a nut-free treat.

PISTACHIO ROSE POPCORN

Makes 10 cups

10 cups popped popcorn
1 cup chopped pistachios
2 cups granulated sugar
¾ cup whole (3.25%) milk
1 tablespoon clear corn syrup
¼ teaspoon salt
1 teaspoon rose water
1 drop soft pink gel food
  colouring

Add a touch of class to your next gathering with our Pistachio Rose Popcorn. Since this popcorn has such a unique flavour, it will be a delightful surprise for guests at a baby shower, girls' movie night, or Galentine's Day event. For extra points in the presentation department, package the popcorn in cellophane bags and tie them with some pretty ribbon.

1. Preheat the oven to 350°F. Line 2 baking sheets with parchment paper.

2. Place the popped popcorn in a large, heat-resistant bowl and remove and discard any kernels that did not pop.

3. Arrange the pistachios in an even layer on one of the prepared baking sheets. Bake for 5 to 8 minutes, or until lightly toasted and golden. Lower the oven temperature to 175°F.

4. In a medium saucepan over medium-high heat, cook the sugar, milk, corn syrup, and salt until a candy thermometer inserted into the middle of the mixture reads 230°F. Remove from the heat, whisk in the rose water and food colouring, then immediately pour the mixture over the popcorn. Using a spatula, stir to coat evenly. Sprinkle with the toasted pistachios and stir to evenly disperse the nuts.

5. Transfer the candy-coated popcorn to the second prepared baking sheet and spread it in an even layer. Bake for 30 to 40 minutes. Let cool to room temperature (see Baker's Tip).

6. Break the popcorn into bite-size pieces and store in an airtight container at room temperature for up to 1 week.

BAKER'S TIP

Instead of baking the popcorn in the oven, you can leave it to dry on the baking sheet at room temperature for 24 to 48 hours.

PEANUT CARAMEL NOUGAT BITES

PEANUT NOUGAT

1½ cups granulated sugar
1 cup white corn syrup
½ cup water
2 egg whites
¼ teaspoon salt
1 cup creamy peanut butter

PEANUT CARAMEL

2 cups granulated sugar
1 cup whipping (35%) cream
1 cup white corn syrup
½ cup unsalted butter,
 room temperature
¼ teaspoon salt
2 cups chopped peanuts,
 toasted
1 tablespoon pure vanilla
 extract

COATING

4 cups (880 g) dark couverture
 chocolate (if tempering)
 or dark chocolate melting
 wafers (if not tempering)
2 cups toasted chopped
 peanuts

Bet you can't eat just one! Nougat, caramel, and peanuts are enrobed in chocolate and garnished with chopped peanuts. This chewy, salty, sweet, and nutty treat hits every flavour note you'd hope for in a bite-size piece of deliciousness.

PEANUT NOUGAT

1. Spray a 13- × 9-inch baking dish generously with cooking spray. Line it with parchment paper and spray again with cooking spray.

2. In a medium saucepan over medium-high heat, bring the sugar, corn syrup, and water to a boil. Boil until a candy thermometer inserted into the middle of the mixture reads 250°F.

3. While the sugar mixture heats, in the bowl of a stand mixer fitted with the whisk attachment, whip the egg whites and salt on high speed until stiff peaks form, about 3 to 4 minutes.

4. Once the sugar mixture reaches 250°F, with the mixer on medium speed, slowly pour the mixture into the egg whites and whip until combined. Turn off the mixer and replace the whisk attachment with the paddle attachment. Add the peanut butter and beat on medium speed until well combined.

5. Transfer the nougat to the prepared baking dish. Using your hand or an offset spatula sprayed with cooking spray, press it firmly into the pan.

PEANUT CARAMEL

6. In a medium saucepan over medium-high heat, cook the sugar, cream, corn syrup, butter, and salt until a candy thermometer inserted into the middle of the mixture reads 245°F. Remove from the heat and, using a heat-safe spatula, stir in the peanuts and vanilla.

ASSEMBLY

7. Immediately pour the Peanut Caramel over the Peanut Nougat base. Let set at room temperature for 12 hours, or overnight, until the caramel is firm to the touch.

8. Line a baking sheet with parchment paper.

9. Transfer the nougat and caramel bar to a cutting board by lifting the edges of the parchment paper. Pull the parchment paper away from the sides of the bar. Using a sharp chef's knife, cut into 2-inch squares. Transfer the squares to the prepared baking sheet and place in the fridge to harden for at least 30 minutes.

10. Temper the couverture chocolate (see instructions on page 267) or melt the chocolate wafers in a heat-resistant bowl in the microwave in 30-second intervals, stirring after each interval, until smooth but not hot. Pour into a deep small bowl.

11. Remove the chilled squares from the fridge. Using a dipping fork, submerge a square in the chocolate to cover completely. Lift it out of the chocolate and let drip, tapping the fork on the edge of the bowl to help remove excess chocolate. Return it to the baking sheet and immediately sprinkle with peanuts. Repeat until all squares are covered.

12. Store in an airtight container at room temperature for up to 2 weeks. Make sure not to leave it in a sunny area or the chocolate will melt!

BAKER'S TIP

For a different look, try dipping only half of each square in chocolate and then sprinkling it with peanuts.

LAVENDER LEMON TRUFFLES

A bright and creamy treat, our Lavender Lemon Truffles combine the velvety texture of a chocolate ganache truffle with the refreshing and refined palette of lavender and lemon. Make these truffles for your next brunch potluck and wow all who try them.

**WHITE CHOCOLATE
TRUFFLE GANACHE**

¼ cup whipping (35%) cream

1 teaspoon dried lavender, more for garnish

1 cup + 2 tablespoons (245 g) white couverture chocolate

2 teaspoons unsalted butter, room temperature

1¼ teaspoons cocoa butter

2 tablespoons fresh lemon juice

COATING

4 cups (880 g) white couverture chocolate (if tempering) or white chocolate melting wafers (if not tempering)

3 to 4 drops oil-based purple liquid chocolate colouring (see Baker's Tip)

WHITE CHOCOLATE TRUFFLE GANACHE

1. In a small saucepan over medium heat, cook the cream and dried lavender until it just begins to boil. Remove from the heat and let steep for 5 to 10 minutes, depending on how much lavender flavour you want your truffles to have.

2. Meanwhile, in a heat-resistant medium bowl, melt the white couverture chocolate in the microwave in 30-second intervals, stirring after each interval, until smooth.

3. Using a fine-mesh sieve, strain the lavender from the cream. Return the cream to the saucepan and place over medium heat. Add the butter and cocoa butter, stirring often until melted. Remove from the heat and stir in the lemon juice.

4. Pour the cream mixture into the bowl of melted chocolate and whisk to combine. Transfer the ganache mixture to a small container and cover with plastic wrap placed directly on the surface of the mixture to prevent a skin forming. Place in the fridge to set until firm to the touch, about 1 hour.

ASSEMBLY

5. Line a baking sheet with parchment paper.

6. Once the ganache mixture is firm, remove it from the fridge and scoop tablespoon-size dollops onto the prepared baking sheet. Once all ganache has been scooped, place the baking sheet in the fridge so that the truffles stiffen to a rollable consistency, about 30 minutes.

7. Remove the truffles from the fridge and use your hands to roll them into balls. If your hands are usually quite warm, run them under cold water and dry them before rolling to help prevent melting. Return the rolled truffles to the baking sheet and refrigerate to harden.

8. Temper the couverture chocolate (see instructions on page 267), making sure to add the chocolate colouring when the chocolate first begins to melt, or melt the chocolate wafers in a heat-resistant bowl in the microwave in 30-second intervals, stirring after each interval, until smooth. Pour into a deep small bowl.

9. Remove the truffles from the fridge. Using a chocolate fork, submerge a truffle in the chocolate to cover completely. Lift it out of the chocolate and let drip, tapping the fork on the edge of the bowl to help remove excess chocolate. Return it to the baking sheet, using another fork to help it slide smoothly into place. Sprinkle with dried lavender. Repeat until all truffles are covered.

10. Let stand at room temperature for about 1 hour, until the chocolate hardens completely. Store in an airtight container in the fridge for up to 2 weeks until ready to serve.

BAKER'S TIP

It is important to use an oil-based chocolate colouring in this recipe. A water-based colouring will cause your chocolate to seize and become gritty and rough. If you are having trouble finding chocolate colouring at your local craft or bulk food store, try ordering it online.

SALTED CARAMEL TRUFFLES

Have you ever seen an adult beg for more chocolate? Our rich and creamy chocolate ganache is paired with luxurious salted caramel and the result is addictive. If you only ever attempt to make one truffle in your life, this should be the one.

**MILK CHOCOLATE
TRUFFLE GANACHE**

½ cup + 1 tablespoon whipping
   (35%) cream
⅓ cup granulated sugar
1 tablespoon water
1 tablespoon unsalted butter,
   room temperature
½ teaspoon salt
1½ cups (330 g) milk
   couverture chocolate

COATING

4 cups (880 g) milk couverture
   chocolate (if tempering)
   or milk chocolate melting
   wafers (if not tempering)

GARNISH

1 teaspoon fleur de sel
Edible gold leaf flakes
   (optional)

MILK CHOCOLATE TRUFFLE GANACHE

1. In a heat-resistant medium bowl, heat the cream in the microwave in 30-second intervals, stirring after each interval, until warm to the touch.

2. In a large saucepan over medium-high heat, bring the sugar and water to a boil and boil until the syrup caramelizes and turns a warm amber colour (see Baker's Tip). Remove from the heat and slowly pour in the warm cream, whisking constantly to prevent the mixture from bubbling over. Add the butter and salt and whisk until fully incorporated.

3. In a heat-resistant bowl, melt the milk couverture chocolate in the microwave in 30-second intervals, stirring after each interval, until smooth. Pour the caramel mixture over the chocolate and whisk to combine (see Baker's Tip).

4. Cover with plastic wrap placed directly on the surface of the mixture to prevent a skin forming. Refrigerate until firm to the touch, about 1 hour.

ASSEMBLY

5. Line a baking sheet with parchment paper.

6. Once the ganache mixture is firm, remove it from the fridge and scoop tablespoon-size dollops onto the prepared baking sheet. Once all ganache has been scooped, place the baking sheet in the fridge so that the truffles stiffen to a rollable consistency, about 30 minutes.

7. Remove the truffles from the fridge and use your hands to roll them into balls. If your hands are usually quite warm, run them under cold water and dry them before rolling to help prevent melting. Return the rolled truffles to the baking sheet and refrigerate to harden.

8. Temper the couverture chocolate (see instructions on page 267) or melt the chocolate wafers in a heat-resistant bowl in the microwave in 30-second intervals, stirring after each interval, until smooth. Pour into a deep small bowl.

9. Remove the truffles from the fridge. Using a chocolate fork, submerge a truffle in the chocolate to cover completely. Lift it out of the chocolate and let drip, tapping the fork on the edge of the bowl to help remove excess chocolate. Return it to the baking sheet, using another fork to help it slide smoothly into place. Sprinkle with fleur de sel and gold leaf flakes, if using. Repeat until all truffles are covered.

10. Let stand at room temperature for about 30 minutes, until the chocolate hardens completely. Store in an airtight container in the fridge for up to 2 weeks until ready to serve.

BAKER'S TIP

1. If the ganache separates when you combine it with the caramel, add 1 teaspoon cold whipping (35%) cream and whisk until it comes together. **2.** When making the ganache use a larger pot than you think you'll need. When you add the cream, the mixture will bubble and you don't want it to boil over.

Makes about 100 (¾-inch)
mini meringues

1 cup caster sugar or superfine
    granulated sugar
½ cup egg whites (about
    4 eggs)
1 dash cream of tartar
1 teaspoon flavouring of
    your choice (optional)
2 drops gel food colouring
    of your choice (optional)

MINI MERINGUES

A tasty delight for those who follow a gluten-free diet, mini meringues can be enjoyed on their own or added to another dessert like a cake or a tart to make it a little extra special. We love topping cakes with these little cuties.

1. Preheat the oven to 400°F. Line a 13- × 9-inch baking dish with parchment paper. Line 2 baking sheets with parchment paper.

2. Spread the sugar in an even layer in the prepared baking dish. Bake for 5 minutes, or until the edges of the sugar are just starting to brown but not melt. Remove from the oven and reduce the oven temperature to 175°F.

3. In the bowl of a stand mixer fitted with the whisk attachment, whip the egg whites and cream of tartar on high speed until stiff peaks form, about 4 minutes. Reduce the speed to medium-high and slowly add the sugar, making sure not to add any browned or melted bits. Increase the speed to high and whip until the mixture is stiff and glossy, about 5 to 8 minutes.

4. Add the flavouring and/or food colouring (if using) and whip on high speed until fully incorporated. To create meringues with a striped pattern, mix the flavouring and colouring in a small dish and, using a paintbrush, brush the mixture on the inside of a piping bag in vertical stripes.

5. Transfer the meringue to a piping bag fitted with the tip of your choice. We used No. 2D, 4B, and 199 tips.

6. Secure the parchment paper to the baking sheets by dabbing a small amount of meringue onto each corner of the baking sheets and then pressing the paper into it. Pipe desired shapes onto the paper. Bake for 2 hours. Turn off the oven and keep the oven door shut. Let the meringues cool in the oven overnight.

7. Store in an airtight container at room temperature for up to 2 weeks.

BAKER'S TIP

Caster sugar is superfine sugar (also known as "berry sugar"). It can sometimes be hard to find in a regular grocery store, so we recommend purchasing it from your local bulk food store. Alternatively, you can pulse granulated sugar in a coffee grinder to reduce the size of the granules by one-half.

COTTON CANDY LOLLIPOPS

Makes 12 (2-inch) lollipops

1 drop white gel food colouring
1 drop soft pink gel food
  colouring
¾ cup granulated sugar
½ cup glucose syrup
¼ cup water
½ teaspoon JRC Liquid Cotton
  Candy or cotton candy
  flavouring
12 standard 4-inch lollipop
  sticks

If you've ever been interested in creating your own lollipops, we've got your new go-to recipe. It is simple and will create delicious cotton candy lollipops for any occasion.

1. In a small dish, combine 1 very small drop of white food colouring and 1 even smaller drop of soft pink food colouring.

2. In a medium saucepan over medium-high heat, bring the sugar, glucose syrup, and water to a boil until a candy thermometer reads 295°F. Remove from the heat and stir in the cotton candy flavouring. Continue to stir until the mixture is no longer bubbling.

3. Using a toothpick, add a small drop of the food colouring to the mixture. Stir to combine. If you'd like the colour to be darker, add another small drop of food colouring until the desired shade of pink is achieved.

4. Carefully transfer the hot syrup to a metal candy funnel and immediately pour into lollipop moulds (see Baker's Tip). Add the sticks and let set until the lollipops have cooled to room temperature and the candy has hardened.

5. Wrap in candy wrappers and store in an airtight container at room temperature, away from sunlight, for up to 2 months. Humidity will cause the lollipops to become sticky, so it's best to wrap them as soon as you can!

BAKER'S TIP

1. Make sure that the candy funnel you're using is made entirely of metal, or metal and silicone. Many funnels contain plastic and will melt from the high temperature of the hot syrup. If you can't find a metal funnel, you can very carefully pour the hot syrup from the pot directly into the moulds. 2. To make cute party favours, simply toss the lollipops in acrylic bags and close each bag with a piece of ribbon tied in a bow.

FILLINGS &
BUTTERCREAM

BAKER'S NOTES

From our Kitchen to yours
xo

AS YOU EXPLORE DIFFERENT RECIPES IN THE BOOK, this is a section that will become increasingly familiar to you. Our unique fillings and flavours—and the wide range of them—are what set apart our treats and make them stand out in a world where flavour combinations are endless. But it's not just our creative combinations that people are attracted to. If we could show you our direct messages on Instagram, you would see how often we are asked for our Vanilla Buttercream recipe (page 296). Most buttercream recipes call for the paddle attachment of a stand mixer to be used, but we have always used the whisk attachment for an extra-fluffy buttercream that is light, sweet, and perfect for cupcakes, cookie sandwiches, macarons, cakes—and anything else that demands a generous dollop. We hope that our go-to filling recipes become your favourites as well, and that they spur you to create your own renditions of your favourite treats.

CHECK YOUR RECIPE

It's really important to read recipes closely to determine how much of each filling you'll need to make. Some recipes ask you to prepare a full batch or a double batch of a buttercream or a filling, whereas others will instruct you to make a half-batch or even a quarter-batch, depending on how it's being used.

SHELF LIFE

While following recipes carefully will ensure that you don't make more or less filling than you'll need, many of our fillings have quite a long shelf life, so making extra does not necessarily mean it will go to waste. It's never a bad thing to have leftover crumble (pages 305 and 306) to sprinkle on pancakes the next morning or extra Salted Caramel (page 299) to slather on toast!

VANILLA BUTTERCREAM

When you open a bakery, you go through so many buttercream variations before finding "the one." We love our buttercream for its delicious taste, perfect pipability, and versatility. We get asked to share the recipe all the time, and now it's yours to use!

Makes 4 cups

2 cups unsalted butter, room temperature
3 cups icing sugar
1½ teaspoons vanilla bean paste (see Baker's Tip)

1. In the bowl of a stand mixer fitted with the whisk attachment, whip the butter on low speed for 30 seconds. Increase the speed to high and whip for 2 minutes. Reduce the speed to medium and add the icing sugar. Whip for an additional 30 seconds. Increase the speed to high and whip for 2 minutes, until the mixture looks light and fluffy. Scrape down the sides of the bowl. Add the vanilla bean paste and whip on high speed for 1 minute.

2. Use immediately or store in an airtight container in the fridge for up to 2 weeks. Remove from the fridge 1 hour before using.

BAKER'S TIP

If you can't find vanilla bean paste, substitute 1 tablespoon pure vanilla extract and the seeds from 1 whole vanilla bean.

MAKE IT

Vanilla Sprinkle Cookie Sandwiches (page 25),
Vanilla Cupcakes (page 60),
Vanilla Sprinkle Cake (page 130),
Vanilla Sprinkle Cream Puffs (page 206),
and many, many more!

MILK CHOCOLATE BUTTERCREAM

This recipe combines the melt-in-your-mouth goodness of milk chocolate with our signature, fluffy Vanilla Buttercream for a frosting you won't be able to resist.

Makes 4 cups

¼ cup + 1 tablespoon whipping (35%) cream
1 cup (220 g) chopped milk baking chocolate (see Baker's Tip)
1¼ cups unsalted butter, room temperature
3 cups icing sugar
¼ cup cocoa powder
½ teaspoon pure vanilla extract

1. In a medium saucepan over medium-high heat, heat the whipping cream until it begins to steam and small bubbles form on the surface.

2. Place the chocolate in a medium heat-resistant bowl. Pour the cream over the chocolate and let sit for 30 seconds. Whisk until the chocolate is melted and the mixture is creamy and smooth. Let cool to room temperature.

3. In the bowl of a stand mixer fitted with the whisk attachment, whip the butter on low speed for 30 seconds. Increase the speed to high and whip for 2 minutes.

4. With the mixer on low speed, slowly add the icing sugar and whip for an additional 30 seconds. Add the chocolate mixture and cocoa powder. Increase the speed to high and whip for 2 minutes, until the mixture looks light and fluffy. Scrape down the sides of the bowl. Add the vanilla and whip on high speed for 1 minute.

5. Use immediately or store in an airtight container in the fridge for up to 1 week. Remove from the fridge 1 hour before using.

BAKER'S TIP

1. For an even richer buttercream, use dark baking chocolate instead of milk baking chocolate. **2.** If you're not a fan of dark chocolate, feel free to substitute this buttercream in any recipe that calls for our Chocolate Lover's Buttercream!

MAKE IT

S'mores Cookie Sandwiches (page 43),
S'mores Cupcakes (page 71), and
S'mores Cake (page 174).

CHOCOLATE LOVER'S BUTTERCREAM

Rich. Decadent. Mouth-watering. We could basically look up "delicious" in a thesaurus and all of the synonyms would describe our Chocolate Lover's Buttercream. The addition of cream cheese makes this buttercream extra smooth.

Makes 4 cups

¼ cup + 2 tablespoons whipping (35%) cream
¾ cup (165 g) chopped dark baking chocolate
¼ cup cream cheese, room temperature
1 cup unsalted butter, room temperature
3 cups icing sugar
½ teaspoon pure vanilla extract
½ cup cocoa powder, sifted

1. In a small saucepan over medium heat, bring the whipping cream just to a boil.

2. Place the dark chocolate in a medium heat-resistant bowl. Pour the cream over the chocolate and let sit for 30 seconds. Whisk until the chocolate is melted and the mixture is creamy and smooth.

3. In the bowl of a stand mixer fitted with the paddle attachment, beat the cream cheese for 1 minute on medium high speed. Add the butter and beat until fully incorporated, scraping down the sides of the bowl often.

4. With the mixer on medium-low speed, slowly pour the chocolate mixture into the bowl and beat until combined. Add the icing sugar, vanilla, and cocoa powder and beat until combined. Increase the speed to medium-high and beat until the mixture looks light, creamy, and well combined. Scrape down the sides of the bowl and beat for an additional minute.

5. Use immediately or store in an airtight container in the fridge for up to 1 week. Remove from the fridge 1 hour before using.

BAKER'S TIP

This buttercream is extremely rich. If you're looking for a softer chocolate taste, substitute our Milk Chocolate Buttercream.

MAKE IT

Brownie Batter Cookie Sandwiches (page 30),
Chocolate Lover's Cupcakes (page 62),
Nanaimo Cupcakes (page 74), and
Chocolate Lover's Cake (page 162).

CREAM CHEESE BUTTERCREAM

Our classic and delicious Cream Cheese Buttercream doesn't form a crust and is the perfect match for anything red velvet.

Makes 4 cups

¾ cup cream cheese, room temperature
½ cup unsalted butter, room temperature
½ cup vegetable shortening
3½ cups icing sugar
1 tablespoon vanilla bean paste (see Baker's Tip)

1. In a stand mixer fitted with the whisk attachment, whip the cream cheese on high speed for 3 to 5 minutes, scraping down the sides of the bowl every minute, until smooth. Add the butter and shortening and mix on high speed for 2 to 3 minutes, scraping down the sides of the bowl every minute, until smooth.

2. With the mixer on low speed, slowly add the icing sugar and mix for an additional 30 seconds. Increase the speed to high and mix for 3 minutes, until the mixture looks light and fluffy. Scrape down the sides of the bowl. Add the vanilla bean paste and mix for an additional minute.

3. Use immediately or store in an airtight container in the fridge for up to 1 week. Remove from the fridge 1 hour before using.

BAKER'S TIP

1. If you can't find vanilla bean paste, substitute 1 tablespoon pure vanilla extract and the seeds from 1 whole vanilla bean. 2. Cream Cheese Buttercream is naturally soft because of the liquid in cream cheese. We help firm up this buttercream for piping by adding shortening. 3. When icing a cake with this buttercream, it is difficult to create crisp edges, so we recommend attempting a lined or rustic design to make it easier on yourself!

MAKE IT

Red Velvet Cookie Sandwiches (page 50),
Carrot Cake Cupcakes (page 66),
Pumpkin Spice Cupcakes (page 83),
Red Velvet Cupcakes (page 87),
Red Velvet Cake (page 171), and
Carrot Cake with Spiced Candied Walnuts (page 191).

MILK CHOCOLATE GANACHE

Our milk chocolate ganache will leave you feeling like you're eating a delicious chocolate bar! Keep some in the fridge to drizzle on fruit for a quick and easy summer treat.

Makes 1½ cups

½ cup + 2 tablespoons whipping (35%) cream
2 cups (440 g) chopped milk baking chocolate

1. In a medium saucepan over medium-high heat, heat the whipping cream until it begins to steam and small bubbles form on the surface.
2. Place the chocolate in a medium heat-resistant bowl. Pour the cream over the chocolate and let sit for 30 seconds. Whisk until the chocolate is melted and the mixture is creamy and smooth. Let cool to room temperature.
3. Use immediately or transfer to a squeeze bottle or an airtight container and store in the fridge for up to 1 week. Before using, heat the ganache in the microwave in 15-second intervals, until a runny consistency is achieved.

MAKE IT

S'mores Cookie Sandwiches (page 43) and S'mores Cake (page 174).

DARK CHOCOLATE GANACHE

Our rich chocolate ganache is a Jenna Rae Cakes kitchen staple. We always have fresh bottles in our fridge ready to use. Store this ganache in your fridge as the perfect addition to pancakes, waffles, and ice cream or to drizzle on top of whipped cream in hot chocolate.

Makes 1½ cups

1 cup whipping (35%) cream
1¼ cups (275 g) chopped dark baking chocolate (see Baker's Tip)

1. In a medium saucepan over medium-high heat, heat the whipping cream until it begins to steam and small bubbles form on the surface.
2. Place the chocolate in a medium heat-resistant bowl. Pour the cream over the chocolate and let sit for 30 seconds. Whisk until the chocolate is melted and the mixture is creamy and smooth.
3. Use immediately or transfer to a squeeze bottle or an airtight container and store in the fridge for up to 1 week. Before using, heat the ganache in the microwave in 15-second intervals until a runny consistency is achieved.

BAKER'S TIP

We always recommend using high-quality chocolate when baking, especially when making ganache. The better the chocolate, the better the result.

MAKE IT

Chocolate Lover's Cupcakes (page 62), Chocolate Lover's Cake (page 162), Cookie Dough Cake (page 166), and Chocolate Hazelnut Cake (page 179).

WHITE CHOCOLATE GANACHE

We use white chocolate ganache tinted in various colours to decorate many of our creations. With a few drops of food colouring, this ganache will bring a colourful pop to your homemade treats.

Makes 1¾ cups

½ cup whipping (35%) cream
2¼ cups (495 g) chopped white baking chocolate
2 drops gel food colouring (optional)

1. In a medium saucepan over medium-high heat, heat the whipping cream until it begins to steam and small bubbles form on the surface.
2. Place the chocolate in a medium heat-resistant bowl. Pour the cream over the chocolate and let sit for 30 seconds. Add the food colouring (if using) and whisk until the chocolate is melted and the mixture is creamy and smooth.
3. Use immediately or transfer to a squeeze bottle or an airtight container and store in the fridge for up to 1 week. Before using, heat the ganache in the microwave in 15-second intervals until a runny consistency is achieved.

MAKE IT

Cinnamon Apple Crumble Cake (page 151) and Pistachio White Chocolate Cake (page 182).

SALTED CARAMEL

This classic salted caramel is a feature in many of our recipes. Its consistency makes it perfect for filling, drizzling, and spreading.

Makes 2 cups

1½ cups granulated sugar
¼ cup water
¾ cup whipping (35%) cream
½ cup unsalted butter, room temperature, cut into 1-inch cubes
1 teaspoon salt

1. In a medium saucepan over medium-high heat, combine the sugar and water and cook, without stirring, until the syrup turns a deep golden brown and is bubbling slowly. Keep close watch to avoid burning it.
2. Remove the saucepan from the heat. Very slowly, whisk the cream into the pot. The mixture will bubble a lot as you add the cream. You may want to wear oven mitts while you whisk to prevent any splatters or steam from burning your skin.
3. Add the butter and salt and whisk until combined. Let cool for at least 30 minutes.
4. Transfer to a squeeze bottle or an airtight container and store in the fridge for up to 2 weeks.

BAKER'S TIP

1. This recipe requires your full attention so that you don't burn or undercook the caramel. Be sure to avoid distractions when preparing it and be cautious around the boiling sugar. It's best to keep little ones out of the kitchen while preparing this sauce!
2. To soften cold caramel that has been stored in the fridge, it can be warmed in the microwave until the desired consistency is achieved.

MAKE IT

Toffee Salted Caramel Cookie Sandwiches (page 26), Pumpkin Spice Cupcakes (page 83), Cashew Praline Party Squares (page 111), Sticky Coconut Cake (page 159), and Salted Caramel Macarons (page 256).

MERINGUE MARSHMALLOW FLUFF

This dreamy fluff tastes just like marshmallows and, when toasted, tastes just like you're eating marshmallows that were freshly roasted over a bonfire.

Makes 6 cups

1¼ cups granulated sugar, divided
1¼ cups white corn syrup
½ cup water
4 egg whites

1. In a medium saucepan over medium-high heat, bring 1 cup + 2 tablespoons granulated sugar, the corn syrup, and water to a boil. Cook over medium-high heat until a candy thermometer placed in the mixture reaches the soft-ball stage, or 240°F. Remove the saucepan from the heat.

2. In the bowl of a stand mixer fitted with the whisk attachment, whip the egg whites and the remaining 2 tablespoons granulated sugar on high speed until soft peaks form, about 3 minutes.

3. With the mixer on medium speed, slowly pour the hot syrup into the egg white mixture so that it trickles down the inside edge of the bowl, taking care not to pour it directly on the whisk. Increase the speed to high and whip for 4 to 5 minutes, until stiff.

4. Meringue Marshmallow Fluff is best used fresh. Store any leftover fluff in an airtight container at room temperature for up to 2 days.

BAKER'S TIP

When it's ready, transfer the fluff directly to a piping bag, as it's easiest to scoop when it's fresh! We love dropping leftover fluff by the tablespoon into hot cocoa or lattes at home.

MAKE IT

S'mores Cookie Sandwiches (page 43),
Lemon Meringue Cookie Sandwiches (page 44),
S'mores Cupcakes (page 71),
Lemon Meringue Party Squares (page 115),
S'mores Cake (page 174),
Lemon Meringue Cream Puffs (226),
Lemon Meringue Macarons (page 250), and
S'mores Macarons (page 252).

BROWNED BUTTER FUDGE

The key to this fudge is to get the browned butter just right. You want the butter to caramelize, turn brown and frothy, and have a lot of little brown specks. Don't be scared to overdo it—just don't let it burn. The more the butter caramelizes, the more delicious this fudge is!

Makes 2 cups

½ cup unsalted butter, melted
4 cups icing sugar
1½ teaspoons pure vanilla extract
¼ cup whole (3.25%) milk

1. In a small saucepan over medium-high heat, cook the butter until it is browned. The butter will look frothy and have little brown specks.

2. In the bowl of a stand mixer fitted with the paddle attachment, add the icing sugar. With the mixer on low speed, slowly pour in the browned butter. Add the vanilla. Add the milk, 1 tablespoon at a time, until the fudge is thick and spreadable but not too creamy. Increase the speed to high and beat for 2 minutes, until smooth. Use immediately.

BAKER'S TIP

A little goes a long way with this decadent fudge! A thin layer is all you need to top your favourite banana bread, blondie, or brownie.

MAKE IT

Cashew Praline Party Squares (page 111) and
Banana Bread Party Squares (page 112).

BROWNIE BATTER

Thick, creamy, and chocolatey—what more could you want in a brownie batter? This recipe tastes just like you're eating straight from a bowl of brownie batter that's about to be baked into a delicious treat, but don't worry, it's meant to be eaten raw.

Makes 3 cups

½ cup unsalted butter, room temperature
1 cup granulated sugar
¾ cup whole (3.25%) milk
1 teaspoon pure vanilla extract
2 cups all-purpose flour, heat treated (see Flour, page 7)
¼ cup cocoa powder
¼ teaspoon salt

1. In the bowl of a stand mixer fitted with the paddle attachment, cream the butter and sugar on high speed for about 2 minutes, until the mixture looks light and fluffy. Add the milk and vanilla and mix until combined. Scrape down the sides of the bowl. Add the flour, cocoa powder, and salt. Mix on medium speed until fully combined. Scrape down the sides of the bowl and mix for an additional 30 seconds. If the batter is too thick to pipe, add up to 2 tablespoons whole milk, 1 tablespoon at a time, until a thick and creamy consistency is achieved.

2. Use immediately or store in an airtight container in the fridge for up to 2 days. Remove from the fridge 1 hour before using.

BAKER'S TIP

Use leftovers to top off your favourite ice cream—it's Ashley's favourite way to use up the scraps!

MAKE IT

Brownie Batter Cookie Sandwiches (page 30) and Brownie Batter Macarons (page 246).

COOKIE DOUGH

Eating raw cookie dough is one of the greatest small pleasures in life. As kids, we always ate as much of it as we could before the cookies were baked, and if you're anything like us, as adults those tubes of cookie dough at the grocery store still call your name. Make this egg-free cookie dough for a safe and delicious treat.

Makes 2 cups

½ cup unsalted butter, room temperature
½ cup packed brown sugar
¼ cup granulated sugar
½ teaspoon pure vanilla extract
2 tablespoons whole (3.25%) milk
1 cup all-purpose flour, heat treated (see Flour, page 7)
¼ teaspoon salt
½ cup mini chocolate chips

1. In a stand mixer fitted with the paddle attachment, cream the butter, brown sugar, and granulated sugar on high speed for about 2 minutes, until the mixture looks light and fluffy. Add the vanilla and milk and mix until combined. Scrape down the sides of the bowl.

2. Sift together the heat-treated flour and salt. Add the dry ingredients to the wet ingredients and mix on medium speed until fully combined. Scrape down the sides of the bowl. Add the chocolate chips and mix for an additional 30 seconds.

3. Use immediately or store in an airtight container in the fridge for up to 5 days. Remove from the fridge 1 hour before using.

BAKER'S TIP

Cookie Dough makes a perfect treat on its own! Prepare the batter, then scoop it into bite-size balls. Roll each ball in mini chocolate chips and serve cookie dough truffles to last-minute guests!

MAKE IT

*Cookie Dough Brownie Cookie Sandwiches (page 52),
Cookie Dough Cupcakes (page 81),
Cookie Dough Cheesecake Party Squares (page 96),
Cookie Dough Cake (page 166), and
Cookie Dough Macarons (page 239).*

APPLE FILLING

This filling made from perfectly spiced, buttery apples makes an appearance in some of our favourite seasonal recipes in the book, but it is also a delicious treat on its own.

Makes 3½ cups

6 cups peeled, cored, and chopped Granny Smith apples
1 cup packed brown sugar
¼ cup unsalted butter, room temperature
½ teaspoon cinnamon
⅛ teaspoon ground nutmeg
1 tablespoon cold water (optional)
2 tablespoons cornstarch (optional)

1. In a medium saucepan over medium-low heat, cook the apples, brown sugar, butter, cinnamon, and nutmeg, stirring frequently, until a fork can easily be inserted into the apples and the mixture is thick and bubbly, about 8 to 10 minutes.
2. If you would like to thicken the filling, use a fork to mix the cold water and cornstarch in a small bowl, until no clumps remain. Pour the cornstarch mixture into the filling and stir over medium heat for about 2 minutes, until the mixture goes from looking cloudy to looking clear again.
3. Use immediately or transfer to an airtight container and let cool to room temperature. Store in the fridge for up to 5 days.

BAKER'S TIP

Granny Smith apples are the best variety to use in this recipe. They are naturally tart, which contrasts nicely with the sweetness of the brown sugar and complements the flavour of the delicious warming spices.

MAKE IT

Apple Crumble Cookie Sandwiches (page 33) and Cinnamon Apple Crumble Cake (page 151).

LEMON CURD

We use this curd in so many recipes! We stuff it in cupcakes, spread it on cakes, and use it as the base for our Lemon Meringue Party Squares (page 115). We're sure this will quickly become your favourite lemon curd recipe, too.

Makes 2 cups

½ cup fresh lemon juice (about 3 lemons; see Baker's Tip)
1 cup water, divided
½ cup granulated sugar
¼ cup cornstarch
⅛ teaspoon salt
5 egg yolks
1 tablespoon unsalted butter, room temperature

1. In a small saucepan over medium-high heat, bring the lemon juice and ½ cup water to a simmer.
2. In a medium bowl, whisk together the sugar, cornstarch, and salt. Add the egg yolks and the remaining ½ cup water and whisk to combine. Slowly pour the lemon juice mixture into the sugar mixture, whisking constantly to temper the egg yolks, until fully combined.
3. Return the mixture to the saucepan and cook over low heat, whisking constantly to prevent burning and to ensure a smooth and creamy consistency. Continue whisking until the mixture thickens and lifting the whisk out of the mixture creates a thick ribbon of lemon curd. Remove from the heat and whisk in the butter until fully combined.
4. Pour the mixture into a medium shallow dish and cover with plastic wrap placed directly on the surface of the mixture to prevent a skin forming. Refrigerate for at least 1 hour, or until ready to use. Store in the fridge for up to 1 week.

BAKER'S TIP

For a lemon curd with even more zing, zest the lemons before juicing them and add the zest to the lemon juice and water mixture.

MAKE IT

Lemon Meringue Cookie Sandwiches (page 44),
Lemon Bar Cupcakes (page 78),
Lemon Meringue Party Squares (page 115),
Lemon Wildberry Cake (page 135),
Lemon Meringue Cream Puffs (page 226), and
Lemon Meringue Macarons (page 250).

RASPBERRY REDUCTION

Our Raspberry Reduction is a staple in the Jenna Rae Cakes kitchen. This reduction brings sweet and tart flavours to buttercreams and batters.

Makes 1 cup

2 cups fresh raspberries (see Baker's Tip)
2 tablespoons water
2 tablespoons granulated sugar
1 teaspoon fresh lemon juice

1. In a small saucepan over low heat, simmer the raspberries, water, sugar, and lemon juice, stirring frequently, until the mixture has reduced by about half.
2. Using a fine-mesh sieve, strain the mixture into an airtight container. Discard the solids. Cover and refrigerate to cool.
3. Store in an airtight container in the fridge for up to 1 week.

BAKER'S TIP

If fresh raspberries aren't in season, use frozen raspberries instead—they work wonderfully in this recipe! An equal amount of blueberries or strawberries will work well, too.

MAKE IT

Raspberry Cheesecake Cream Puffs (page 209) and Raspberry Rose Macarons (page 263).

STRAWBERRY COMPOTE

A compote is fruit cooked in syrup. This compote features the bright flavour of strawberries made slightly sweeter with the addition of sugar, along with some lemon juice that leaves a vibrant taste on your palette.

Makes 1 cup

3 cups hulled and sliced fresh strawberries (see Baker's Tip)
2 tablespoons granulated sugar
2 tablespoons water
1 teaspoon fresh lemon juice

1. In a small saucepan over low heat, simmer the strawberries, sugar, water, and lemon juice, stirring frequently, until the mixture has reduced by about half. Transfer to a bowl of a food processor and pulse until smooth.
2. Transfer the mixture to an airtight container and place in the fridge to cool.
3. Store in an airtight container in the fridge for up to 1 week.

BAKER'S TIP

The resulting taste might be less pronounced, but you can substitute frozen strawberries in this recipe if fresh strawberries are not in season.

MAKE IT

Strawberry Shortcake Cookie Sandwiches (page 46) and Strawberry Shortcake (page 138).

STRAWBERRY JAM

Here's a strawberry jam you can use for the recipes in this book or on toast. No matter how you choose to use it, we're sure it will become one of your new favourite recipes! Skip the store-bought stuff and make your own. You can even use it as a host gift. Jam takes 24 hours to make, so be sure to prepare this recipe in advance.

Makes 3 cups

3 cups hulled and sliced strawberries (see Baker's Tip)
1½ cups granulated sugar
¼ cup + 1 tablespoon powdered pectin
2 tablespoons fresh lemon juice
¼ teaspoon pure vanilla extract

1. Place the strawberries in a medium bowl. Use a fork to mash the berries until pulverized, or purée with an immersion blender. Transfer to a small saucepan.

2. In a small bowl, whisk together the sugar and powdered pectin. Add the sugar mixture to the saucepan. Add the lemon juice. Bring the mixture to a boil over medium heat. Boil for 5 minutes, stirring constantly and reducing the heat as necessary so that the fruit doesn't catch on the bottom of the pan. Remove from the heat and stir in the vanilla.

3. Transfer the mixture to an airtight container (an old jam jar works well!) and refrigerate overnight to thicken. Store in an airtight container in the fridge for up to 2 weeks.

BAKER'S TIP

Swap out the strawberries for an equal amount of blueberries, raspberries, or another favourite fruit.

MAKE IT

Peanut Butter and Jam Cookie Sandwiches (page 36).

WILDBERRY REDUCTION

This Wildberry Reduction is another staple in the Jenna Rae Cakes kitchen. Make extra and add it to your morning oatmeal or enjoy it over a big scoop of vanilla ice cream.

Makes 1 cup

1 cup fresh blueberries
1 cup fresh raspberries
1 cup hulled and chopped fresh strawberries
1 teaspoon fresh lemon juice
2 tablespoons sugar
2 tablespoons water

1. In a medium saucepan over low heat, simmer the blueberries, raspberries, strawberries, lemon juice, sugar, and water, stirring frequently, until the mixture is reduced by about half, about 20 minutes.

2. Using a fine-mesh sieve, strain the mixture into an airtight container to remove any seeds from the berries. Place in the fridge to cool.

3. Store in an airtight container in the fridge for up to 1 week.

BAKER'S TIP

If you don't have access to fresh berries, use 3 cups frozen mixed berries instead.

MAKE IT

Wildberry Cupcakes (page 84),
Lemon Wildberry Cake (page 135), and
Pavlova Cream Puffs (page 216).

GRAHAM CRACKER CRUMBLE

This Graham Cracker Crumble adds the crunchy, buttery taste of graham crackers to our s'mores-inspired treats.

Makes 1 cup

3 tablespoons melted salted butter
1 teaspoon pure vanilla extract
1 cup graham cracker crumbs (see Baker's Tip)
¼ cup packed brown sugar
Pinch of salt
Pinch of cinnamon

1. Preheat the oven to 350°F. Line a baking sheet with parchment paper.
2. In a small heat-resistant bowl, melt the butter in the microwave. Add the vanilla.
3. In a medium bowl, combine the graham cracker crumbs, brown sugar, salt, and cinnamon. Add the butter mixture to the dry ingredients and stir until evenly coated.
4. Spread the mixture in an even layer on the prepared baking sheet. Bake for 5 minutes. Remove from the oven and stir. Return to the oven and bake for an additional 3 minutes. Let cool to room temperature.
5. Store the crumble in an airtight container at room temperature for up to 1 week.

BAKER'S TIP

If you can't find graham cracker crumbs at your local grocery store, you can crush some graham crackers yourself.

MAKE IT

S'mores Cake (page 174) and S'mores Macarons (page 252).

SHORTBREAD CRUMBLE

Our Shortbread Crumble adds a deliciously crispy, buttery texture to whatever you sprinkle it on. We dye this crumble pink because, well, we like pink. But feel free to leave yours au naturel!

Makes 2 cups

1 cup all-purpose flour
½ cup granulated sugar
2 tablespoons cornstarch
Pinch of salt
¼ cup + 2 tablespoons melted unsalted butter
½ teaspoon pure vanilla extract
1 to 2 drops electric pink gel food colouring (optional)

1. Preheat the oven to 325°F. Line a baking sheet with parchment paper.
2. In a medium bowl, mix the flour, sugar, cornstarch, and salt. Add the butter, vanilla, and food colouring, if using. Stir until the dry ingredients are evenly coated.
3. Spread the mixture in an even layer on the prepared baking sheet. Bake for 5 minutes. Remove from the oven and stir. Return to the oven and bake for an additional 3 minutes. Let cool to room temperature.
4. Store the crumble in an airtight container at room temperature for up to 1 week.

BAKER'S TIP

This recipe also makes a delicious topping for your favourite yogurt or ice cream!

MAKE IT

Strawberry Shortcake Cookie Sandwiches (page 46), Lemon Bar Cupcakes (page 78), and Strawberry Shortcake (page 138).

CHOCOLATE SHORTBREAD CRUMBLE

This crumble adds the perfect slightly salty crunch to our Chocolate Lover's Cake (page 162), but don't stop there! Top any of our chocolate cupcakes with a sprinkling of this crumble for additional texture and flavour.

Makes 2 cups

¾ cup all-purpose flour
½ cup granulated sugar
2 tablespoons cocoa
Pinch of salt
⅓ cup unsalted butter, melted
¼ teaspoon pure vanilla extract

1. Preheat the oven to 350°F. Line a baking sheet with parchment paper.

2. In the bowl of a stand mixer fitted with the paddle attachment, add the flour, sugar, cocoa, and salt and mix on medium speed for 1 minute, until combined. Scrape down the sides of the bowl. Add the butter and vanilla and beat on medium high speed for an additional 30 seconds.

3. Spread the mixture in an even layer on the prepared baking sheet. Bake for 5 minutes. Remove from the oven and stir. Return to the oven and bake for an additional 2 to 4 minutes. Let cool to room temperature before using.

5. Store the crumble in an airtight container at room temperature for up to 1 week.

MAKE IT

Chocolate Lover's Cake (page 162).

SUGAR AND SPICE CRUMBLE

If you're a pumpkin spice lover, this crumble is for you. We can't get enough of this recipe in the fall at our shop; we use it to add crunch to just about everything! Leftover spiced crumble is a great topper for anything from pancakes to pies and give your favourite spiced treats some extra spice and extra crunch!

Makes 2 cups

½ cup granulated sugar
½ cup unsalted butter, room temperature
¼ teaspoon pure vanilla extract
1 cup all-purpose flour
2 tablespoons cornstarch
2 teaspoons pumpkin pie spice (see Baker's Tip)
1 teaspoon cinnamon
Pinch of salt

1. Preheat the oven to 350°F. Line a baking sheet with parchment paper.

2. In the bowl of a stand mixer fitted with the paddle attachment, cream the sugar and butter on high speed for 2 minutes, until the mixture looks light and fluffy. Scrape down the sides of the bowl. Add the vanilla and beat on high speed for an additional 30 seconds.

3. Add the flour, cornstarch, pumpkin pie spice, cinnamon, and salt and beat on low speed until combined and the mixture has the texture of wet sand. Scrape down the sides of the bowl and mix for an additional 30 seconds.

4. Spread the mixture in an even layer on the prepared baking sheet. Bake for 5 minutes. Remove from the oven and stir. Return to the oven and bake for an additional 2 to 4 minutes. Let cool to room temperature before using.

5. Store the crumble in an airtight container at room temperature for up to 1 week.

BAKER'S TIP

1. If you like your spices strong, feel free to add one more teaspoon of pumpkin pie spice. **2.** If you don't have pumpkin pie spice on hand, substitute ½ teaspoon cinnamon, ½ teaspoon ground nutmeg, ¼ teaspoon ground ginger, ¼ teaspoon allspice, and a pinch of ground cloves.

MAKE IT

Pumpkin Spice Cupcakes (page 83) and Cinnamon Apple Crumble Cake (page 151).

PEANUT BUTTER MARSHMALLOW SQUARES

Your favourite childhood square is ready to stuff cookie sandwiches, top cakes, and more! This recipe is quick and easy, and you may even have leftovers to enjoy on their own.

Makes 48 (1½-inch) squares

1 cup creamy peanut butter
½ cup unsalted butter, room temperature
1 cup butterscotch chips
5 cups mini multicoloured marshmallows

1. Grease a 13- × 9-inch baking dish with shortening or cooking spray.

2. In a medium heat-resistant bowl, heat the peanut butter and butter in the microwave in 30-second intervals, stirring after each interval, until melted and smooth. Add the butterscotch chips and stir to combine. Heat again in the microwave in 30-second intervals, stirring after each interval, until melted and smooth. Do not overheat. Let cool for 10 minutes. Add the marshmallows and gently fold to coat.

3. Pour the mixture into the prepared baking dish and press into an even layer. Let cool to room temperature.

4. Use immediately or store in an airtight container at room temperature for up to 1 week.

BAKER'S TIP

The multicoloured marshmallows give this treat its distinctive taste—you wouldn't think peanut butter and fruity marshmallows would go together, but they work so well in this recipe!

MAKE IT

Peanut Butter Marshmallow Cookie Sandwiches (page 29), Peanut Butter Marshmallow Party Squares (page 119), and Peanut Butter Marshmallow Cake (page 154).

SPICED CANDIED NUTS

Spiced, sweet, and easy to make. This recipe is perfect for candy-coating and spicing any of your favourite nuts—from pecans to almonds to walnuts to cashews. Just substitute an equal amount of your preferred nut for the pecans.

Makes 1 cup

1 cup raw pecans, roughly chopped
½ cup granulated sugar
2 tablespoons water
¼ teaspoon cinnamon
⅛ teaspoon ground nutmeg

1. Preheat the oven to 350°F. Line a baking sheet with parchment paper.

2. Spread the pecans in an even layer on the prepared baking sheet. Toast for 7 minutes. Let cool.

3. In a small saucepan over medium-high heat, bring the sugar and water to a boil. When the mixture is bubbling slowly but has not yet begun to caramelize, add the nuts and stir using a heat-resistant spatula, until the sugar begins to crystallize. Add the cinnamon and nutmeg and continue stirring until the nuts no longer stick together. Remove from the heat and return the nuts to the prepared baking sheet to cool.

4. Store in an airtight container at room temperature for up to 1 week.

MAKE IT

Carrot Cake Cupcakes (page 66) and Carrot Cake with Spiced Candied Walnuts (page 191).

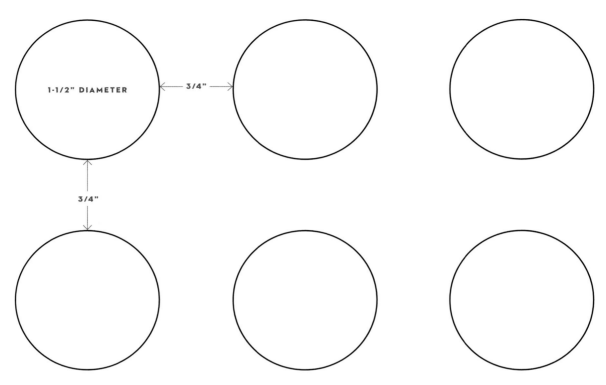

1-1/2" DIAMETER

3/4"

3/4"

MACARON SHELLS PIPING TEMPLATE

Use this template to trace perfectly sized and spaced guides onto your parchment paper.

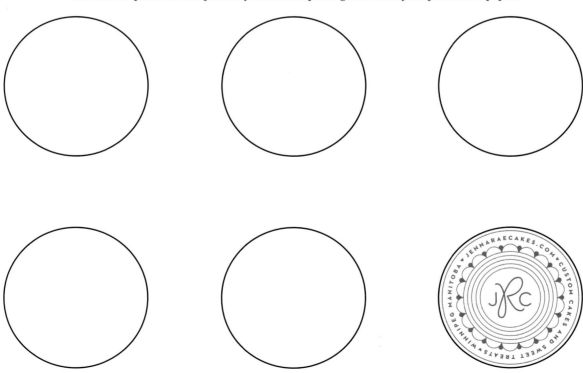

PÂTE À CHOUX PIPING TEMPLATE

Use this template to trace perfectly sized and spaced guides onto your parchment paper.

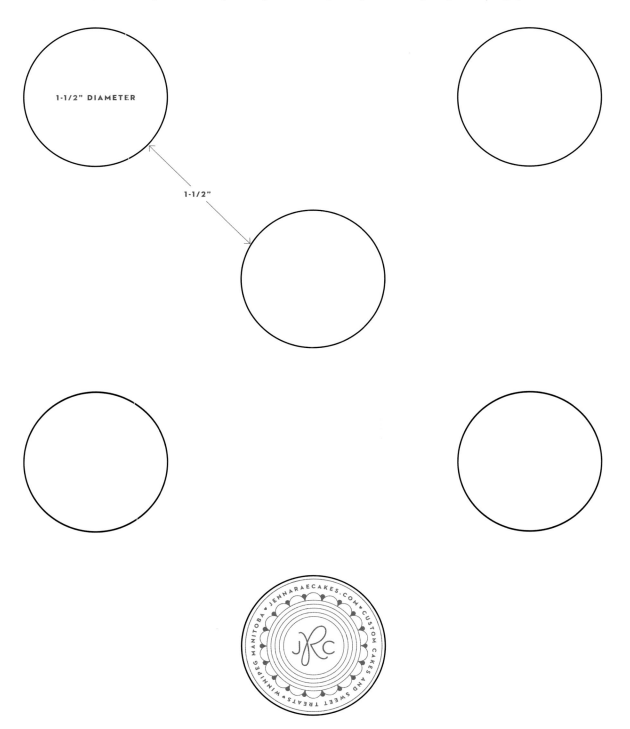

1-1/2" DIAMETER

1-1/2"

ASHLEY'S LITTLE BLACK BOOK

AS A PHOTO STYLIST, I've collected a lot of favourite props, serving dishes, and utensils along the way. My cupboards at home are full to the brim with unique plates, bowls, and the tiniest spoons. I'm always on the hunt for the perfect vessel to serve or shoot with, and if you love to style, you can use this list to track down some of the items you see popping up on our Instagram feed.

BACKDROPS, PAPER, AND STONE TILES

I get a lot of questions about what kind of backgrounds I shoot on for flat lays. I get custom-made printed coloured paper that's finished with a protective, non-shiny coating, which makes it perfect for food. I also find that mat boards from framing shops make great, large backdrops. For a more textural backdrop, my go-tos are cement and marble tiles, which are available at most flooring stores—just make sure they're not shiny or you'll be dealing with annoying reflections!

CAKE STANDS

After working so hard on a cake, you need to proudly display it on a cake stand! The sturdy cake stands from Sarah's Stands are simple, strong, and beautiful. Most of the stands we rent out in our shop are from Sarah's Stands. I collect marble pedestals whenever I can find them for home and in-store use.

CERAMICS

Lot 50 is my favourite place to get perfectly imperfect ceramic plates, and Pepo Ceramics makes our popular pink and gold JRC mug, which is available online.

CUTLERY

I've sourced a lot of my cutlery and cake lifters from vintage shops, so I don't have any specifics on where to find them. I suggest taking your time to browse thrift stores and garage sales, as well as visiting boutique shops when you travel.

FLOWERS

Fresh flowers and foliage are the perfect finishing touch to any sweets table, and they provide a great pop of colour in photos! Our go-to in Winnipeg is Academy Florist.

PACKAGING

I spend a lot of time conceptualizing and designing our packaging at Jenna Rae Cakes. Pink boxes, colourful tape, and shiny metallic foil make quite a few appearances in our photos and help to brand our image while also adding a nice aesthetic touch.

EQ3

This modern furniture and houseware chain has roots right here in Winnipeg, Manitoba. We love their furniture, and their kitchen accessories are some of our favourites. They do a lot of work in marble and natural stone, and we can't get enough of it.

GREAT JONES

Their pots and pans are gorgeous, heavy duty, and affordable. They don't ship to Canada, however, so be prepared to ship your items to the border.

HOMESENSE

One of my favourite pastimes is walking around Homesense, searching for imported treasures. Their natural wood and stone pieces are my favourite finds.

JUNE HOME SUPPLY

Owned by a husband and wife duo in Winnipeg, the houseware items this company carries are timeless and classic. Their linen aprons are some of our personal favourites.

OH HAPPY DAY SHOP

We love their simple paper plates, which are available in every colour imaginable! They're an affordable way to add colour to your table and photos.

MERCI

I fell in love with this shop while visiting Paris a few summers ago. Their linen napkins and tablecloths are my favourite.

the
Kitchen Crew

Hi Dad!

Our little families

Baking with mom

SPECIAL THANKS

THIS BOOK IS THE RESULT of more than five years of hard work and the efforts of a large number of talented people. This process has truly been a team effort, made better by every baker who has worked in our kitchen and shared their knowledge with us over the years. Jenna Rae Cakes is a team, and this was truly a team effort!

To our head baker, Jordain Houdayer, your work ethic still floors us after all these years! Thank you for the endless hours you spent perfecting, tweaking, and testing. Every recipe shines because of your expertise and passion.

To Brittany Mahood, our dear, dear friend. You capture all of our special life moments—from weddings to babies—and there is no one else in the world we would have trusted to capture the images for this book. We spent countless hours crammed into a small room styling and photographing every image with you, and we enjoyed every second of it. We love you so much!

To Aelea, Jenna Rae Cakes would not be where it is today without your creativity, writing skills, and incredibly organized mind. Thank you for being our first non-family hire, for whipping our processes and procedures into shape, and for helping us put these recipes down on paper. We're so happy you continue to stick with us as your career evolves. You are still such an integral part of Jenna Rae Cakes.

We want to extend a huge thank you to our team of amazing bakers who all had a hand in testing and perfecting the recipes in this book. Jenna Reid, Tori Langdon, Kimberly Sy, Amirah Mansilla, Alyssa Houston, Darleen Tolentino, Dennilyn Raymundo, Jeremy Hutsebaut, Taylor Navitka, Beatriz Romarate, Jana Badenhorst, and Marcel Carriere—thank you all for your hard work, dedication, and creativity!

To our editor, Laura Dosky, and to everyone at Penguin Random House Canada, thank you for your tireless guidance throughout this process. We would have been completely lost without your patience and expertise! A special thanks to Rachel Brown, who approached us about writing a book. We remember getting your first email and jumping up and down with excitement! Thank you for making our dreams of writing a cookbook come true.

To Trevor, we're so thankful you chose to join the family business. It just wouldn't be the same without you! You keep us focused and on track with your spreadsheets and numbers, while also keeping everyone laughing with your amazing dad jokes and one-liners. You don't get nearly enough recognition for the success of Jenna Rae Cakes. We love you!

To our mom, thank you for instilling a love of baking in us at an early age. You taught us that anything is possible, and you lead by example every day. We love you!

To our dad, we feel so lucky to work with you every day. Thank you for being the best delivery driver, office assistant, and maintenance manager around. You're the best guy we know, and we got our work ethic from you. You're our biggest fan, and we're definitely yours.

To our siblings, Chelsea and Brendyn, your sweet tooth suggestions have led us to so many bestselling creations. Chelsea, we'll always look back fondly on the first year Jenna Rae Cakes was open and you took a year off of school to work side-by-side with us for 17-hour days in a tiny hot kitchen. We loved every second of it!

To our kids, you're our whole world. We hope to lead by example and show you that you can do whatever you set your minds to! Stay kind, curious, and humble and never let anyone dull your shine.

And to you, the reader! Thank you from the bottom of our hearts for purchasing this book. We hope you put it to good use and build many beautiful memories while baking for your loved ones.

INDEX